INTERVENTIONISM

Other Books in the Current Controversies Series:

The Abortion Controversy
The AIDS Crisis
Alcoholism
Drug Trafficking
Energy Alternatives
Ethics
Europe
Free Speech
Gun Control
Illegal Immigration
Iraq
Nationalism and Ethnic Conflict
Police Brutality
Pollution
Sexual Harassment
Violence Against Women
Women in the Military
Youth Violence

INTERVENTIONISM

David L. Bender, *Publisher*
Bruno Leone, *Executive Editor*

Katie de Koster, *Managing Editor*
Scott Barbour, *Senior Editor*

Paul A. Winters, *Book Editor*

Library of Congress Cataloging-in-Publication Data

Interventionism / Paul Winters, book editor.
p. cm. — (Current controversies)
Includes bibliographical references and index.
ISBN 1-56510-232-0 (pbk.) — ISBN 1-56510-233-9 (library)
1. Intervention (International law)—
[1. Intervention (International law)] I. Winters, Paul A., 1965–
II. Series.
JX4481.I554 1995
341.5'84—dc20 94-28197
CIP
AC

Contents

Foreword 12

Introduction 14

Chapter 1: Is Humanitarian Intervention Effective?

Chapter Preface 18

Yes: Humanitarian Intervention Can Be Effective

Humanitarian Intervention Can Protect Human Rights *by Massoud Barzani, interviewed by* Harvard International Review 19

Military intervention to stop massive human rights violations is becoming an accepted norm in international relations. The United Nations should lead the way to a new world order in international relations based on the protection of human rights.

Humanitarian Intervention Can Save Lives *by Matthew Rothschild* 24

Leftists in America raised many objections to U.S. intervention in Somalia, but saving Somalis from starvation outweighs all these objections. A more democratic and less bureaucratic United Nations is the ideal body to make intervention decisions.

There Is a Christian Duty to Intervene *by Kenneth R. Himes* 29

Though the Roman Catholic Church has championed the "just war" tradition, which is based on the primacy of state sovereignty, Pope John Paul II has argued that human rights outweigh state sovereignty in considerations of military intervention. To Roman Catholics, the international community has a duty to intervene in the affairs of nations to stop human rights abuses, and failure to do so is a further crime against human rights.

Moral Considerations Should Outweigh Political Arguments on Intervention *by Jane Sharp* 35

Bosnia presents a good case for intervention. The political and military arguments against intervention are outweighed by the moral arguments for it. Western nations ignore conflicts such as the one in Bosnia at the peril of abandoning international treaties on human rights.

No: Humanitarian Intervention Is Not Effective

Humanitarian Intervention Is Not Effective *by Adam Roberts* 39

The end of East-West rivalry in the UN Security Council and the decline of the rule of nonintervention in international relations have enabled the United Nations to sponsor a number of multilateral humanitarian interventions. However, because the goals of humanitarian intervention are unclear, the results of efforts in Iraq, Somalia, and Bosnia have been disappointing.

Humanitarian Intervention Is Problematic *by Alex de Waal and Rakiya Omaar* 48

Military intervention in the name of humanitarianism has a long history of failure and abuse by powerful states that justify political and military objectives by citing humanitarian concerns. Humanitarian aid, sanctions, and military intervention are all limited in their effectiveness. Military intervention should be a last resort and should meet a set of rigorous preconditions.

Military Intervention Is Always Political *by Caleb Carr* 57

Humanitarian intervention by U.S. or UN military forces cannot be separated from the politicized tasks of peacemaking and nation-building. Regardless of charges of colonialism, it is necessary for the United States to ensure that indigenous leaders are willing and capable of governing; otherwise, the United States should remove them. If American forces are not willing to take on all of these tasks, they ought to stay home.

Humanitarian Aid Undermines Self-Sufficiency *by Michael Maren* 62

Private voluntary organizations (PVOs) that provide food aid are in the business of obtaining U.S. government grants to dump U.S. food surpluses in Third World countries. Free food aid decreases demand for domestically produced crops, creating dependence on foreign aid while ruining Third World agricultural economies. The press presents an uncritical picture of food aid because journalists rely on the relief agencies for information.

Chapter 2: Should Interventions Be Used to Promote Peace and Democracy?

Interventions for Democracy: An Overview *by Jack Hitt et al.* 68

The U.S. foreign policy of democratic "enlargement," as a successor to the strategy of containment of Soviet communism, is debated by policy experts. Some believe that America's national interest should be given precedence, while others believe that altruistic, humanitarian, or democracy-promoting motives should rank more important. The civil war in Bosnia-Hercegovina, and America's reluctance to intervene in it, presents a case study in the debate over whether there is an emerging liberal democratic world order and what America's role should be in that order.

Yes: Interventions Should Be Used to Promote Peace and Democracy

The United Nations Should Intervene to Save Failing States *by Gerald B. Helman and Steven R. Ratner* 77

The end of colonialism and the spread of democracy—the "self-determination of peoples"—led to a proliferation of new states, some of which are now failing at the job of governing themselves. Because the United Nations is responsible for safeguarding international peace and security, it should intervene to save these failing or failed states.

The United Nations Should Foster Self-Government in Africa *by Paul Johnson* 88

The problems twentieth-century African states have in governing themselves are a result of abrupt decolonization, not colonialism. A benign form of colonialism—revival of United Nations trusteeships—is needed to help these African states learn to govern themselves.

The United States Should Protect New Democracies *by Morton H. Halperin* 95

Since the end of the Cold War, there has been a global trend toward constitutional democracy, with democratizing countries requesting UN observation of their elections to guarantee fair results. The United States, under UN auspices, should support this process, with military intervention if necessary to defend against antidemocracy coups.

The West Is Responsible for Peace and Democracy in Africa *by Jennifer Parmelee* 102

Although Westerners are increasingly unconcerned with Africa because the violence there seems unstoppable, the West bears a moral responsibility to try to end that violence. The West's push for multiparty democracy has not been matched by attempts to reform military forces, the biggest opponents of democracy in Africa. The sale of arms and military training to these forces by the West has worsened the violence. The United Nations should work harder to establish cease-fires and protect innocent civilians.

Economic Sanctions Can Be Effective *by Ivan Eland* 107

Economic sanctions, as a middle step between diplomatic and military intervention, can effectively influence the behavior of target nations through both practical and symbolic impacts. Harsh economic sanctions may strengthen the target regimes' political resolve and exacerbate the plight of the poor, but selective and limited sanctions, especially when imposed by a unified bloc of nations, can achieve political aims.

No: Interventions Should Not Be Used to Promote Peace and Democracy

Promotion of Western-Style Democracy Has Encouraged Violence *by Aryeh Neier* 113

Nationalistic majority groups around the world are violently oppressing minorities to defend "majority rights." The majority-rule model of democracy that the United States champions has contributed to this violent religious and ethnic nationalism.

Intervention Should Not Be Used to Solve Regional Conflicts *by Barbara Conry* 116

U.S. military intervention is not a viable solution to regional conflicts.

Military force is of limited usefulness in achieving political goals, and it is difficult for outside parties to remain neutral. In the end, intervention causes more problems than it solves.

The United States Must Cease Its Imperialist Interventions *by* Revolutionary Worker 124

The United States has always used its military forces to further the interests of its capitalist system. Because this system is self-serving, the United States is incapable of using its military for humanitarian or democratic purposes. "Nation-building" by the United States is a codeword for capitalist imperialism. Therefore, all U.S. interventions must be opposed.

Economic Sanctions Are Not Effective *by Gary Hufbauer* 131

Although between the end of World War II and the early 1970s the United States achieved its goals in about half the cases where it imposed sanctions, that success rate has declined. The open global economy has given even small countries the ability to escape the effects of economic sanctions. In the few recent cases where sanctions have worked, they have been supported by multilateral backup mechanisms and a strong political will that may be missing in other cases.

Chapter 3: What Role Should the United Nations Play in Interventions?

United Nations Interventions: An Overview *by Lucia Mouat* 135

There is little agreement on the proper role for the United Nations, in part because the UN's expanded peacekeeping role is becoming more complicated and dangerous. A special Humanitarianism and War Project has studied the UN's problems and concludes that the United Nations lacks a peacekeeping strategy. UN secretary general Boutros Boutros-Ghali believes that the United Nations must continue its present efforts even while reforming.

The United Nations' Role Should Be Broadened

The United Nations Should Be the World's Policeman *by Lincoln P. Bloomfield* 139

The Gulf War, where the United States led a UN-sanctioned coalition to free Kuwait from Iraqi aggression, represented a shift away from the nation's history of mostly unilateral military operations and toward a more collective approach to national security. In response to post–Cold War security threats and humanitarian crises worldwide, the United Nations, with strong U.S. leadership, must set up a law-enforcement-type collective security arrangement able to respond quickly to regional conflicts.

The United Nations Should Keep Peace and Promote Development *by Boutros Boutros-Ghali* 149

With the end of the Cold War, the United Nations has expanded the number and scope of its peacekeeping operations. In order to develop the ability to respond more rapidly to crises, the United Nations should have its own funds to finance operations; member governments should donate a reserve of equipment to be deposited at locations throughout the world; and each member should keep a reserve of specially trained personnel and troops available for UN operations. Economic development must be viewed as an indispensable part of social and political stability and international peace.

The United Nations Should Have Its Own Volunteer Armed Forces 157
by Brian Urquhart
The UN's inability to respond rapidly to crises, despite post–Cold War cooperation within the Security Council, has damaged its credibility. A UN force made up of volunteers would make possible rapid, early intervention in crises. Such a volunteer force could take on a peace-enforcement role—ending conflicts by separating combatants—rather than the traditional peacekeeping role of observing and patrolling cease-fires.

The United Nations' Role Should Be Restricted

The United Nations Should Play a Limited Role in Interventions 163
by Kim R. Holmes
The expansion of UN peacekeeping operations is based on the mistaken belief that state sovereignty and national interests have eroded in the post–Cold War era. Future UN peacekeeping operations will be successful only where peace and humanitarian concerns are in the national interests of warring parties.

The United Nations Should Stress Prevention over Intervention 170
by Thomas G. Weiss
The end of the Cold War has brought an explosion of civil wars. If the United Nations is to deal with these conflicts, it must stress prevention over intervention; it must act decisively and avoid half-measures when it does intervene; and it must be more selective in deciding which battles to fight, choosing those that can be won and avoiding those that are lost causes.

The United Nations Should Not Use Military Force 176
by Michael Clough
Calls for the expansion of the UN's military role are based on the mistaken belief that the end of the Cold War will give the United Nations more responsibility for international peace and security. UN attempts to resolve conflicts will be no more successful than past efforts, will damage the UN's neutrality, and may hinder successful action by others. The United Nations should focus on preventing conflict in the numerous places it is likely to start.

Chapter 4: When and Where Should the United States Intervene?

U.S. Intervention: An Overview *by Stephen Engelberg* 181
The debate over U.S. intervention abroad is divided between new globalists and anti-interventionists. New globalists argue that it is in America's interest to intervene to promote peace abroad, while anti-

interventionists say American interests are limited to American security and prosperity.

The United States Should Undertake Interventions

The United States Must Lead Interventions to Prevent Aggression 185
by Stanley R. Sloan
The United States has turned its attention to domestic issues with the end of the Cold War. This leaves a vacuum of leadership in the world, encouraging some states to commit aggression. If the United States does not take a leading role to stop aggression, anarchy will follow.

The United States Should Intervene to Preserve International Order 188
by Robert G. Neumann
For the foreseeable future, international peacemaking efforts will only succeed with strong U.S. leadership. The United States, therefore, must be willing to forcefully intervene to help new democracies, to end ethnic and nationalist conflicts, and to prevent religious terrorism. Such disorders directly threaten the interests of the United States.

The United States Should Intervene to Promote Democracy 193
by Anthony Lake
U.S. foreign policy should be based on enlarging the number of free-market democracies. To achieve this goal it is necessary to strengthen democracy and the economy in the United States; foster new democracies, especially in Russia; isolate antidemocratic "backlash" states; and promote a humanitarian agenda around the world.

The United States Should Intervene to Protect American Interests 201
by James A. Baker III
To maintain its leadership after the Cold War, the United States must follow a policy of selective engagement. This involves identifying key challenges to America's vital national interests and maintaining the military capability and credibility to support those interests.

U.S. Interventions Should Balance Moral and Practical Principles 207
by James Chace
American foreign policy has always had two components: a moral component that seeks worldwide democracy and a practical need to protect national interests. In order for foreign interventions to succeed, the United States must balance its pursuit of national interests with its democratizing mission.

The United States Should Avoid Interventions

The United States Should Avoid Interventions *by David Fromkin* 210
Military interventions cannot promote peace and democracy without a long commitment of troops. U.S. military force, therefore, should be used only to protect vital national interests, and only in situations in which armed intervention will prove effective at an acceptable cost.

The United States Should Let Its Allies Defend Themselves 214
by Pat Buchanan
Ignoring the advice of past military leaders has left the United States

with the burden of defending South Korea and other allies. The United States should let these nations defend themselves—with nuclear deterrents, if necessary—so long as no vital U.S. interests are threatened.

All U.S. Interventions Should Be Opposed *by Stephen R. Shalom* 217

The end of the Cold War has not changed the nature of interventions. Intervention should still be opposed because it is difficult to distinguish between good and bad interventions, because outsiders cannot solve internal problems, and because military force is counterproductive. Allowing exceptions to the rule of noninterventionism creates dangerous precedents.

UN Interventions by World Region: September 1994 227

Bibliography 233

Organizations to Contact 239

Index 244

Foreword

By definition, controversies are "discussions of questions in which opposing opinions clash" (Webster's Twentieth Century Dictionary Unabridged). Few would deny that controversies are a pervasive part of the human condition and exist on virtually every level of human enterprise. Controversies transpire between individuals and among groups, within nations and between nations. Controversies supply the grist necessary for progress by providing challenges and challengers to the status quo. They also create atmospheres where strife and warfare can flourish. A world without controversies would be a peaceful world; but it also would be, by and large, static and prosaic.

The Series' Purpose

The purpose of the Current Controversies series is to explore many of the social, political, and economic controversies dominating the national and international scenes today. Titles selected for inclusion in the series are highly focused and specific. For example, from the larger category of criminal justice, Current Controversies deals with specific topics such as police brutality, gun control, white collar crime, and others. The debates in Current Controversies also are presented in a useful, timeless fashion. Articles and book excerpts included in each title are selected if they contribute valuable, long-range ideas to the overall debate. And wherever possible, current information is enhanced with historical documents and other relevant materials. Thus, while individual titles are current in focus, every effort is made to ensure that they will not become quickly outdated. Books in the Current Controversies series will remain important resources for librarians, teachers, and students for many years.

In addition to keeping the titles focused and specific, great care is taken in the editorial format of each book in the series. Book introductions and chapter prefaces are offered to provide background material for readers. Chapters are organized around several key questions that are answered with diverse opinions representing all points on the political spectrum. Materials in each chapter include opinions in which authors clearly disagree as well as alternative opinions in which authors may agree on a broader issue but disagree on the possible solutions. In this way, the content of each volume in Current Controversies mirrors the mosaic of opinions encountered in society. Readers will quickly realize that there are many viable answers to these complex issues. By questioning each author's conclusions, students and casual readers can begin to develop the critical thinking skills so important to evaluating opinionated material.

Current Controversies is also ideal for controlled research. Each anthology in the series is composed of primary sources taken from a wide gamut of informational categories including periodicals, newspapers, books, United States and foreign government documents, and the publications of private and public organizations. Readers will find factual support for reports, debates, and research papers covering all areas of important issues. In addition, an annotated table of contents, an index, a book and periodical bibliography, and a list of organizations to contact are included in each book to expedite further research.

Perhaps more than ever before in history, people are confronted with diverse and contradictory information. During the Persian Gulf War, for example, the public was not only treated to minute-to-minute coverage of the war, it was also inundated with critiques of the coverage and countless analyses of the factors motivating U.S. involvement. Being able to sort through the plethora of opinions accompanying today's major issues, and to draw one's own conclusions, can be a complicated and frustrating struggle. It is the editors' hope that Current Controversies will help readers with this struggle.

"What we may be witnessing is not just the end of the Cold War, or the passing of a particular period of postwar history, but the end of history as such."

Francis Fukuyama

Introduction

The end of history, as defined by Francis Fukuyama, an analyst at the RAND Corporation and author of *The End of History and the Last Man*, was the end of the conflict between the ideologies of Soviet-promoted communism and Western-style democracy, inevitably leading to "the universalization of Western liberal democracy as the final form of human government." Western liberal democracy—characterized by free and fair elections, the rule of constitutional law, and respect for human rights—emerged from the Cold War as the only acceptable and viable form of government, in Fukuyama's view. However, the uncontrolled spread of ethnic and nationalist conflict in many parts of the world made some people question the inevitability of the victory of democracy. In the words of Max M. Kampelman, a lawyer formerly with the Department of State, "The question may well be asked: Are we entering an age of democracy or an age of disorder?"

The "universalization" of democracy has been less than the smooth process that Fukuyama's thesis seemed to predict. The promise of democracy in countries formerly under authoritarian rule has prompted many subnational ethnic groups to clamor for official recognition and representation, seek redress for discrimination, and press claims to historic lands, according to *New Yorker* writer Robert Cullen. Many have discovered, writes Cullen, that "transitions to democracy, rather than ameliorating conflicting claims to collective rights, can exacerbate them." Ethnic war, the breakdown of government, and the rise of military dictatorship—typified by the cases of Bosnia, Somalia, and Haiti—stand out as stumbling blocks on the road to the "end of history."

In former Yugoslavia in 1991, the republics of Slovenia, Macedonia, and Croatia declared independence, precipitating a war between Croatia and what was left of the federal Yugoslav government in Serbia. As a UN-brokered cease-fire was signed in January 1992, European governments quickly extended diplomatic recognition to these newly independent countries. Following the others' lead, in 1992 the republic of Bosnia and Hercegovina also declared independence from Yugoslavia. Bosnian Serbs who wanted to remain part of Yugoslavia then began a civil war and rapidly took control of more than two-thirds of Bosnian territory. The Bosnian Serbs defend their action in the civil war by asserting their right to live in a nation-state that unites all of Yugoslavia's Serbs. Others perceive their campaign as an especially violent instance of nationalist extremism. *Los Angeles Times* reporter Carol J. Williams, for example, describes the civil war as a "nationalist quest to force an ethnic division with bombs and bullets." UN forces entered the country in May 1992 to protect civilians and relief efforts, but as of October 1994 had been unable to negotiate a lasting settlement.

In Somalia, the overthrow of Mohammed Siad Barre, who ruled from 1969 until 1991, plunged that country into anarchy, with so-called warlords from various clans vying to succeed Siad Barre as dictator. According to Michael W. Doyle, writing in *Dissent*, "Three hundred thousand Somalis died in 1991–1992 in a famine brought about by the murderous competition of the Somali warlords." Throughout 1991 and 1992, the United Nations attempted to mediate a cease-fire and resolution. The failure of the cease-fire and the worsening of the famine caused by the civil war prompted the United States to intervene in December 1992 to protect the flow of relief supplies. In October 1993, U.S. forces clashed with Somalis, resulting in the deaths of 18 U.S. soldiers and hundreds of Somalis. U.S. armed forces departed Somalia in March 1994, leaving UN-led forces in their place. As a result of the warlords' struggle for power and the subsequent U.S.–UN intervention, writes Doyle, "the population was divided into rival clans and united only in their rejection of foreign rule."

In Haiti in September 1991, military generals deposed President Jean-Bertrand Aristide, who had been elected the previous December. Fearing that the military would execute him, Aristide fled Haiti and formed a government in exile in the United States. The United States and the Organization of American States implemented an embargo against Haiti, with the aim of restoring the democratically elected government. But because the embargo failed to produce results, in January 1993 the United Nations imposed trade sanctions on Haiti. Under pressure from the United States, the military rulers of Haiti signed the Governor's Island Accord in June 1993, agreeing to allow Aristide to resume his presidency. The military broke the accord, however, and in October 1993 new, stronger sanctions were imposed. According to Randall Robinson, director of the human rights organization TransAfrica, the military then "unleashed a reign of terror in Haiti," assassinating supporters of Aristide and other political opponents and tightening their grip on power. This political repression prompted thousands of refugees to flee Haiti and seek political asylum elsewhere. However, on September 18, 1994, under the threat of invasion by U.S. military forces, the military rulers once again agreed to observe the Governor's Island Accord. As of October 1994, 17,000 U.S. and multinational troops were monitoring Aristide's resumption of the Haitian presidency.

While there are signs that democracy may succeed in Haiti, conflicts like those in Bosnia and Somalia continue to simmer in many countries, making the spread of disorder sometimes seem more likely than the "universalization" of democracy. Francis M. Deng, a senior fellow at the Brookings Institution, attempts to explain the post–Cold War contradiction between the hopes for

Western-style democracy and the spread of conflict in the Third World. Those countries that were already internally democratic are moving toward a more cooperative, democratic world order with more active international organizations, Deng asserts, while nations emerging from the control of oppressive, totalitarian regimes are struggling to assert self-determination independent from outside interference in their internal affairs. The solution Deng proposes for both a democratic world order and resolution of Third World conflict is "a third party as mediator, moderator, peacemaker, and lawgiver." The most obvious institution to play this role, according to Deng, is the United Nations.

UN Secretary General Boutros Boutros-Ghali also supports this new role for the United Nations and envisions expanded duties for UN peacekeeping forces. The traditional role for these peacekeepers involves lightly armed troops from UN member countries who observe agreed-upon cease-fires and separate the combatants, but only use force to protect themselves. Boutros-Ghali believes that UN troops should be prepared to take on a more assertive role, forcibly intervening to impose cease-fires and protect civilian populations. In his words, "Protecting the flow of relief supplies, preventive deployment, and sanctions on commerce and communications are only part of what may be involved in the future. Beyond these measures, when established rules of engagement are no longer sufficient, United Nations forces may need authorization to use force."

Many of those writing on foreign policy are opposed to such an expanded role for UN forces. Among them is Stephen John Stedman, assistant professor at the Johns Hopkins University School of Advanced International Studies, who sees a danger in the "new interventionism." According to Stedman, new interventionists "believe that active international intervention is necessary to bring about a semblance of order to the post–Cold War world, based on the dubious presumption that the Cold War's end makes internal violence somehow more tractable." In his view, those who call for interventions lack an understanding of ethnic war, government breakdown, and military dictatorship and how to resolve these conflicts. Intervention through aid to civilians or imposed cease-fires, according to Stedman, by protecting and feeding weaker groups, may simply prolong resistance to an inevitable military or political solution, and may cost more lives. In his words, "Most civil wars become amenable to settlement only after they have played themselves out with ferocity. . . . There are no panaceas for internal conflicts."

There is strong debate over Francis Fukuyama's thesis that the end of the Cold War has resulted or will result in the "universalization" of Western-style democracy, with its emphasis on law and human rights. Western countries have attempted to promote democracy by intervening to uphold human rights and constitutional law in some Third World countries but have had mixed results so far, as exemplified by the cases of Bosnia, Somalia, and Haiti. Whether Western countries should intervene to promote democracy and protect human rights is among the issues debated in *Interventionism: Current Controversies*.

Chapter 1

Is Humanitarian Intervention Effective?

Chapter Preface

The International Committee of the Red Cross, an emergency relief and aid organization, defines humanitarian action as "action to prevent and alleviate human suffering wherever it is found." Others, among them *Médecins sans Frontières*, a private organization of doctors who provide medical services in humanitarian emergencies, stretch the definition to include a right to intervene in the internal affairs of sovereign nations during times of crisis to prevent and ease suffering. For some, though, even the right to intervene is not enough; they believe that the international community has a duty to prevent humanitarian tragedies.

Among those who support the right to intervene is Pope John Paul II, as leader of the Roman Catholic Church. The pope believes that the ethical consciences of people all over the world call for intervention in humanitarian crises. He states, "The conscience of humankind . . . asks that humanitarian interference be rendered mandatory in situations which gravely compromise the survival of entire peoples and ethnic groups: this is an obligation for both individual nations and the international community as a whole." According to the pope, "nations no longer have the right to be indifferent" to human rights abuses and humanitarian emergencies.

Others argue that an unrestricted right to intervene in humanitarian emergencies is likely to overload the international community and undermine the tradition of sovereignty. According to Stanley Hoffmann, a professor of French civilization at Harvard University, "Humanitarian crises . . . often result from serious political flaws and troubles. If the political causes are not removed, victims will remain in danger and the intervention will risk, at best, being no more than a band-aid." Moreover, Hoffmann asks, if intervening countries begin to change the political situation of countries with humanitarian crises, "what would happen to the sacrosanct notion of sovereignty and domestic jurisdiction?"

Washington Post reporter Keith B. Richburg notes that "the world seems to be moving toward acceptance of 'humanitarian intervention' as a principle of diplomacy." Others, like Hoffmann, would introduce a note of caution to those who accept this new principle. Viewpoints in the following chapter examine whether intervention can effectively provide humanitarian aid and relief.

Humanitarian Intervention Can Protect Human Rights

by Massoud Barzani, interviewed by *Harvard International Review*

About the author: *Massoud Barzani is president of the Kurdistan Democratic Party of Iraq and a member of the Presidential Council of the Iraqi National Congress.* Harvard International Review *is published quarterly by the Harvard International Relations Council, Inc.*

Questions of humanitarian intervention are often considered in a theoretical context by persons who can declare opinions without having to deal with the practical consequences. The perspective of the victims of human rights violations offers a different look at the intervention issue which complements that of the theorists. As a leader of the Iraqi Kurds, Massoud Barzani considers his people's experiences when analyzing the intervention problem. He agreed to answer the following questions for the *Harvard International Review.*

Humanitarian Intervention Defined

Harvard International Review: *How do you define "humanitarian intervention"?*

Massoud Barzani: We understand humanitarian intervention to be the right of the international community to act militarily upon verified and well-documented evidence of massive human rights violations by a sovereign member of the United Nations (UN) against its people, especially when the level of such atrocities reaches a point of humanitarian crisis that endangers peace and stability beyond the boundaries of the given nation.

We also understand this principle as the use of collective military intervention after exhausting diplomatic means to deliver humanitarian assistance to civilians affected by man-made or natural disasters. We add that preventive deployment is the essence of humanitarian intervention, either to check the spread of an armed conflict or to deter an outlaw regime from committing genocide.

For years, dictators have barricaded themselves behind the sovereignty of

"Hope Restored: Benefits of Humanitarian Intervention," an interview with Massoud Barzani, *Harvard International Review*, Fall 1993. Reprinted with the permission of the *Harvard International Review*.

their states to justify gross human rights violations and have considered their mistreatment and abuses as purely internal matters out of reach of the civilized world. The Kurds, who are unrepresented at the "club of nations," have been the victims of this attitude. In Iraq, the Kurdish people, numbering 3.5 million, were the target of a genocidal campaign by the Iraqi regime. They had nowhere to go to make their voices heard and present their case except for the UN Human Rights Commission, chaired at the time, ironically, by the Iraqi representative at UN Headquarters in Geneva.

"UN Security Council Resolution 688 . . . demands an end to repression of civilian populations by their sovereign governments."

In 1988, Iraq used poison gas to decimate whole communities of Kurds. Our cries and pleas over this flagrant violation of international law went unheard except by a few decent Western journalists who called for intervention.

The Kurds are proud that through the cruelty and barbarity perpetrated upon them by the Iraqi regime, they have moved the consciousness of the world to introduce the principle of humanitarian intervention as a precedent in international relations. This historical and unique principle now has a legal foundation embodied in UN Security Council Resolution 688, which demands an end to repression of civilian populations by their sovereign governments.

The Use of Military Force

Under what circumstances must military force, as opposed to other means, be used to achieve humanitarian goals, such as halting massive violations of human rights within a country?

Military force should be used to deter a government from committing gross violations of human rights and to ensure the delivery of humanitarian assistance to civilians under siege through the protection of supply lines and the provision of physical security for aid workers and aid agencies' installations and centers, whenever they are threatened by combatants. Military force should also be employed to prevent a conflict from spreading into a volatile area where the interests and stability of other nations are threatened. It can be applied to guarantee compliance with UN resolutions or international criteria, particularly to stop a nation from illegally acquiring weapons of mass destruction.

Why should the sovereignty of a nation be violated by other nations in the name of humanitarian intervention? Under what conditions is it justified? How is the "slippery slope" argument relevant to the humanitarian intervention dialogue?

The sovereignty of a nation should not be sacred and untouchable when its rulers pursue a systematic policy of massive human rights violations and follow a deliberate course of flouting international conventions and threatening regional or international peace and order. I believe that sovereignty can no longer be asserted in isolation, but rather in a context of greater international integration that guarantees national self-expression. The international community has a moral responsibility to intervene to stop a sovereign nation from taking international law into its own hands and behaving irresponsibly toward other nations. I believe that if the principle of humanitarian intervention is entrenched further it will lead to the development of democratization processes, assist the human rights cause and bring a stronger sense of responsibility to many nations around the world for their international obligations and commitments.

The "slippery slope" argument has been used to counter the humanitarian intervention principle. However, I believe that if the goal of the intervention is well-defined and a clear mandate is established by the participants, open-ended involvement will be prevented. It is also important to supplement the deployment of military forces or peacekeeping missions with sanctions, political isolation and other diplomatic means. It is true that the root causes of many humanitarian crises are political; therefore it is imperative to consider a viable and lasting political solution through the UN to overcome the source of humanitarian crises.

United Nations Leadership

If justified, should humanitarian intervention be conducted under UN auspices?

It is important that humanitarian intervention be conducted under UN auspices. The nature of the mission is the use of collective deployment of military force by a number of nations, which requires the authorization of the UN. In the new world order that is emerging after the collapse of communism and the end of the Cold War, the UN is confronted with mounting challenges to maintain peace and order. The UN should rise to the challenges, modernize its machinery and be more flexible in dealing with new situations that require different approaches to new realities. There should be a break with the standardized set of rules that deal only with sovereign member states. The UN should devise mechanisms that deal with internal conflicts and uphold the principle of humanitarian intervention. The new challenges faced by the UN require new thinking to be applied to its administration, in which all nations are both accounted for and are held accountable.

> ***"[National] sovereignty can no longer be asserted in isolation, but rather in a context of greater international integration."***

The Somali people seem to have rejected the UN efforts in their country. Do you believe that the Kurds of Iraq would have reacted in the same way?

When the [Operation Desert Storm] coalition forces started to pull out of Iraqi Kurdistan in July 1991, after they had established a security zone and left behind some security arrangements on the ground, the Kurdish people sent home the withdrawing forces with tears and flowers and demonstrations of gratitude and appreciation. Though deep down they felt that the job was half-done, they felt reassured by the continued commitment to their physical security from renewed Iraqi attacks.

The Kurdish people and their leadership have supported Operation Provide Comfort [relief effort begun in April 1991 following the failed rebellion of Kurds against Saddam Hussein's government] and cooperated to assist this unprecedented humanitarian operation. The aim and limitations of the mission were well understood by the Kurdish people and their leadership. Though there were certain stereotypes and misconceptions about the tribal nature of the Kurds and disunity among the Kurdish parties, we have proven that we have a united leadership and that we are a mature and experienced political movement that enjoys the support of the majority of the people. Our commanders in the field worked very closely with the allied forces to lay down the security arrangements.

What is happening in Somalia is very disappointing, and it is disturbing to see that Operation Restore Hope did not go as smoothly as Operation Provide Comfort. There is a great deal of difference between the two situations, and any arbitrary comparison would be misleading. We saw the coalition forces who intervened to extend humanitarian assistance to the Kurdish refugees, resettle them in a secure environment and deter the Iraqi regime from committing massive human rights violations, as saviors and liberators, not as occupiers. In Somalia, though, it seems that certain sectors of the public are viewing the UN peacekeeping forces as invaders and occupiers. In Somalia there has been a lack of unified leadership, and due to civil war and famine a number of tribal leaders, warlords and parties emerged and failed to achieve unity and cooperate with the mission. I assume that our people have a higher degree of education, a better standard of living and greater maturity and realism.

"The UN should devise mechanisms that deal with internal conflicts and uphold the principle of humanitarian intervention."

Operation Provide Comfort was a resounding success, mainly because the goal of the mission was clear. Also, its leadership was decisive, had a specific mandate, gained the confidence of the population and dealt with a united Kurdish leadership. The Kurds of Iraq supported the mission; therefore they would never have rejected the UN efforts in their country.

A Bona Fide Solution

Is the use of military force for humanitarian purposes simply a means of avoiding a moral duty to deal with more basic problems in the international arena, or is it a bona fide *solution to humanitarian crises?*

I think the use of military force for humanitarian purposes is a *bona fide* solution to humanitarian crises, but it is difficult to disassociate it from morality. However, each humanitarian intervention operation should be judged by the concrete realities of each crisis. In the case of the Kurds, for decades we were at pains to draw the attention of the civilized world to the plight of our people. We were deeply hurt by the lack of response from the international community to the use of chemical weapons by Saddam Hussein's regime against the Kurdish population, his systematic policy of mass disappearance of persons, the uprooting of whole communities and genocide. Sadly, economic considerations and commercial greed by Western governments always took priority over humanitarian concerns.

> ***"The use of military force for humanitarian purposes is a* bona fide *solution to humanitarian crises."***

There was, in my view, a moral failure by the international community to respond and act decisively. When the US-led coalition forces successfully liberated Kuwait and rolled back the Iraqi aggression, our people were encouraged by public statements from Western leaders to rise up against the Iraqi regime but were then abandoned to the mercy of the Iraqi army and air force. Subsequently there was a moral obligation involved in the humanitarian intervention by the victorious coalition forces. It was indeed the international media that steered the consciences of the decision makers to move and respond through unconventional means to a very serious humanitarian crisis.

Having exhausted diplomatic means of attempting to resolve a crisis, why should the international community decide to intervene rather than do nothing at all?

The international community has a responsibility and a duty to resolve serious humanitarian crises, and should not stand idle when diplomatic means fail. The UN is now confronted with a challenge to assume the leading role in the resolution of conflicts. It has the opportunity to impose an order on the emerging new world based on the ideals of common security, justice, democracy and the free market.

The end of the Cold War has produced more trouble spots, more conflicts and more humanitarian crises. The UN should undertake peacekeeping missions and intervene not only on behalf of its member states, but also on behalf of people who face serious injustice by man-made or natural disasters. It has a challenge to modernize its machinery and be more responsive in assuming a leading role in the new world order.

The old world order, based on the exercise of power, must now give way to a new order in which nations respond to the pressing needs of humankind. The UN must take a central role if that order is to be realized.

Humanitarian Intervention Can Save Lives

by Matthew Rothschild

About the author: *Matthew Rothschild is publisher of the* Progressive *magazine.*

I supported the U.S. mission to Somalia. I supported it, even though I have opposed every U.S. invasion of my conscious lifetime, from Vietnam to El Salvador, from Nicaragua to Iraq, from Libya to Panama, and all parts in between.

Despite Objections

I supported it, even though I knew the overwhelming responsibility the United States bears in supporting the brutal Somalia government of Siad Barre, which killed tens of thousands of its people and reduced much of Somalia to a land of famine.

I supported it, even though I knew the atrocious record of the United States in causing starvation and death elsewhere in the world.

I supported it, even though I knew the Pentagon will no doubt continue to use it as propaganda—a pretext for continuing to sop up U.S. taxpayer dollars that should be better spent for domestic needs.

I supported it, even though I would have much preferred the United Nations itself to have taken a more prominent role in mounting the effort.

I supported it for one simple reason: I believed it would save thousands of lives. That was—and is—reason enough for me. The left should be in the humanity business, not the ideology business. When our ideology obstructs our humanity, I worry.

In the case of Somalia, leftist critics of the U.S. role got most of the analysis right, but their conclusions struck me as almost cruel.

Yes, George Bush had ulterior motives in sending in the military.

Yes, he was bored and depressed after losing the [1992] election and he wanted a diversion.

Yes, he saw the need for projecting U.S. force in a "humanitarian" effort as a

Matthew Rothschild, "Why I Supported the U.S. Military in Somalia," *Peace & Democracy News*, Summer 1993. Reprinted with permission.

public relations move to buttress the Pentagon budget.

Yes, he realized that the Pentagon could use a base on the horn of Africa.

But these ulterior motives, and the overwhelming hypocrisy of U.S. policy, should not make us callous to the Somalis who were literally starving to death.

The lives of poor Africans had long gone neglected by U.S. policymakers. Many critics—in the United Nations, on the left, and in the African-American community in the United States—had contended that the U.S. policy was racist in its unconcern for African lives. That's one reason why Randall Robinson of TransAfrica and Jesse Jackson supported the U.S. mission in the first place.

The "They're-Dead-Anyway" Argument

By contrast, some conservatives condemned the U.S. mission on the coldest of grounds. "True, starving children are temporarily being fed," wrote Edward Luttwak in the *New Republic* of January 25, 1993, "but because of all that is not being done, that only gives them a chance to grow up into *khat*-chewing teenage gunmen, or their victims." This is the heart of immorality: to cheerfully let people starve to death today because of what they might turn into tomorrow.

Opposition on the left was not so crude, and was surely better intentioned, but still I find it chilly. Some leftist critics, such as Stephen Rosskamm Shalom, argued that the U.S. military presence was unnecessary in part because the worst of the crisis had passed. In the February 1993 issue of *Z Magazine*, Shalom wrote that "in Baidoa, for example, the epicenter of the famine, death rates had dropped from 300 a day in September [1992] to under 100 a day in November and early December (in part because many of the young, old, and sick had already died). And it was at the end of November [1992] that George Bush announced his offer to the United Nations to send U.S. troops to Somalia."

I must say I'm not persuaded by this they're-dead-anyway argument. First of all, Shalom's figure of fatalities of "under 100 a day" still makes the corpses pile up quickly in Baidoa alone. And secondly, this is not an argument against intervening at all, but an argument for intervening sooner. When Somalis were dying at a rate of 300 a day in Baidoa, the case for intervention by Shalom's own logic was more compelling. But he and other leftist critics didn't face that logic, much less endorse a U.S. intervention had it been more timely.

> ***"[George Bush's] ulterior motives . . . should not make us callous to the Somalis who were literally starving to death."***

This raises the fundamental question: Is there any amount of human suffering that would justify intervention by the United States? Assume that the most cataclysmic estimates on Somalia were accurate: as many as one million Somalis were at imminent risk of starvation. Would saving these one million people be wrong in the left's eyes simply because it spells a public relations victory for the Pentagon? Or forget about Somalia for a minute: Assume that famine threatens one million people in another country, where U.S. policy may not have been so complicit. Would saving these one million people be similarly wrong?

For me, that's an easy one. At some point, the sheer humanitarian urgency of saving lives should overwhelm the need to cling to the correct line.

The "Lending-Respectability" Argument

Shalom and other leftist critics have tried to get around this point by arguing that in the long run more people will suffer because U.S. imperialism has been given a face-lift. "If Somalia lends respectability to the Pentagon," Shalom wrote, "many Third World people will pay the price."

But some Third World people in Somalia were paying the ultimate price before the United States intervened, and I am leery of letting some people die in the here-and-now for fear that more will die somewhere down the road.

I find two other flaws with this "lending-respectability" argument. First, it is possible to hold the Pentagon to its own rhetoric of humanitarianism when it or its clients behave brutally. Many leftists have long asked that the United States base its foreign policy on humanitarian concerns, not cold geopolitics; in Somalia, the United States did that, at least in the rhetorical realm. Activists could perhaps use this departure from the geopolitical norm to pressure the government to adhere to a higher standard. It is the ultimate hypocrisy to go to Somalia to save people from starvation when U.S. policy helped induce that starvation and is inducing it elsewhere, as in Haiti and East Timor. Such a contradiction is a call to action.

> ***"The sheer humanitarian urgency of saving lives should overwhelm the need to cling to the correct line."***

Second, when Shalom argues that Somalia lends respectability to the Pentagon, he assumes that were it not for Somalia, the Pentagon would be trimmed and its conduct altered. This belief seems naive. Because of the way power is arranged in the United States today, the Pentagon may well continue to dominate regardless of Somalia; it is not at a loss for pretexts, and it has the clout to get its way. Shalom and other leftist critics have posited a false alternative.

And yet I've had grave second thoughts about my own position on Somalia. I've cringed as reports have come in of U.S. soldiers killing unarmed Somali youths. I've cringed as reports have come in of U.S. soldiers disrupting food distribution in the process of trying to disarm the Somalis. I fear that the U.S. effort may end up further distorting the Somali economy, making it more dependent on emergency relief and less self-reliant. And I dread the ever-present prospect of waking up one day to hear that the U.S. military has gone on the offensive, killing hundreds of Somalis whom the United States was ostensibly trying to save.

Do these doubts, then, concede the argument? I don't think so. When faced with suffering on a biblical scale, as with Somalia in 1992, the world community had an obligation to respond. The United Nations unfortunately was not up to the task, so it fell to the United States, with all its complicit history and imperialistic motives correctly noted, to intercede. Inaction was unjustifiable. And diplomacy was short on time.

Some on the left contend that the United States should have allowed diplomatic efforts to continue for a longer period; ironically, some of these same critics blame the U.S. military for waiting a week to get the food to the crisis centers once the intervention began. But you can't blame the United States for not acting quickly enough when you didn't want it to act at all or when you wanted it to take a slower route.

> ***"Inaction was unjustifiable. And diplomacy was short on time."***

As a person of the left, and as a member of the world community, I was and still am willing to take a chance that the U.S. effort in Somalia will have done more good than harm. To me, the risks of not intervening outweighed the risks of intervening. Not intervening would have spelled certain and imminent death for an intolerable number of people. Intervening at least raised the possibility of saving lives on a grand scale. The United States may end up botching the effort, but that is not certain. Starvation was certain.

The Somalia case brings up several basic questions: When, if ever, is sovereignty not sacrosanct? When, if ever, is force justified? When, if ever, should an outside power intervene? Who should do the intervening?

Reluctantly, I am not a pacifist. For years, I've read and listened to and mulled over the arguments of my pacifist colleagues, and I just don't find them persuasive. Nonviolent resistance would not have stopped Hitler or [Cambodia's] Pol Pot, and letting Hitler and Pol Pot continue their massacres would have been unbearable. At some point, in some cases, force is necessary to beat back a ruler willing to use all measures of brutality.

When a government is committing genocide against its own people—as Hitler and Pol Pot did—it seems callous and arbitrary to cling to notions of sovereignty. Human beings come before flags, lives before boundaries.

And when wholesale human suffering is occurring as in Somalia, I believe it is again justifiable for outside powers to intervene.

Who Has the Right to Intervene?

But who has the right to intervene? The ideal vehicle is the United Nations—or, more precisely, a more democratically controlled and less bureaucratically ossified United Nations. When one country so violates the norms of the international community, or when human suffering becomes so crushing in one country, it is up to the community as a whole to take action.

In an imperfect way, this is what happened in Somalia. True, the United States used its superior position to demand control of the military action and supply most of the early troops. But for the longest time it was the United Nations seeking a greater U.S. involvement and not the other way around.

And there is a hopeful sign: Under the UN plan, most of the U.S. troops left Somalia [by May 1993] and were replaced by a multinational force—15,000 to 20,000 troops, about 20 percent American—under the control of a Turkish general. Such a force breaks with American policy that has always resisted placing its troops under international command and offers the hope, however faint, that the United Nations will begin to assume the role it was originally heralded to play.

Some on the left are wary of working within the United Nations, viewing it as a puppet of the U.S. government and the West. There is something to this argument, and that's why the institution needs to give more power to its Third World members. Others on the left view strengthening the military arm of the United Nations as a grave mistake, contending that it will only add more ordnance and combatants to an already-overmilitarized world. Here, too, the argument makes some sense. But what are the alternatives? By not going through the United Nations, we give in either to the most powerful nation or to the most barbaric one, and we cede the argument that there are universal standards of behavior that are worth upholding.

> ***"Human beings come before flags, lives before boundaries."***

We need to envision the world we would like to inhabit, a world without genocide, a world without starvation, a world without torture and rape. And we need to start constructing institutions that can bring this world into being. It is no longer enough to reflexively oppose U.S. actions when those actions may, unwittingly or not, be part of that construction process. And it is no longer enough to reflexively oppose U.S. actions when those actions may directly save thousands of lives.

Editor's note: The UN-sanctioned U.S. mission to Somalia, given the name Operation Restore Hope, began in December 1992 with more than 20,000 U.S. troops. By February 1993, the United States was pressuring other UN members to send troops so that U.S. forces could be brought home. In June 1993, General Cevik Bir of Turkey took over command of the UN forces in Somalia. In October 1993, following the deaths of 18 U.S. soldiers, President Bill Clinton announced that he would send an additional 7,000 U.S. troops to Somalia in order to facilitate the withdrawal of all U.S. forces by March 31, 1994. All U.S. forces were withdrawn by this deadline, at which time a new UN mission in Somalia began.

There Is a Christian Duty to Intervene

by Kenneth R. Himes

About the author: *Kenneth R. Himes, of the Order of Friars Minor, is an associate professor at the Washington Theological Union in Silver Spring, Maryland, and is coauthor of* Fullness of Faith: The Public Significance of Theology.

It has become a commonplace to note that we live in a new context for thinking about international relations. The cold war is over. The bipolar mind-set that saw the world as essentially a contest between two superpowers with allies arrayed behind both the United States and the Soviet Union is no longer helpful for understanding foreign or military policy. For its time, whatever its deficiencies, the bipolar viewpoint was elegant in its simplicity. Now things are a good deal more messy, as any suitable theory of international relations must encompass a variety of important actors, pose a new slate of concerns and offer a more complicated notion of power than in the past.

The Weakening of "Sovereignty"

Among the most dramatic shifts in the way we must reflect upon the global situation is the weakening of one of the very pillars of Western political theory—namely, the presumption of state sovereignty. The idea that a state has absolute sovereignty within a set of territorial borders has been a given for centuries. This idea was the basis for arguments against intervention in the internal affairs of a nation-state. Indeed, the United Nations Charter makes state sovereignty a near absolute. Many commentators would remove the word "near" from that statement. But this viewpoint and the framework it provided for foreign policy have come under attack from several sources.

It is not difficult to list the various "pressure points" impinging on the traditional view of state sovereignty. Certainly the entire nuclear age has challenged the idea of sovereignty, since no nation today is capable of insulating its civilian population from the threat of nuclear destruction. And while the term "global

From Kenneth R. Himes, "Just War, Pacificism, and Humanitarian Intervention," *America*, August 14, 1993. Reprinted with the author's permission.

marketplace" may be a bit hyperbolic, it still is at least a half-truth. Increasingly, it is the case that capital, products, consumption, jobs and even labor do not respect territorial boundaries. Economic interdependence is growing, and no nation can isolate itself from other nations on this level. In the past, a national government would have understood its task to be, at the minimum, protection of its citizenry from attack as well as protection of its domestic economy from manipulation by outside forces. That it is no longer possible to accomplish these fundamental tasks demonstrates the shift in the role of the nation-state.

"Certainly the entire nuclear age has challenged the idea of sovereignty."

More recently, with the collapse of the "logic of the blocs," there has been increasing pressure on the state from above and below. From below, we find the rise of ethnic groups seeking self-determination and wishing to break away from existing political entities. In these cases the nation-state appears too large to accommodate the desires of people. From above, we see new alliances on regional bases—for example, the developing Common Market in Europe and the movement to a North American free-trade zone. Such developments illustrate that in important ways the nation-state is too small to match the ambitions of its people. Another pressure from above on state sovereignty comes from transnational problems such as global population or pollution of the oceans. No nation can address these questions unilaterally. There are also transnational actors—corporations, religious institutions, social movements—that claim the loyalties of people and present both opportunities and problems to nation-states.

The Just War Tradition

One of the most significant of the transnational actors is the human rights movement, composed of formal and informal organizations as well as individuals motivated by a powerful vision of human dignity and rights. In the name of human rights a state's sovereignty may be challenged, as when the Kurds are provided a protected enclave within the state borders of Iraq.

But the most dramatic example of how the idea of state sovereignty is weakening may be seen in calls by governments for humanitarian intervention involving armed force within the territory of another nation. What would have been unthinkable as a topic to put before the United Nations only a few years ago is now regularly discussed in U.N. Security Council meetings. This shift in thinking about state sovereignty provides a new context for the theory of the just war. The just war tradition has always been dynamic and open to revision and refinement. Dramatic political change demands creative response from those who espouse some version of this tradition as a helpful politico-ethical framework for analyzing international relations.

Pope Pius XII (1939–1958) provided an example of the continuing reflection process that occurs within the just war tradition. His reduction of the criterion of "just cause" to "national defense against aggression" was encouraged by the papacy's sense that modern warfare [during World War II] was so costly in human life and suffering that other arguments for "just cause" were no longer persuasive. Changes in the nature of military weaponry and the conduct of war provoked this development in just war theory, but a fundamental part of the political context for the just war continued—that is, state sovereignty.

Today, the political change extends beyond what Pius XII could have foreseen. An argument for a just war based on national defense accepts the presumption of state sovereignty, a presumption that of late has been losing its hold on the political imagination of many, especially among Catholics in the peace movement. By contrast, arguments for just war based on humanitarian intervention presume a human rights theory that exercises increasing power over the political imagination of Catholics, especially those conversant with the social teachings of the church. What one finds, then, is that a traditional presumption that justified war is eroding even though there is nothing yet to replace a nation's right to self-defense. At the same time a new argument for justified use of armed force, humanitarian intervention, is gaining credence. . . .

Pacifism and Nonviolence

No development has been more significant for the Catholic Church's examination of war than the legitimation of pacifism by Vatican II. [Vatican II was an ecumenical council held in four sessions between 1962 and 1965 to update Catholic teachings.] But pacifism, like the just war tradition, is not uniform. There are theories within each tradition, and the debates can be as intense within the traditions as between them. One of the striking aspects of the discussion about humanitarian intervention is that certain pacifists are sounding like just war theorists, and vice versa. This is not surprising once the pluralism within these two traditions is understood.

Properly understood, pacifism is not the same as nonviolence. The claim of nonviolence embraces all relationships—personal, interpersonal, societal and international. The truly nonviolent person can be no more comfortable with a police officer carrying weapons than he or she is with a soldier bearing arms. Pacifism is a subspecies of nonviolence that rejects the specific form of violence known as war. It is perfectly reasonable, therefore, for a pacifist to engage in an act of personal self-defense by violent force or to assist, through violent means, an innocent third party under attack. Pacifists can even accept the validity of police actions employing violent force. What a pacifist cannot permit is the large-scale violence of war, with its indiscriminate destruction and killing, as well as the culture of militarism bred by the modern state.

"In the name of human rights a state's sovereignty may be challenged."

In other words, not all violence, but the specific form of violence called war, is what must be opposed by pacifists. All adherents of nonviolence are pacifists, but not all pacifists subscribe to nonviolence in all situations. Thus, the question often put to pacifists about whether they would defend a loved one being attacked by a street criminal has always missed the mark. Pacifists can condone controlled and limited uses of violent force without being inconsistent in their opposition to warfare.

Just war adherents may also differ in a variety of ways. In recent decades certain adherents accepted the legitimacy of some wars but never of a nuclear war. Confusingly, members of this group were sometimes called nuclear pacifists, but it is more accurate to think of them as one family within the just war clan. Other disputes within the just war tradition entail differences about the criteria for determining a just war, the weight to be given to each of these criteria, and their interpretation.

Pacifism and Humanitarian Intervention

After these clarifying remarks, it is now possible to analyze the framework of discussion within the Catholic community when the topic of humanitarian intervention arises. If one starts by analyzing the deployment of soldiers in Somalia, it is apparent that there are considerable parallels between this military assignment and police action. Most of the military's work was to provide protection for relief workers and Somalis seeking to enter the camps where aid was available. The relatively few incidents of violence usually involved encounters with snipers and other agents of the social chaos that goes under the name of civil war. In truth, a good number of the alleged combatants in the civil war are brigands and marauders seeking no clear political goal but only personal gain. The intervention achieved a certain restoration of domestic order rather than the destruction of that order which war usually entails. Therefore, it is plausible to argue, as some pacifists have done, that this military action was justifiable precisely because the action had similarities to domestic police activity.

"Not all violence, but the specific form of violence called war, is what must be opposed by pacifists."

In a 1993 issue of *Kerux*, the newsletter of the Metro New York chapter of Pax Christi, there is a report on a discussion, initiated by the National Board, concerning Pax Christi's openness to humanitarian intervention. Many in the New York chapter are unhappy with the board's decision, but that a group like Pax Christi [which advocates nonviolence] would even debate the issue illustrates how human rights theory has complicated assessments of legitimate armed force. People who might be suspicious of war based on defense of state sovereignty now find themselves weighing the idea of military force for the sake of human rights.

There is a similar reaction apparent in the writings of John Paul II. Although the Pope made an explicit statement during the debate on the Gulf War that he was not a pacifist, he was far more skeptical of the war's legitimacy than many other Western observers. In this country his voice was drowned out by the chorus calling for support of the troops. Had John Paul's voice been heard, many American Catholics would have found themselves out of step with the Pope.

"There exist interests which transcend states: they are the interests of the human person, his rights."

Given the general papal denunciation of violence, it is interesting to read John Paul's speech before the diplomatic community in January 1993, the context in this case being former Yugoslavia. Midway through his remarks the Pope urged the international community to be direct in its opposition to "territorial conquest by force" and the "aberration of 'ethnic cleansing.'" He then condemned wars of aggression and, noteworthy considering his audience, denounced "practical indifference" in the face of such aggressive behavior by others as a "culpable omission."

At the end of his speech, the Pope returned to this topic and made his view unmistakably clear. First, he placed the papacy on one side of a debate that has been raging in political philosophy for some time now about whether the state or the individual is the basic unit of analysis in international relations. The papal view is forthright: At "the very heart of international life is not so much states as man. . . . The emergence of the individual is the basis of what is called 'humanitarian law.' There exist interests which transcend states: they are the interests of the human person, his rights." John Paul sides with what can be called the "cosmopolitan" view of international relations rather than the viewpoints of "realism" or "moral statism" held by other commentators. Cosmopolitans stress the rights of the individual person as central, while realists focus on global stability and moral statists see state sovereignty as foundational.

The Duty to Intervene

Following the logic of his premise, John Paul notes that "a new concept has emerged, that of 'humanitarian intervention.'" He distinguishes this from humanitarian assistance, which does not entail violent force, and goes on to state: "Once the possibilities afforded by diplomatic negotiations and the procedures provided for by international agreements and organizations have been put into effect, and, nevertheless, populations are succumbing to the attacks of an unjust aggressor, states no longer have a 'right to indifference.' It seems clear that their duty is to disarm this aggressor, if all other means have proved ineffective."

Striking in Pope John Paul's statement is that 1) he speaks not of a right but of a duty to intervene, and 2) for the Pope it is evident that human rights relativize state sovereignty. Talk about a duty to intervene goes far beyond what is being discussed in the literature of political philosophy or international law. There the debate rages as to whether third parties possess even a right to intervene. But the language of a duty and describing the failure to act on such a duty as a "culpable omission" move the Vatican into a position taken by almost no one else in the debate. Perhaps the language here is that of the prophetic voice underscoring a moral challenge before the international community. Whatever the case, it is not the more cautious and temperate language of political leaders or international jurists.

Human Rights Above Sovereignty

Within Catholic social teaching the state has never been accorded the absolute sovereignty found in commentaries on international law. So the papal view that human rights have preeminence is not novel among Catholic thinkers, but it is a position that others are only beginning to consider seriously. Within the United Nations it was the countries of the so-called third world who most opposed any discussion of intervention. Moving out of the shadow of political colonialism or economic exploitation, these nations feared that acceptance of intervention would lead to the justification of more powerful countries once again dominating the internal affairs of fledgling nations. Since 1987, however, there have been a number of U.N. discussions about such intervention, and the decline of the superpower competition has led to growing consensus within the Security Council that intervention is possible. Indeed, the Council's decision after the Gulf War to establish enclaves for the Kurdish people within Iraq is a strong rejection of any doctrine of absolute sovereignty.

> ***"States no longer have a 'right to indifference.'"***

John Paul recognizes that the international community is venturing into uncharted terrain with the emergence of arguments for humanitarian intervention. At the end of his January 1993 remarks to the diplomatic corps he stated: "The principles of the sovereignty of states and of noninterference in their internal affairs . . . retain all their value." Yet these international norms "cannot constitute a screen behind which torture and murder may be carried out." The Pope acknowledged that "jurists will still of course have to examine this new phenomenon [humanitarian intervention] and refine its contours." In the end, the Pope makes clear that the underlying basis for the Catholic position is human rights, for "the organization of society has no meaning unless the human dimension is made the principal concern, in a world made by man and for man."

Moral Considerations Should Outweigh Political Arguments on Intervention

by Jane Sharp

About the author: *Jane Sharp is a senior research fellow at King's College, and directs the Defense and Security Program at the Institute for Public Policy Research in London.*

"Our silence enables this madness to continue," wrote American lawyer Betsy Midden in the *International Herald Tribune* on January 13, 1993, after visiting Bosnian victims of Serbian violence, deploring that so few people had been willing to speak out against the slaughter. Why has the international community, especially Western democracies, allowed the systematic torture, rape, and murder of Muslims in Bosnia-Hercegovina?

Why Not Bosnia?

If there was a case for intervening with force to "liberate" Kuwait, why was there no case for liberating Bosnia? If the United States could send 30,000 combat troops to escort relief supplies in Somalia, why were U.S. servicemen not part of the U.N. relief effort in Bosnia? If the United States, Britain, and France could bomb Iraq when Saddam Hussein violated the southern air exclusion zone, why did all three powers tolerate daily breaches by Serbia of the U.N.'s "no-fly" zone over Bosnia? Why does the United States so often engage in international conflicts with symbolic gestures that fail to curb the underlying aggression or to punish the obvious aggressors? Who makes the rules, sets the standards, establishes the criteria for military intervention? Do we need a doctrine of "just intervention" to match the doctrine of just war?

Until it decided to act in Somalia, the United States had often cited concerns over the violation of state sovereignty as a bar to intervention for mere "humanitarian" reasons. It would, however, intervene to defend an ally or sphere of in-

Jane Sharp, "The West's Moral Failure." Reprinted, with permission, from the March 1993 *Bulletin of the Atomic Scientists*.

fluence against "outside" aggression (as in Korea and Vietnam)—especially when doing so also maintained free access to vital resources like oil (as in Desert Storm). In 1984 [then] Defense Secretary Caspar Weinberger suggested that five conditions must be met before the United States should intervene: its vital interests must be at stake; political and military objectives must be clearly defined; the operation must be continually monitored and readjusted when required; popular approval must be secured; and, while force must be a last resort, victory must then be the unambiguous goal.

> ***"Who makes the rules, sets the standards, establishes the criteria for military intervention?"***

During the early summer of 1991, when Serbia first invaded Slovenia and Croatia, both of which sought independence from Yugoslavia, President George Bush passed the responsibility for resolving the Yugoslav crisis to the twelve countries of the European Community (EC). In the absence of U.S. leadership, however, the Europeans proved inept and uncertain. A year later, when Yugoslavia had disintegrated into five separate states and Serbian atrocities in Bosnia were reported, President Bush referred to the Bosnian conflict as a mere hiccup.

Even in early January 1993, Bush was still unwilling to intervene in Bosnia. He had, however, sent troops to feed the starving in Somalia, and in two speeches (at Texas A&M University and at [U.S. Military Academy], West Point) he attempted to redefine policy on intervention. In contrast to Weinberger, Bush did not limit the use of force to the protection of vital national interests. He proposed that "military force may not be the best way of safeguarding something vital, while using force might be the best way to protect an interest that qualifies as important but less than vital."

Military, Not Legal, Considerations

Two dominant themes emerged from the many reasons and rationalizations offered in European capitals and in Washington for not intervening in Bosnia: "It's none of our business—this is a civil war and we can't intervene in the domestic affairs of a sovereign state," and, "It would be too difficult militarily—we are not equipped for guerrilla warfare. [Marshal Josip Broz] Tito and his partisans tied the Germans in knots in these mountains in the Second World War."

Was the conflict in Bosnia a civil war? No. The principal aggressor was Serbia, directing proxies in Bosnia after the United States, the European Community, and most of the international community had recognized Bosnia-Hercegovina as an independent state. A Western-led coalition of states had as much right to intervene against Serbian aggression in Bosnia as they did against Iraqi aggression in Kuwait. British legal scholar Christopher Greenwood has said categorically that political and military considerations, not legalities, precluded military measures against the Serbs.

Military intervention would not have been risk free, but it would not have been impossible, either. Those carrying out atrocities against Bosnian Muslims were not Tito's partisans. We do not know how they would have stood up to professional military forces. U.N. peacekeeping forces made little attempt to confront the Serbian aggressors. On the contrary, a report by Thomas O'Brien to the United States Agency for International Development documented that U.N. officers regularly deferred to Serbian authorities in Bosnia, allocated some 23 percent of relief supplies to Serbian warlords, and allowed Serbian commanders to check the ethnicity of convoy drivers.

But suppose that Radovan Karadzic, leader of the Serbs in Bosnia, had been a home-grown Bosnian instead of a carpetbagger from Serbia. Could the West then have justified washing its hands of the atrocities committed against Bosnian Muslims on the grounds that to intervene would violate state sovereignty? On that basis, the West should have tolerated Hitler's killing of Jews as long as they were German Jews. Genocide is wrong whether or not it crosses international borders. There is no justification for passivity and indifference in the face of the systematic killing, torture, and rape of a people because they belong to a religion, race, or nation that has been declared "unclean."

Prevention and Punishment of Genocide

Until World War II, genocide was considered largely a matter of domestic concern and not subject to interference by other states. The Convention on the Prevention and Punishment of the Crime of Genocide, which came into force in 1951, was a response to the wholesale murder of Jews by Nazi Germany. Since then, genocide has been a crime under international law. From Bosnia we learn that systematic rape must also be added to the list of war crimes.

During the Cold War, the principle of non-intervention dominated relations between East and West. Western nations did not interfere in Eastern Europe. With the collapse of the Soviet Union and the Warsaw Pact, the principle of non-intervention is now giving way to one of humanitarian intervention at both the United Nations and at the Conference on Security and Cooperation in Europe (CSCE).

> ***"Political and military considerations, not legalities, precluded military measures against the Serbs."***

And yet there remains the matter of political will. The cause may be just, but the price may be deemed too high. Are fat and complacent Western states willing to risk casualties in support of the human rights of others when their own vital national interests are not at stake?

Western nations obviously have much to lose by military intervention in Bosnia. NATO [North Atlantic Treaty Organization], the European Community, and the European Free Trade Area comprise a security community, the members of which do not even think of settling disputes between them by force. Western governments would prefer to retain current levels of military stability and security and continue to act as though they are insulated from the problems of their eastern neighbors. But this insulation, a legacy of the Cold War, is no longer tenable. In weighing the costs of intervention, governments must also calculate the high costs of inaction. Can any nation that has taken no action to stop the Serbian practice of ethnic cleansing continue to call itself civilized?

The Cold War Is Over

It was plausible to believe during the Cold War that to intervene in Hungary in 1956 or in Czechoslovakia in 1968 would have been imprudent, because it risked a wider war that could go nuclear. The West, therefore, collaborated with the Soviet Union in a policy of mutual deterrence, partly resting on the fear of nuclear war, but more on the acceptance of tacit spheres of influence. The West was insulated from occasional bouts of turbulence in the East by the iron grip of the Soviet Union on its satellites. Although it was an unjust peace it served the interests of global survival.

But intervention in former Yugoslavia no longer carries the risk of nuclear war. Conversely, without Western intervention, the prognosis is for the conflict to eventually engulf the entire Balkan peninsula and risk involvement by the wider community of Muslim nations.

> ***"In weighing the costs of intervention, governments must also calculate the high costs of inaction."***

Western indifference may also encourage land grabbing and ethnic cleansing elsewhere. By allowing the Serbs to profit from their aggression against the Bosnian Muslims, the so-called civilized Western nations have said to potential aggressors, "We no longer respect the Charter of the United Nations or the November 1990 Paris Charter of the CSCE, and we do not take seriously the group and individual human rights laid down in the 1948 Genocide Convention, the 1948 U.N. Universal Declaration of Human Rights, the 1950 European Human Rights Convention, or the 1966 U.N. Covenant on Civil and Political Rights."

In effect, we are morally bankrupt.

Humanitarian Intervention Is Not Effective

by Adam Roberts

About the author: *Adam Roberts is Montague Burton Professor of International Relations and a fellow of Balliol College at Oxford University, England.*

After the euphoria, the hangover. In 1991 and 1992, the United Nations was involved to varying degrees in the initiation of three major operations involving elements of humanitarian intervention—in northern Iraq, the former Yugoslavia and Somalia. The results of these operations expose fundamental flaws in the impulse for and practice of humanitarian intervention, to the extent that the whole concept needs to be reconsidered. The question is not so much the endlessly debated one of whether there ought or ought not to be any right of humanitarian intervention in any circumstances. Rather, it is whether any actual or imaginable presence of foreign military forces is properly described by so anodyne [innocent] a term.

Short-Lived Results

A central problem of the recent cases is that the results of foreign military involvement in the name of humanitarianism do not endure and fail to provide a framework for security. The situation is roughly analogous to what one might expect in the medical field if the focus was largely on the delivery of emergency first aid at the site of major disasters, rather than on long-term treatment. The two approaches, of course, often have to be combined, but in the field of international relations that combination has proved peculiarly difficult.

The first flush of enthusiasm for humanitarian intervention is now having to yield to a more sober appreciation of the difficulties of forceful military involvement in societies torn by deep ethnic, tribal, religious or regional conflicts. What general lessons can be learned from these experiences?

Increasingly, the term "humanitarian intervention" seems a misnomer. It is a form of justification, and one which deserves to be viewed skeptically. It carries

Adam Roberts, "The Road to Hell . . . : A Critique of Humanitarian Intervention," *Harvard International Review*, Fall 1993. Reprinted with the permission of the *Harvard International Review*.

the implication that a military intervention in another country can be humanitarian in four respects: in its original motives, in its stated purposes, in its methods of operation and in its actual results. Recent practice confirms doubts as to whether it can really be humanitarian in all of these ways. There is indeed wisdom in the old saying, "The road to Hell is paved with good intentions."

The Rule of Non-Intervention

"Humanitarian intervention"—the idea that a military intervention within another sovereign state might in certain extreme circumstances be permissible, even without the agreement of the government of that state—has a distinguished lineage in international legal and moral discourse. To use a phrase that recurs in the literature, the circumstances in which such intervention might be justified are those which "shock the conscience of mankind." In other words, intervention might be justifiable as a response to such horrors as systematic attacks by a government on its own people, genocide, widespread starvation or complete failure of government to ensure the most elementary conditions of life.

In the past, the most common objection to advocacy of "humanitarian intervention" has been based on commitment to the rule of non-intervention—that is, the strong consensus against uninvited military incursions into states. Non-intervention makes the world go round. It has not served badly as an ordering principle of international relations and has both practical and moral claims to being taken seriously. It appeals, if in different ways, to both realists and liberals. It provides a clear rule for limiting the uses of force by states and for reducing the risks of war between the armed forces of different states. It acts as a brake on their territorial and imperial ambitions. It involves respect for different societies and their religions, economic systems and political arrangements.

Because non-intervention remains so important a principle, it is not surprising that the idea of "humanitarian intervention" has never been formally accepted in any general legal instrument, but the continued life of humanitarian intervention in international scholarly debate (and, to a lesser extent, in practice) is evidence of the seriousness and perennial character of the issues with which it deals.

The actual observance of the non-intervention rule has been very imperfect. States have violated it on many occasions and for many reasons, including the protection of nationals, the prevention of changes to the balance of power and counter-intervention in response to another state which is deemed to have intervened first. Yet the rule has not collapsed: evidence, perhaps, that a robust rule can outlive its occasional violation.

> ***"Non-intervention . . . has not served badly as an ordering principle of international relations."***

The idea of humanitarian intervention is not necessarily the incorrigible enemy of the general rule of non-intervention. Even the stoutest defender of non-intervention must concede one of its more glaring weaknesses. Can that rule really apply when the situation in a country is so serious that it is an affront to the moral conscience of mankind? What is the ethical or logical foundation of the rule that makes it so rigid, so uncomprehending of the evidence of misery, that it cannot allow for exceptions? One might even say that if a coherent philosophy and practice of humanitarian intervention could be developed, it could have the potential to save the non-intervention rule from its own logical absurdities and occasional inhumanities.

> ***"The main foundations of the non-intervention rule have been concerns about states' acting unilaterally."***

There can be no disputing the sheer force of circumstance which brought about the new practice, and doctrine, of humanitarian intervention. The age-old problem of whether military intervention in another state to protect the lives of its inhabitants can ever be justified became politically sensitive in recent years when harrowing situations, especially when reported on television, led to calls for action and when the UN Security Council, no longer hamstrung by East-West disagreement, was able at last to reach authoritative decisions, giving a degree of legitimacy to interventions that might otherwise have been hotly contested.

Authorization by the UN

Any possibilities of developing a coherent notion of humanitarian intervention involve crucial questions about the authorization of such intervention. The possibility that the society of states as a whole might in some way authorize particular acts of intervention significantly weakens the traditional objection to humanitarian intervention. The issue of authorization looms especially large since the main foundations of the non-intervention rule have been concerns about states' acting unilaterally, pursuing their own interests, dominating other societies and getting into clashes and wars with each other. If an intervention is authorized by an international body and has specific stated purposes, all these concerns begin to dissolve.

In the past half century there has been a particularly strong tendency for a wide range of military interventions to be conducted on a multilateral basis, or at least with multilateral fig-leaves: hence the frequent use of regional organizations to sanctify such interventions as those of the Soviet Union into Czechoslovakia, of Syria into Lebanon or of the United States into Grenada. Now that the UN Security Council is more capable than before of reaching decisions on major matters, it is emerging as the main instrument for sanctifying interventions, including humanitarian ones, and for enunciating their purposes. In this matter the United Nations has obvious advantages over bodies with more limited membership. If intervention were permitted only with UN Security Council authorization, the risks of competitive chaos and insecurity, and of pursuit of unilateral advantage, would be greatly reduced.

The role of the United Nations Security Council is the principal new element in recent acts of intervention. Its decisions giving legitimacy to the use of force have been crucial, but it has not yet been involved in a textbook case, in the sense of authorizing humanitarian intervention against the stated opposition of the government of the target state. In each of the three main cases in which it has used a humanitarian justification for a military involvement— Iraq, the former Yugoslavia and Somalia—the whole question of the consent of the host state has proved to be far more subtle in fact than ever it was in legal theory.

In Iraq, the UN required in the Delphic terms of Resolution 688 of April 5, 1991, that "Iraq allow immediate access by international humanitarian organizations to all those in need of assistance in all parts of Iraq," which was less than a formal authorization of intervention, but was nevertheless of considerable help to the Americans and their coalition partners. The operation has to be seen partly in the special context of post-war actions by victors in the territory of defeated adversaries. Further, there were elements of Iraqi consent in the subsequent presence of UN guards in northern Iraq.

In the former Yugoslavia, although the initial deployment of the United Nations Protection Force (UNPROFOR) in February 1992 was with the consent of the parties to the conflict, successive UN Security Council resolutions were so phrased as to suggest that the UN might actually require the states involved to accept the continued presence of peacekeeping forces with a humanitarian role whether they wanted them or not, and there were also suggestions in these resolutions that if UNPROFOR and its humanitarian activities were obstructed, further measures not based on the consent of the parties would be taken to deliver humanitarian assistance.

"Action must be premised upon a legal determination of the existence of a threat to international peace and security."

In Somalia, the US-led invasion of December 9, 1992 had the full blessing of UN Resolution 794—the first resolution to authorize explicitly a massive military intervention by member states within a country without an invitation from the government. However, there was no Somali government to give or refuse consent, so the UN-authorized intervention by the Unified Task Force in December 1992, and its continuation by the United Nations Operation in Somalia II in May 1993, was hardly a classical case of humanitarian intervention.

Intervention and the UN Charter

Even if these are not textbook cases, they all contain very strong elements of humanitarian intervention. They also raise questions about the consistency and seriousness of recent UN practice.

The first question has to do with the terms of the UN Charter. It is sometimes suggested that the Security Council is a structurally flawed body when it comes to considering the matter of humanitarian intervention, because under the Charter and its own past practices it cannot authorize a military action purely on the grounds of the existence of grave human rights violations. In order to act under Chapter VII of the Charter, as it did in each of these cases, the Security Council's action must be premised upon a legal determination of the existence of a threat to international peace and security. The contrast between the legal and the real grounds of action is clearest in Resolution 794 of December 3, 1992, on Somalia. It mentions "a threat to international peace and security" once, almost ritualistically, as if to get over a necessary legal hurdle; it mentions the word "humanitarian" no less than eighteen times—a dismal record for a UN Security Council resolution, but an indication of the reasoning and intentions behind the authorization of intervention. In general, it would be hard to argue that the need to prove a threat to international peace and security has seriously distorted UN practice in the matter of humanitarian intervention. Once a consensus has emerged that action is warranted (whether on humanitarian or other grounds), this requirement has not proved a major obstacle.

"It is extremely hard to divine anything like a doctrine from so variegated a set of cases and approaches."

Double Standards

A second ground for doubt about recent UN practice has to do with selectivity and so-called "double standards." Undoubtedly, the conscience of mankind was shocked by the plight of Iraqi Kurds, the vicious fighting and sieges in the former Yugoslavia, and the starvation in Somalia. But there have been other perhaps equally shocking situations in the past few decades. The fact that mass slaughter in Cambodia, shootings in Beijing, ruthless dictatorship in Myanmar (Burma) or catastrophe in Sudan did not lead to humanitarian interventions suggests that some other factors are involved in decision-making.

Humanitarian intervention seems for the most part to be confined to cases in which there has been extensive television coverage, where there is some particular interest in intervention, and in which there is not likely to be dissent among powers or massive military opposition. In short, it may largely be confined to highly publicized situations of chaos and disintegration, Somalia and Yugoslavia being prime examples. It will not be an answer to the often more serious problem of the over-powerful and brutal state. True, the operation in northern Iraq in 1991 was an intervention in a state with an all-too-powerful government, but that was in the exceptional circumstance of a state recently defeated in war, and about which the victors felt an unusually high degree of responsibility, not least because of the US encouragement to the people of Iraq to engage in an ill-starred and brutally suppressed rebellion.

Overall, the practice of the Security Council does suggest a high degree of selectivity about the situations in which humanitarian intervention might be authorized—and the selectivity involves many factors other than the human rights plight of the people whom an intervention might be intended to assist. This is the exact equivalent of the Security Council's familiar selectivity in certain other spheres, such as in the question of which invaded states it assists with forceful measures. The same defense can be made of Security Council practice in both cases: that prudence is not a bad guide to action, and it is better to uphold basic principles selectively than not at all.

Absence of a Doctrine

A third problem with recent UN practice involving elements of humanitarian intervention is that it is extremely hard to divine anything like a doctrine from so variegated a set of cases and approaches. Security Council resolutions have moved the matter forward inch by inch, in a thoroughly pragmatic way. There are plenty of references to exceptional circumstances, but no general defense of humanitarian intervention. When the Security Council passed Resolution 794 of December 3, 1992, authorizing Operation Restore Hope in Somalia, the following wording was put at the beginning of the preamble at the express wish of African states: "Recognizing the unique character of the present situation in Somalia and mindful of its deteriorating, complex and extraordinary nature, requiring an immediate and exceptional response." In other words, they did not want the invasion of Somalia to be viewed as a precedent for invasions of other sovereign states.

The real difficulties in the contemporary practice of humanitarian intervention have to do with its uncertainty of purpose and its questionable consequences. In these matters, the very factor which led to the new practice of humanitarian intervention—namely, the possibility of agreement in the Security Council—has also contributed to the difficulties regarding purposes and methods of operation. The Security Council is better at agreeing upon formulae than it is at clear strategic direction of an operation.

> ***"The repeated emphasis on the word 'humanitarian' has been a natural corollary of the complete absence of a serious long-term policy."***

What on earth does the word "humanitarian" mean, and does it accurately describe anything beyond the original supposed motive of an action? How does such a motive translate into actual policies to transform a situation? Does it make sense to call an intervention in a country "humanitarian" when the troops involved may have to fight and kill those who, for whatever reasons, seek to obstruct them? Or when the troops involved fail to provide what the inhabitants most desperately need—especially security?

In all the recent cases involving humanitarian intervention, the repeated emphasis on the word "humanitarian" has been a natural corollary of the complete absence of a serious long-term policy in respect of the target country. It reflects the natural desire to do *something* in the face of disaster, and a tendency to forget that in all these cases the disaster has been man-made and requires changes in institutions, even sometimes in the structure of states and their boundaries. The absence of any precise idea as to what kind of state or political structures might resolve the crisis results in the fudge-outcome of endless repetition of the word "humanitarian," with which no one wants to quarrel.

Vague Goals

The vague and incomplete aims of recent cases are striking. In northern Iraq, there has been ambiguity about the extent to which Kurdish autonomy is or is not supported. In former Yugoslavia, the aims of UNPROFOR have varied from place to place and from time to time but have been widely viewed by the inhabitants as inadequate. In Somalia, the mandates of the forces intervening under UN auspices have never been clear on the key matters of who is supposed to be in charge in Somalia, and what is supposed to be done about the weapons and warfare of the clans and warlords. In all these cases, there are understandable reasons for the vagueness of aims. What is deplorable, though, is the pretense that, in the absence of serious long-term purpose, it suffices to call an action "humanitarian."

"While [humanitarian intervention] has undoubtedly saved many lives, there have been serious defects."

The mixed character of the outcome of recent humanitarian intervention cases reflects their unclear goals. Only in the first of the recent cases, Operation Provide Comfort in northern Iraq, have the results shown signs of enduring; and even there, such modest security for the Kurds as has been achieved is under constant threat, with great apprehension about whether Saddam Hussein's government and armed forces can be kept indefinitely from wreaking vengeance in the region.

A further worry about northern Iraq is that it provides some evidence in support of the proposition that intervention is a step onto a slippery slope, reducing the inhibitions against further interventions: from August 1991 onwards, in a purely unilateral move, Turkish forces launched attacks in northern Iraq against their foes in the Kurdish Workers' Party; similarly, in 1993 Iran attacked some targets in northern Iraq.

In the former Yugoslavia, UNPROFOR has fulfilled at least some humanitarian purposes, but it has conspicuously failed to actually protect the inhabitants—at least in Bosnia. To the extent that UN action in Yugoslavia can be considered a case of humanitarian intervention, it is one which cruelly exposes the limitations of the idea.

In Somalia, the follow-up to Operation Restore Hope of December 1992 has been sadly reminiscent of colonial policing, and deserves the name Operation Abandon Hope. The words of the UN military spokesman in Mogadishu on September 10, 1993, the day after yet another incident in which UN troops had killed a number of civilians, are an appropriate epitaph for a short-sighted optimism about humanitarian intervention: "Everyone on the ground in that vicinity was a combatant, because they meant to do us harm." A strong risk is emerging of a UN involvement's ending in a unique manner, with a peacekeeping operation being forced to an inglorious conclusion by troop-contributing states' withdrawing their contingents.

Problems and Defects

Recent practice involving elements of humanitarian intervention has reflected real and urgent problems. It has also introduced innovative features, of which the most significant is the emphasis on the UN Security Council as the authorizing body. While it has undoubtedly saved many lives, there have been serious defects.

1. In the current state of international society, there is absolutely no possibility of securing general agreement among states about the legitimacy of humanitarian intervention. It will, and perhaps should, remain in a legal penumbra: something which may occasionally be approved by the Security Council or by other bodies, may reluctantly be tolerated by states, but cannot be given a sort of generic advance legitimation—not only because it involves breaking a valued norm, but also because it would be impossible to spell out in advance the circumstances in which it might conceivably be justified.
2. It is not enough to call an intervention "humanitarian." It has to be based on well-considered policies on a range of issues which are likely to arise. In fractured societies, it may need to take on governmental functions.
3. The claim that an intervention by one's own forces is "humanitarian"—the provision of assistance to unfortunate peoples incapable of providing for themselves—appeals too easily to the ethnocentrism that lurks in all of us. In particular it appeals to a streak of unilateral universalism—a belief that certain truths are not only self-evident but also that they should be actively applied abroad—which is a hardy perennial element of the American worldview and is not entirely lacking in that of others, including the British.
4. Any intervention is liable, sooner or later, to provoke local opposition. Even humanitarian assistance can provoke strong local resentment, especially if the very necessity for its presence cruelly exposes failings in the target society, or if the forces involved are substantially ignorant of, or arrogant toward, local forces and customs with which they have no long-term relationship.
5. A multilateral intervention, authorized by the Security Council, is especially at risk in several respects. These derive partly from inevitable features of the way the UN does its collective business: compromise, inertia and avoidance of difficult issues. In this sense, the end of collectivism in the Soviet empire has had the paradoxical effect of encouraging its applica-

> tion, faults and all, to the field of international relations. There may be a lack of clear strategic direction in any operation, a lack of knowledge of the country and its languages and a lack of any deep commitment or sense of responsibility on the part of troop-contributing states. In the absence of these qualities, an operation may be characterized primarily by a sense of moral rectitude—of operating, on behalf of the UN, on a higher plane than the local forces. This mix of factors quickly transforms itself into arrogance, anger, bathos and despair. In the absence of a convincing public role, private interests take over. What begins as humanitarian intervention may well end in humiliating exit.

The growing disillusion with UN-authorized interventions, including those initiated in the name of humanitarianism, was reflected in President Clinton's address to the UN General Assembly on September 27, 1993. He was right to stress that there will have to be a more cautious approach and a clearer definition of the goals and purposes of UN actions. However, it may be salutary to remember that all recent actions under UN auspices have been launched with the approval of the US and other governments. Any faults in recent practice are not faults of the UN alone, but also of its leading member states and their foreign policy decision-making processes. The whole idea of humanitarian intervention needs to be rethought and indeed renamed, not only in New York, but also in national capitals.

Humanitarian Intervention Is Problematic

by Alex de Waal and Rakiya Omaar

About the authors: *Alex de Waal and Rakiya Omaar are codirectors of Africa Rights, a human rights organization based in London.*

"Humanitarian intervention," the violation of a nation-state's sovereignty for the purpose of protecting human life from government repression or famine or civil breakdown, is an old concept that has been given a new lease on life with the end of the Cold War. It is [as of March 1994] being practiced in Somalia and parts of Iraq, and has been discussed, with varying degrees of seriousness, with regard to Bosnia, Angola, Mozambique, Liberia, Zaire, Sudan and Haiti.

The Roots of National Sovereignty

The concept of national sovereignty has long been the chief legal and political obstacle to military intervention in pursuit of humanitarian objectives. This principle of sovereignty was established in modern times with the Treaty of Westphalia of 1648, which brought an end to the Thirty Years' War [a conflict between Catholics and Protestants that became a major-power land grab] and a century of destructive religious conflict in Europe. Under the original formulation of this principle, the religion of the ruler was to be the religion of his or her subjects: dissent was a privilege, not a right, and appeal to any authority higher than the ruler (such as the Pope) was not permitted. The benefit of the principle of sovereignty, and its corollary of non-interference in the affairs of another state, was the end to confessional wars [wars between religious denominations]. The negative result was the growth of absolutist government: sovereignty was located in the person of the ruler. The idea that sovereignty resides in a people rather than a ruler was a product of 19th-century romantic nationalism, put into practice by leaders such as [Germany's] Bismarck, [Italy's] Garibaldi and Victor Emmanuel [also of Italy].

"Can Military Intervention Be 'Humanitarian'?" by Alex de Waal and Rakiya Omaar, *Middle East Report* (pp. 3-8), no. 187/188, March/June 1994. Reprinted by permission of MERIP/*Middle East Report*, 1500 Massachusetts Ave. NW, #119, Washington, DC 20005.

One of the sovereign rights accorded to a ruler was the right to declare war. The principle of sovereignty was applied by and for the powerful states (not, for instance, on behalf of Poland) and was never extended to territories and societies outside Europe. African and Asian nations (not nation-states) were invaded and conquered, sometimes in the name of civilization and humanitarianism. With the spread of the nation-state system to the world beyond Europe and North America, the principle of national sovereignty was extended as well.

"The underlying rationale [behind formation of the UN] was that respect for human rights would be a check on arbitrary power."

In the recent period, the behavior of the Nazi regime in Germany posed a great challenge to the notion of national sovereignty because the principle of non-interference allowed practices which became genocidal. It was only when the Third Reich invaded other countries, submitted their populations to appalling abuses, and threatened to dominate Europe that a coalition of states emerged to confront and defeat the Nazis. The contemporary debates around intervention in Bosnia and even in Iraq reflect the same sorts of hesitations to intervene when the main issue is a regime's treatment of its own subjects.

The United Nations (UN) was founded following the defeat of Germany and Japan, and one of its guiding principles was linking respect for human rights with world peace. This link was jettisoned, in practice, with the Cold War, but it informed the Universal Declaration of Human Rights [1948] and similar international instruments. The underlying rationale was that respect for human rights would be a check on arbitrary power, thereby allowing for the preservation of the principle of sovereignty and non-interference. The UN envisioned that sovereignty would be exercised by governments on *behalf* of the people, more or less democratically.

Sovereignty thus became the cornerstone of human rights legislation. Starting with the Universal Declaration of Human Rights, that legislation was binding on sovereign governments in their relations with their people. Sovereignty lost some of its absolute power to the extent that the UN was seen to reflect the community of nations and, as such, a higher authority.

Humanitarian Justifications for Military Intervention

Customary international law has always recognized a principle of military intervention on humanitarian grounds. The classic examples of 19th-century military "humanitarian intervention" occurred when Britain, France and Russia cited persecution of Christians in Muslim-ruled territories of the Ottoman Empire. Britain intervened in Greece in 1830; France sent a military expedition to Syria and Lebanon in 1860; Britain sent troops to Crete in 1866. The motives of European rulers were influenced by public opinion at home, but strategic interests also played a crucial role. The European occupation of Africa was spurred to a significant extent by pressure from Christian missionary societies to suppress the slave trade and idolatry, and to spread Christianity and "civilization." The philanthropic imperialism with which the European powers entered Africa was regarded as benign at the time, but history allows us to take a more skeptical view with regard to the interests at stake.

Nonetheless, the theoretical and legal debate was sophisticated. In a formulation that has rarely been bettered, W.V. Harcourt, writing in the mid-19th century, described intervention as "a high and summary procedure which may sometimes snatch a remedy beyond the reach of law. . . . [I]n the case of intervention as that of revolution, its essence is illegality, and its justification is its success."

European confidence in its "civilizing mission" was severely tested by the experience of fascism, beginning with the Italian invasion of Ethiopia in 1935. The alleged abuses suffered by ethnic Germans were cited as a reason for the Nazi invasion of Czechoslovakia [in 1939]. The UN Charter was therefore drawn up in the context of extreme skepticism about "humanitarian" justifications for intervention. The Charter expressly prohibited the use of force, or threats of the use of force, by states except in self-defense. No article of the Charter, nor subsequent international legal instrument, makes reference to the use of force for humanitarian purposes.

"Few if any cases of military [humanitarian] intervention . . . come close to the ideal."

Critics of military humanitarian intervention argue that this is no accident; that the doctrine of humanitarian intervention in customary law was so abused that it had become worthless. Advocates argue that the UN Charter is designed to restrict the use of force to self-defense *and* collective action in support of peace and human rights. The use or threat of force in pursuit of humanitarian goals, when sanctioned by the UN, is by this interpretation within the spirit of the Charter.

Over the last 40 years, a number of governments have justified unilateral military action with reference to the customary law of military humanitarian intervention in one form or another. Without exception, the international community has refused to recognize these actions as legitimate. Clear instances are Vietnam's invasion of Cambodia and Tanzania's invasion of Uganda, both in 1979. Related examples of military action ostensibly taken in defense of foreign nationals in the countries concerned include the US invasion of the Dominican Republic and the US-Belgian action in the Congo, both in 1964. In all these cases, the absence of UN sanction of the military action has been of paramount importance in the wider refusal to condone the actions as true cases of humanitarian intervention.

The Revival of Intervention

Military humanitarian intervention has [in the 1990s] undergone a revival in circumstances where national sovereignty has manifestly failed to serve the citizens of a given state. Recent instances (Iraqi Kurdistan and Somalia) have been undertaken under the auspices of the UN. Intervention in Bosnia has been considered under a similar mandate.

If an abusive government such as Iraq or Sudan cites "sovereignty" to defend actions involving mass violations of human rights (or, *in extremis*, genocide), then it is clearly failing to exercise that power on behalf of the people to whom it is supposed to be accountable. When the US-led coalition states occupied part of the Kurdish area of northern Iraq, they were violating only the very debased form of sovereignty exercised by the Iraqi government.

UN blessing for such military actions has been crucially important, as is the fact that this endorsement be seen as the outcome of a genuine international consensus, and not the outcome of manipulation by one or more powerful countries. In fact, however, the UN is increasingly seen as a tool of the US. In Somalia, the international forces were routinely referred to as "the Americans" by both Somalis and foreigners. This confusion is dangerous. If UN resolutions, and even UN instruments such as the Universal Declaration of Human Rights, are no longer seen to represent the collective will of the community of nations but rather the foreign policy concerns of Western states, sovereignty will again become a more plausible defense by abusive governments. It is no accident that the government of Sudan was the most outspoken opponent of US intervention in Somalia.

The legal status of military humanitarian intervention is thus problematic. There is an ideal form of such intervention that few would object to: when a governing power is so tyrannous that its crimes can be remedied only by external intervention, and the world community is united in demanding such action. The problem is that few if any cases of military intervention which cite this doctrine come close to the ideal.

Intervention in Practice

Humanitarian intervention can, in fact, take a variety of forms: material assistance (through relief aid), sanctions (coercive, non-military pressure to end abusive practices) and, finally, the dispatch of military forces to remedy a human disaster.

Intervention in the form of material relief is difficult and rarely done well. This fact is obscured by the uncritical publicity given to the efforts of relief organizations. Assistance given for the best motives can have counterproductive consequences. For example, generous aid to help refugees, just like other forms of aid, can be used to prop up an authoritarian government or to enrich elites. The list of major recipients of US aid in sub-Saharan Africa—Sudan, Zaire, Liberia, Ethiopia and Kenya, with Somalia receiving the highest amount per capita—scarcely testifies

"Food aid has fed wars in Africa wherever it has gone."

to success in promoting stability or long-term economic development.

In situations of conflict, assistance is even more problematic since it is likely to have strategic military significance. The large-scale provision of aid to Ethiopia in the mid-1980s helped to make possible counterinsurgency campaigns that were deeply damaging to the rural poor. Food aid has fed wars in Africa wherever it has gone. Both sides in most conflicts feed their armies, at least in part, from food aid, and armies use food to attract civilian populations to areas they control. The presence of Western relief agencies can give spurious humanitarian credentials to military operations designed to displace and impoverish rural communities.

"Many conventional interventions—sanctions are a case in point—actually contribute to human suffering."

Where relief programs in wars have been successful, they have been implemented in concert with attempts to address the strategic context as well. In 1989, Operation Lifeline played a key role in restoring a degree of normality to southern Sudan, devastated by war and famine. There was a simultaneous ceasefire brought about by internal political processes in Sudan. The ceasefire made it possible for rural people to return home, plant crops and herd their animals in confidence that they would not be attacked. Trade and labor migration also became possible. The economic benefit of these activities was far greater than the provision of relief, though the latter received much more international publicity. . . .

Military Intervention

The third level of humanitarian intervention—the use of military force in violation of sovereignty and in pursuit of humanitarian goals—is fraught with problems. It is never "clean" nor quick. For these reasons, consideration of military humanitarian intervention should be subject to rigorous preconditions which have rarely if ever been met in practice.

- *Military intervention, if acceptable at all, should be a last resort.* Where military intervention is contemplated or implemented, there has always been a history of inept or damaging diplomacy and peacekeeping, and inadequate or incompetent relief programs by the international community. Alternatives, if tried, rarely have been tried properly. In every case in which military intervention has been tried or is contemplated, observers with detailed knowledge of the situation can point to missed opportunities and serious blunders.

  Mean-spirited refugee policies often underlie crises that military intervention is supposed to resolve. The unwillingness of Turkey to host Iraqi Kurdish refugees prompted the crisis that led to military intervention in northern Iraq [in 1991]. Had Turkey responded as did Iran, with hospitality and a well-managed relief program, massive human suffering could have been averted. Similarly, US unwillingness to receive Haitian boat people is a key factor in US policy towards Haiti. The claim that "all else has failed" should therefore always be treated with skepticism. The conventional routes are always open, but they are often slow and fraught with complications. Diplomacy of this kind may appear a luxury when there is an urgent humanitarian crisis, but may in the long run be the most effective international response.

- *There must be an accurate and independent evaluation of the scale and nature of humanitarian needs.* In Africa, humanitarian crises are rarely as severe as the relief agencies and media make out. In the Sahel [the southern Sahara] in the early 1970s, demographic investigations show that at most 100,000 people died; contemporary press reports put the figure in the millions. In Ethiopia in 1984–85, the predicted death toll ranged as high as six million; most relief agencies claimed that one to two million died, but the scanty mortality figures available put the toll at probably about 500,000. Those in the relief business are familiar with such exaggeration, but it has always been considered bad taste to draw attention to it, for fear of sounding callous.

In practice, it is the media's assessment of the severity of a crisis that prompts action. Given the wildly inaccurate diagnoses of the severity of famines or refugee crises common in the media, this is deeply disturbing. Reporters and editors must pay much more attention to the reliability of their assessments of disasters.

"The claim that 'all else has failed' should . . . always be treated with skepticism."

It is important to accurately calibrate humanitarian emergencies for planning an appropriate response. If it had been true, as the UN claimed, that two million faced death by starvation in Somalia in December 1992, a military occupation capable of responding to such need would have been unobjectionable. The reality did not warrant the degree of panic displayed and manipulated. Relief agencies repeatedly confuse the efficiency of their own operations with the degree to which famine is being overcome. It is quite possible for relief to become more difficult just as a harvest is gathered in and the famine comes to an end. This is indeed what was happening in Somalia at the end of 1992.

This is not an argument for universal skepticism about impending disasters, but accurate intelligence is not a luxury. It is vital for effective emergency relief operations.

Can the Military Do the Job?

- *The most important question concerning intervention is: can military forces do the job?* This covers several distinct questions. The first is whether the forces can remain militarily intact, sustaining a low, politically acceptable level of casualties. Most modern military forces are equipped for and trained to fight high-technology wars with the aim of securing a quick victory. Events in Somalia have demonstrated the inappropriateness of such equipment and training for humanitarian missions. Humanitarian intervention demands a different set of military skills. It is akin to counterinsurgency. The very few successful counterinsurgency campaigns—for example, the French in Morocco in 1910–25 and the British in Malaya in the 1950s—were necessarily comprehensive and constructive. They stressed extreme patience, a high level of confidence between troops and people, and a military strategy that was an intrinsic part of an overall political and economic plan. At the time these two colonial campaigns were waged, furthermore, it was politically acceptable for intervening forces to sustain a relatively high level of casualties. Military commanders on peacekeeping missions almost always feel unduly constrained by the rules of engagement which, for instance, prevent them from firing first. On the other hand, an aggressive and insensitive force can quickly alienate local people, as happened in Somalia. Radical changes in military doctrine and training will be needed if armies are to carry out humanitarian tasks. But the demands made upon Western armies by politicians and constituents at home for quick fixes and low casualties make the required changes difficult.

Military Agenda vs. Civil Society

A separate question is whether the military can accomplish the tasks at hand. Military assistance can help with relief logistics. There is a tendency to assume that escorting relief convoys is an end in itself. But food assistance is invariably a relatively small factor in alleviating the hardship and death caused by famine. Most people die from epidemic disease, hence public health programs are the single most important factor in saving lives. Concentrating people in protected zones without adequate public health facilities inevitably facilitates the spread of communicable diseases and increases death rates. Moreover, people's self-help efforts are cumulatively more important than external aid. Undermining self-reliance is disastrous under any conditions; enabling people to carry out economic activities is by far the most effective form of relief. If the troops confine themselves to protecting relief convoys and creating safe distribution zones, they may actually do more harm than good.

> ***"Humanitarian crises are rarely as severe as the relief agencies and media make out."***

Military intervention has its own logic. The troops may go in because relief agencies call for them, but once there they follow commands from military structures, not relief agencies. Their operations are dictated by military strategy, which puts the security of military personnel as the first priority. This means that the troops will move slowly, with their own massive logistical backup. In Somalia, the early weeks of the intervention diverted transport resources and port space from the relief effort. In Bosnia, security of UN forces has often proved the paramount concern, and risks to European ground forces the critical factor militating against US air strikes. If the threat is in the form of guerrilla insurgency, commanders will adopt counterinsurgency "safe zones" which oblige people to abandon homes and farms and congregate in camps in order to receive relief. The troops may fulfill a narrow humanitarian mandate, but only at the expense of creating larger problems. Relief agencies must realize that military intervention does not make the job of fighting famine any easier; it merely makes it different.

"Radical changes in military doctrine and training will be needed if armies are to carry out humanitarian tasks."

- *Military intervention does not necessarily address the strategic context of a disaster.* The logic of military occupation and the demands of peacemaking and reconstructing a society are very difficult to reconcile. Foreign military commanders deal with local military commanders. This is their training and the requirement for protecting their troops. Intervention may thereby confer on local commanders a degree of legitimacy that is, in political or human rights terms, unwarranted. The alternative to negotiating with warlords is fighting, defeating and disarming them, and then creating a civilian administration under the protection of the intervention forces. Fighting a war of this sort is likely to be politically unacceptable to the international community and the countries sending the troops.

Is there a middle way? Can civil initiatives be nurtured under the umbrella of an intervention force, which keeps the warlords at bay in the meantime? The problem is that while the interventionary forces are there, they constitute the major factor in the political equation. When they are removed, the premises of negotiations change. Civil structures built up by an interventionary force are unlikely to survive the withdrawal of that force. Military intervention does not solve diplomatic problems; it merely changes the diplomatic agenda.

Neutrality and Accountability

- *Intervening military forces should strive for neutrality, and must be accountable.* The case for military intervention is always made on the basis of the failure of diplomatic interventions. The governments that send troops invariably have sorry records on relief and diplomacy. The UN may be just as bad. As a result, the intervening forces are already a party to the tragedy when they arrive. It is a delusion to think they are neutral or above the fray. Under all circumstances, intervening forces should be accountable. An independent body, consisting of representatives of the international and local community, should monitor the neutrality of and respect for human rights by the intervention forces. This body should work in the public realm and have the power to follow up complaints. Intervening forces should respect the Geneva Conventions and other laws of war. Indeed, propagating knowledge about international humanitarian law should be one of their tasks. In Somalia, the UN justified violations of the Geneva Conventions by claiming that its authority stemmed solely from the Security Council resolution authorizing them to take "all necessary measures" to capture or punish General Muhammad Farah Aideed. Putting international forces above the Geneva Conventions is an extremely dangerous precedent that must be challenged.

The entry of international military forces represents a failure of the international community's earlier efforts. The UN's standing is lowest precisely where it matters most, where it has been most needed and has bungled the job. One reason for the UN Secretariat's support for intervention in Somalia was to cover its previous shameful record. The organization is now widely reviled by Bosnians and held in contempt by Cambodians and Iraqis. The UN has been unwilling to submit itself to independent or public scrutiny. A necessary component of any military intervention should be a thorough, public and independent examination of what went wrong beforehand.

"Civil structures built up by an interventionary force are unlikely to survive the withdrawal of that force."

Relief operations and diplomatic interventions should be done earlier and better than they have been in the past, so as to make military intervention unnecessary. No reasonable person could object to the idea that when a human rights or humanitarian emergency reaches a state of massive loss of life, sovereignty should not be an obstacle to international intervention. But situations of mass starvation or genocide do not happen overnight. They invariably follow from a history of culpable negligence or equally culpable complicity by the international community. Conventional solutions continue to be possible in most instances, but require more persistence, imagination and professionalism than is commonly brought to bear.

When military intervention does take place, for whatever reason, there are certain standards of independent verification of facts, accountability and human rights that must be respected. Above all, the international community must recognize that military intervention cannot solve humanitarian or conflict resolution problems; it can only alter them.

In a seemingly intractable situation, it is tempting to throw up one's hands in horror and cry "do something!" Sending in the Marines is a satisfyingly dramatic "something," but the respite it gives is extremely brief.

Military Intervention Is Always Political

by Caleb Carr

About the author: *Caleb Carr is a contributing editor of* MHQ: The Quarterly Journal of Military History *and author of* The Alienist.

If American leaders glean nothing else from the troubled U.N. adventure in Somalia, they ought at least and at long last to recognize the unattainability of that often-sought grail of U.S. foreign policy, the "purely humanitarian" (or "nonpolitical") military intervention. Any military action abroad that involves combat is essentially an act of war, and thus governed by Karl von Clausewitz's axiom that war is policy by different means. The notion of a nonpolitical military intervention is therefore worse than chimerical: it is oxymoronic, carrying with it from the start the seeds of its own eventual frustration.

Political Escalation in Somalia

The U.N. action in Somalia—a country that, with the end of the Cold War, has lost any shred of geopolitical significance it might once have possessed—is a particularly clear case in point. The multilateral intervention was prompted not by big-power jockeying but by widespread public discomfort, in a broad range of nations, with the images of famine and disease that the international media relentlessly brought out of the strife-torn African nation during the course of 1992. Particularly in the United States, there was a strong feeling that something simply *had* to be done for the Somalis: that if other nations could only offer those suffering people food and the chance for an equitable domestic political arrangement, they would seize both and be grateful to the agents who brought them. In addition, the prospect of intervention in Somalia seemed politically cost-free. Unlike such tangled humanitarian crises as those in Indonesia or the former Yugoslavia, the Somali situation appeared devoid of allies or enemies who might resent American action. "We came to your country for one reason only," President Bush told the Somali people in December 1992, "to enable the

Caleb Carr, "The Consequences of Somalia," *World Policy Journal*, Fall 1993. Reprinted by permission of the World Policy Institute, New York.

starving to be fed." The U.S. and U.N. troops that joined together in a resulting expedition to the Horn of Africa seemed predestined for the status of heroes.

Very quickly, however, it became clear that starvation and its attendant malaises were not *causes* of the strife in Somalia, but *weapons* in the civil war; for in fact there was no shortage of food and relief supplies in the country. The population was suffering because various armed clans (at war since the deposition of the last Somali strongman, Siad Barre, in 1991) saw those supplies merely as additional tools with which to slaughter their enemies—not through use, but through deprivation. In addition, the clan leaders (Mohammed Farah Aidid, his chief antagonist, Mohammed Said Hersi "Morgan," and their various lieutenants and confederates), who had initially seemed willing to put their differences aside and work with the United Nations, turned out to be blatant liars whose true purpose was to prostitute the U.N. effort to their own purposes. Obviously, the general Somali population could not be helped in any systematic way unless the feuding clans were disarmed; but the U.N. forces declared that the task of disarmament exceeded the terms of their mandate.

"Gang Leaders" Become Representatives

A peace conference was convened in March 1993 in the Ethiopian capital of Addis Ababa. Hoping for the emergence of a trustworthy Somali leader, the United Nations treated the gang leaders who had abused and starved their own people for nearly two years as respectable, legitimate representatives at the conference. But it was not long before these men were feuding and then warring again, and this time the U.N. troops could not stay above the conflict. Faced with the true and brutal nature of the Somali warlords, the multinational force began to seize arms from the clan members, and subsequently came under fire themselves. Inevitably, charges of "colonialism" began to be made against the U.N. forces; and the most powerful clan leader in the capital of Mogadishu, Farah Aidid, became a hunted outlaw who just as inevitably tried to portray himself as a fugitive resistance leader standing tall against the forces of imperialism.

Somali gangs now [as of Fall 1993] ambush U.N. detachments, threaten international workers, and murder foreign journalists with impunity. At least one of the nations contributing forces to the multilateral effort, Italy (former colonial master of Somalia), has questioned the United Nations' new, more forceful policy and undermined the multilateral action by talking bilaterally with the gangs. A man whose "army" would not be able to defy the police force of any major American city now pretends to the rank of an international figure of consequence. Relief workers, their job rendered impossible by the fighting, call for an end to the U.N. presence, but European and American citizens continue to believe that the

> ***"Starvation and its attendant malaises were not* causes *of the strife in Somalia, but* weapons *in the civil war."***

innocent victims of Somali violence—the elderly, as well as women and children—must be assisted. Yet ironically, many women and children in Somalia participate in the violence against foreigners, by hiding weapons on their persons and transporting them to the sites of ambushes.

In short, the intervention is a failure that stands on the brink of becoming a true disaster.

How could such noble motives produce such catastrophic results?

Who Was the Enemy?

First and foremost, the United States and the United Nations entered the affair believing that they could place combat troops in a foreign country and then direct them to ignore existing political realities and pursue extra-military—which is to say extra-political—ends. The U.N. forces established famine, not the gangs and their leaders, as the enemy: the coalition members were unwilling or unable to recognize that famine, in Somalia, is not a natural disaster akin to the flooding of the Mississippi. It is (like war) policy by different means, a policy that in this case has been carefully orchestrated by each of the clan leaders in an effort to destroy those citizens who will not lend allegiance to their respective sides.

> ***"The U.N. forces established famine, not the gangs and their leaders, as the enemy."***

Recognition of this fact came too late in the international effort, and acknowledgment of its implications is proving just as tardy. We hunted Farah Aidid like the criminal he has always been; yet our delay in beginning that hunt, along with the ludicrous spectacle of the peace conference in Addis Ababa, gave him the time, the media attention, and a setting in which to portray himself as a legitimate Third World leader. His seizure, along with that of "General Morgan" and the other gang leaders, as well as the immediate disarmament of their followers, should have been the first order of business for the intervention: if famine was the enemy, then the agents of famine should have been quickly and severely chastised. Such a military (and thus political) goal would have been no more than an appropriate object for a military operation.

Many in the West are uncomfortable with such an approach, however, echoing Aidid's claim that it amounts to colonialism. Quite possibly—but it also represents the only real cure for Somalia's ills. Proofs of this claim are spotted all over Somalia, most notably in towns like Baardheere, where American marines quickly established a "weapons-free zone," neutralized the gangs, and helped the citizens rebuild their lives. . . . Colonialism, no doubt; but we must remember that the local indigenous leaders were the agents of famine and disease. Again, bloodshed and famine are not natural disasters in Somalia; they are rife because many powerful Somalis and their followers *prefer* bloodshed and famine to a loss of power.

By (at least initially) treating those warlords like responsible leaders, the

United States and the United Nations implicitly acknowledged that the turf war in which they were engaged was a valid reason for tearing their country to shreds. Apparently, we have changed our point of view in this regard; but we ought to have been clear on this point, among ourselves, *before* our troops ever reached Somali shores. . . .

> ***"Military intervention, by definition, cannot be nonpolitical."***

But the consequences of Somalia extend far beyond the fate of that small desert nation, and beyond the troubled continent of Africa more generally. In the realm of American foreign policy, they encompass the long-overdue recognition that military intervention, by definition, cannot be nonpolitical: if we send American and U.N. forces abroad because of a "humanitarian" crisis, we will *necessarily* come into conflict with those indigenous political leaders who are not capably addressing—or, as in the case of Somalia, are actively abetting—that crisis. We must determine *before going in* the legitimacy of those leaders, as well as (should they be at war with each other) the validity of their various positions in the conflict.

Such a shift in policy would have obvious regional implications, not only in the developing world, but in Europe as well: Do we accept the legitimacy of the leaders of the Bosnian-Serb conflict? Do we believe that the nationalistic, cultural, and religious bases of their dispute are valid grounds for war and slaughter? If not, we must be prepared, should we choose military intervention, to arrest such leaders, disarm their followers, and create a U.N. protectorate whose term may be far longer even than that in Somalia—for there may be no indigenous leaders who truly believe in peace and compromise in either Bosnia or Serbia, and it may take many generations to foster such. The alternative, of course, is to allow the fighting to continue; a thoroughly available option for the Western powers, but one that dooms many civilians to violent death. There is no middle road in such a conflict, as the absurd airlift to Bosnia demonstrated: if we enter the fray we become political players, whereas any attempt to portray a political conflict as a humanitarian crisis is simply sidestepping the terrible choice before us.

"War in Any Event"

In April 1914, Woodrow Wilson, in response to the arrest of several American sailors by a brutally repressive and—to Wilson—illegitimate Mexican dictator, was preparing to send U.S. marines to the port of Veracruz. Calling a group of congressional leaders in for a conference on the subject, Wilson said that he intended to cite an insult to America's national honor, as well as the Mexican dictator's illegitimacy, as bases for the military action. But Senator Henry Cabot Lodge, one of the notable realists in the history of American foreign policy, questioned whether such nebulous philosophical considerations were adequate justifications for so forceful an act, and urged the president to base his move on the need to protect the lives and property of American citizens. Wilson demurred, saying that such a statement "would widen too much and lead to war"; Lodge quickly snapped that he "thought it war in any event."

The clarity of Lodge's logic has continued to escape interventionist American presidents throughout the twentieth century, a trend that Bill Clinton will perpetuate if he does not allow the U.N. mandate in Somalia to fully evolve toward protectorate status or if he agrees to dispatch American troops to the former Yugoslavia for "humanitarian" reasons. Whether we are "peacemaking" or ensuring the delivery of food and medicine, we will be at war when our troops hit the ground in Bosnia, just as surely as we were at war in Somalia; and it will be our responsibility, as one of the combatants, to know—*before* any of our soldiers die—just who we want to see disarmed, who we want to see jailed, and what kind of peace we want to see forged by the conflict. Then, we must be ready to pick up the burdens of administration—and to suffer the inevitable accusations of colonialism—that will accompany the tasks of pacification and reconstruction, should we finally judge the country's indigenous leaders incompetent to perform those tasks.

If we are not prepared for these responsibilities and eventualities, we would do well to stay at home and spare our consciences by shutting off our televisions. For half-measures aimed at anything less than a thorough reordering of the way tribal, ethnic, and religious factions in the former Yugoslavia (or Somalia, or Cambodia, or anywhere else) do business with each other will ultimately do no more than give those factions the sustenance they need to keep killing each other for yet another generation.

Humanitarian Aid Undermines Self-Sufficiency

by Michael Maren

About the author: *Michael Maren, a former aid worker for the Peace Corps, Catholic Relief Services, and the United States Agency for International Development, is a journalist whose work on Africa, and Somalia in particular, often appears in* The Village Voice.

From a speech delivered in March [1993] by Michael Maren to the Camel Breeders, a group of Cornell University graduate students from various disciplines who are preparing to work in international development. [Editors of Harper's Magazine*]*

As you [graduate students] prepare for and look forward to careers in international development, I am compelled to issue a warning. With the hindsight of someone who spent five years in the development business, I'm going to tell you that the development industry hurts people in the developing world. Its greatest success has been to provide good jobs for Westerners with graduate degrees.

Personal Experience in Aid Programs

I don't expect that any of you will take my advice and start looking for careers elsewhere. And I'm in no position to criticize you for going ahead and working in development even after you hear me out. You see, I had a pretty wonderful career in the aid business. I can't remember ever having more fun. In fact, I was having so much fun that I didn't want to stop, even after I realized that our programs were hurting the very people they were supposed to help.

In 1980, when I was twenty-five years old, I was hired by Catholic Relief Services (CRS) to administer food-for-work programs—programs that feed people in exchange for their work on local development projects—in Kenya. I was given a beautiful garden apartment in a nice neighborhood in Nairobi, a brand-new Land Cruiser, a great office, and almost a million dollars in a U.S. Agency for International Development (AID) grant to oversee the programs. As I began the job, shiploads of U.S. government surplus rice were leaving a port in Texas and heading to Mombasa. Meanwhile, CRS notified the country's parish priests and government officials that this rice was available. All they had to do to receive it was fill out a one-page application describing their proposed project and specifying the number of "recipients"—the number of the project's workers who would receive sacks of rice in exchange for their labor. Thousands of applications were submitted.

"I knew nothing about agriculture, forestry, road building . . . or any of the projects I was approving."

I took some of the U.S. AID money and customized the Land Cruiser, adding extra-large fuel tanks and a really nice stereo system, and then I set off across Kenya to inspect the proposed projects. It was a dream come true. I was driving absolutely free across one of the world's most beautiful landscapes. I was so awestruck by my own good luck that sometimes I'd stop in the middle of a huge empty wilderness, or beside a herd of giraffes or elephants, and just yelp with delight.

I was having so much fun running around starting food-for-work projects—water projects, agriculture projects, forestry projects—that I completely overlooked the most obvious problem: I knew nothing about agriculture, forestry, road building, well digging, dam building, or any of the projects I was approving. But nobody seemed to care. Only once did anyone in authority at CRS ever go and look at a project. When I'd return to Nairobi every few weeks, my boss, who let me work completely unsupervised, had only one question: How many more recipients did you sign on? More recipients meant more government grant money, which meant we could buy more vehicles and hire more assistants.

Relief Agencies Are Businesses

When I slowed down for a moment to consider what was happening, it became clear: aid distribution is just another big, private business that relies on government contracts. Private voluntary organizations (PVOs) such as CRS are paid by the U.S. government to give away surplus food produced by subsidized U.S. farmers. The more food CRS gave away, the more money they received from the government to administer the handouts. Since the securing of grant money is the primary goal, PVOs rarely meet a development project they don't like.

Of all the aid programs, those involving food delivery are especially prized by PVOs because they generate income, are easy to administer, and are warmly received by the public. Yet most food aid has little to do with need and everything to do with getting rid of surplus food. Kenya was not a country facing starvation when I worked there. Many of the projects I started were in the rich agricultural land of the central and western parts of the country. In fact, around the world, only about 10 percent of food aid is targeted at emergency situations. PVOs publicize situations such as the one in Somalia in order to raise money from the public, but most of their work is done in areas where there is plenty to eat, because there are simply not enough starving people to absorb all of our surplus food. Also, it's easier to distribute large quantities of food in more developed areas.

Harmless as this might at first sound, sending food to areas where there is already food creates serious problems. It decreases demand for locally produced commodities, subsidizes the production of cash crops, and fosters dependence among those who receive the aid. Since PVOs can only operate with the approval of the host government, they typically end up supporting the government leaders' political goals, rewarding the government's friends, punishing its enemies, and providing fodder for a vast system of political patronage.

That's exactly what happened in Somalia, where the government and the generals had been playing games with food aid for more than a decade before the Marines arrived. I was working for U.S. AID in Somalia in 1981, when we started pumping food into that country. It was clear to many of us, even then, that the program was working to prop up a corrupt dictator and turn nomads into relief junkies. Refugees poured over the borders and into camps, where they were fed day after day, year after year, by PVOs, while little effort was made to break their growing dependence. In 1987 a World Food Program report stated that Somalia had actually produced a surplus of food that year, yet PVOs continued to distribute free food and collect U.S. government money for administering the delivery. Inevitably, indigenous food-distribution networks withered and died. The country's economy adapted to foreign aid—not to production. Meanwhile, the PVOs and corrupt government officials got fat and rich.

> ***"Most food aid has little to do with need and everything to do with getting rid of surplus food."***

The Role of the Press

No one questions private voluntary organizations. Not the U.S. government, which needs to get rid of the food and wants to keep its aid bureaucracy functioning. Not the host government, whose officials often profit from the aid racket. Not the public, which sees aid workers as so many Mother Teresas. And not the press—*especially* not the press—which has, in recent years, become an integral part of the aid system.

The press's role in that system is to convey to the West the PVOs' view of Africa. And because the distribution of food aid is first and foremost a business, it is not surprising that the priorities of aid organizations dominate the West's image of the continent—an image of helpless nations in need of our support.

This is not a new phenomenon. Aid workers are simply the latest in a series of recent western vanguards in Africa, each of whom put forward the image of Africa that best suited its own interests. The first Europeans to form a vanguard in Africa were the naturalists. Because of them, early European views of Africa emphasized the continent's natural history. Later, as missionaries began to outnumber explorers, Europe began to see the continent through the eyes of those who were out to save its soul. And as Europe developed political and mercantile interests in Africa, merchants and traders were at the vanguard. At that time, Europeans were concerned with turning Africans into loyal subjects, workers, producers, and citizens of empires. No one really worried about feeding them.

"The press . . . has, in recent years, become an integral part of the aid system."

Historically, the press has been willing to uncritically accept whatever image of Africa the western vanguard has been selling. In the case of the PVOs, the press has bought their line because reporters are as dependent on aid organizations as the organizations are on them. It would have been impossible, for example, for the press to cover Somalia without the assistance of PVOs. There's no Hertz [Rent A Car] counter at the Mogadishu airport, and no road maps available at gas stations. If a journalist arrives in Africa from Europe or the United States and needs to get to the interior of the country, PVOs are the only ticket. Journalists sleep and eat with PVO workers. When they want history and facts and figures, they turn to the PVOs. In press coverage of Somalia or almost any other crisis in Africa, it is always the PVOs who are most often quoted and are regarded as the neutral and authoritative sources—as if they have no vested interest in anything but the truth.

Alternatives to Aid Are Not Discussed

A typical example of the connection between journalism and the aid system is this analysis from a February 22, 1993, story about Africa in the *New York Times:*

> The greatest danger now to Mozambique's tranquillity, almost everyone agrees, is Mozambique's tranquillity.
>
> Lacking scenes of carnage and starvation to disturb Western television audiences, Mozambique is having trouble competing for attention with Somalia and the former Yugoslavia.

The article goes on to quote numerous CARE officials whose primary concern is to raise more money to give more aid to Mozambique. The article never considers any alternatives to aid. No aid worker raises the possibility, for example, that Mozambique's economy might improve if the country focused on exporting goods. No one mentions that in the absence of carnage, Mozambique might be a good place to invest. No one is talking about creating permanent employment for Africans. The only discussion is about raising more money to send experts there and preserve the jobs of expatriates and create more jobs for graduate students from programs like [Camel Breeders at Cornell University]. The people who are called upon to diagnose and comment on Africa's problems are the very people who stand to profit from the diagnoses.

I know that you don't want to be part of this problem. You'll tell me that you can change all of this, that you want to work within the bureaucracy to reform the bureaucracy. But in a couple of years you're going to be in Ouagadougou [Burkina Faso] or Gaborone [Botswana] making a very good salary. The years will pass and you'll find yourself with two kids in an expensive private school in New England, and you're going to have perfected skills that aren't very useful outside of the Third World. You're going to think about quitting, about raising hell, but you won't be able to. Because by then you, too, will have become part of the never-ending cycle of aid.

Chapter 2

Should Interventions Be Used to Promote Peace and Democracy?

Interventions for Democracy: An Overview

by Jack Hitt et al.

About the author: *Jack Hitt is a contributing editor of* Harper's Magazine.

In January 1993, when President Clinton took office, the job of directing "the world's only superpower" seemed an easy one. The phrase promised a global Pax Americana: history was at an end, what remained to be done was routine police work. That rosy scenario, however, was soon overtaken by events, and the White House, without a compass for the new world, has found itself lurching from crisis to crisis, changing strategies with each set of map coordinates.

Amid the flurry of policy shifts, high-level contradictions, and official "clarifications," scant attention has been given to the primary questions of American foreign policy: Should our dealings with other nations be governed by Wilsonian moral precepts or by a strict calculation of interests? How much are we willing to sacrifice to support democracy and human rights in other nations? What, in the end, are our responsibilities outside our borders? By way of encouraging President Clinton to at least consider, if not confront, the questions at hand, Harper's Magazine *gathered six experts to give foreign-policy advice to a domestic-policy president.*

The following forum is based on a discussion held at Le Mistral, a restaurant in Washington, D.C. Jack Hitt served as moderator. Kenneth Anderson is a lecturer at Harvard Law School, where he teaches the laws of war. Jean Bethke Elshtain teaches political philosophy at Vanderbilt University. She is the author of Women and War *and the coauthor of* But Was It Just? *a reflection on the morality of the Persian Gulf war. Kim R. Holmes is the vice president and director of foreign policy and defense studies at the Heritage Foundation. Will Marshall is the president of the Progressive Policy Institute. A former policy director of the Democratic Leadership Council, he is the co-editor of* Mandate for Change, *a manifesto of the "New Democratic" ideas on which President Clinton campaigned. Frank McCloskey represents the Eighth Congressional Dis-*

trict in Indiana. A Democrat, he is a member of the House Armed Services Committee and the House Foreign Affairs Committee. Aryeh Neier is the president of the Open Society Fund and a former executive director of Human Rights Watch and the American Civil Liberties Union.

Jack Hitt: For the purposes of our discussion, let's imagine that I am President Clinton. I've gathered you here as my new team of national-security advisers to help me get out of the mess that I'm in. In January 1993, I was inaugurated with a mandate from the American people to pay as little attention to foreign policy as possible. It seemed to work for a while, but then events in Bosnia, Somalia, Moscow, and Haiti made that position untenable. It's been said that my foreign policy is confused because no one knows what America stands for. Has the time come for me to articulate a clear strategy—a "Clinton Doctrine"—to guide our behavior abroad?

Jean Bethke Elshtain: No. The word "doctrine" implies a comprehensiveness for which we're not prepared. We haven't begun to take the measure of the post–Cold War world. After World War II we were able to talk about a Truman Doctrine, but that's because it was easier then to perceive our interests and concerns.

Will Marshall: I would agree that the international picture is just too inchoate for something as rigid as a Clinton Doctrine. But I would argue that you, as president, have already articulated a general foreign-policy framework—elevating commerce to a strategic interest, revamping our military to meet new threats, and reinforcing the global movement toward democracy and markets. You *have* a policy; it's just that the problems cropping up in the daily headlines don't fit neatly into it.

Elshtain: I disagree. All you and your advisers have been able to come up with is "enlargement"—and that's a nostrum, not a strategy. Of *course* America is in favor of the expansion of democracy and free markets. It's like saying the pope ought to be Catholic.

Kim Holmes: The reason you should not have a doctrine, Mr. President, is that there isn't a single idea that encapsulates all the diverse problems at large in the world. "Containment" worked after World War II because it perfectly melded a concept—a way to see the world—with a guide for action. Now we must be content with setting priorities among our interests and stating which regions of the world are important to us and which are not.

"Of* course *America is in favor of the expansion of democracy and free markets."

Aryeh Neier: What I would propose, instead of a policy based only on "interests," is that you issue a "minimum articulation of principles."

Hitt: What should those be?

Neier: Most basically, certain extremities of suffering inflicted by leaders on their own populations, or on the populations of other countries, will not be tolerated. Of course, we have to accept our limits and recognize that by intervening we may make a bad situation worse. But if the suffering extends to crimes against humanity on a gigantic scale, the United States will consider that it has a responsibility to try to alleviate the situation.

National Interests vs. Altruism

Holmes: The essential division in the debate over American foreign policy has always been between a national-interest approach and a humanitarian approach. We Americans find it difficult to navigate between these two poles, because we confuse our national interest with humanitarian concerns.

Kenneth Anderson: Or even invert them completely. Look at some recent positions taken by the National Conference of Catholic Bishops. The bishops were hesitant about American involvement in the Gulf War, where we were clearly motivated by raw interests in a material sense. Then came Bosnia, where they endorsed military intervention precisely because they felt that there were *no* national interests at stake—only a humanitarian principle. It's a peculiarly American way to think.

Holmes: And it never works in the real world. You can't get a consensus behind a strategy totally devoid of national interest. Not only that; I also think such a strategy is morally corrupt. The American government is elected to represent the interests and values of the American people. To pretend that foreign policy can operate without regard for our self-interest is a breach of the social contract between the U.S. government and the American people.

"We Americans . . . confuse our national interest with humanitarian concerns."

Elshtain: It's a huge mistake to divorce considerations of national self-interest from ethical imperatives. Ethical imperatives historically have also been a part of our national interest. Max Weber made the observation a long time ago that if you have a policy of pure interest severed from ethics, it gets brutal and opportunistic too easily. And if you have a policy that's too idealistic and severed from interests, it becomes naive and Utopian rather quickly. To bring these together in a fruitful mix—that's our challenge.

Neier: What Kim is ignoring is the importance of leadership. Just because the current president tends to follow public opinion doesn't mean that's the way it has to be. When the Marshall Plan was proposed in 1947, it was supported by only about 10 percent of the American people. But the president led the public, through argument, to see that the Marshall Plan was in their self-interest. My premise—that what's needed is a statement of principles—is based on the idea that there is no fixed set of national interests.

Anderson: I would go even further. I believe that there are moments when it is appropriate, just, right, and defensible for one political community to come to the aid of another country without any national-interest calculation at all, out of pure altruism, on exclusively moral grounds. These moments are limited and, as Aryeh said, require extraordinary political leadership. Bosnia, I would argue, is such a case.

Elshtain: There's nothing but trouble in that position, Ken. Pure altruism is notoriously difficult to articulate in foreign policy. It slides too easily into moralistic posturing. What's right isn't necessarily what's pure.

> ***"[America's] principle of preventing genocidal conduct converges with our interest in order and stability."***

Anderson: But I hold it out there because I don't want to be in a position—nor should the country—of always trying to translate our actions into some kind of national-interest talk. The result of that is a confusion of altruism and self-interest, which does neither any good.

Post–Cold War Interests and Principles

Holmes: Our foreign policy works best when our altruistic instincts and national interests coincide. The Cold War made that marriage easy: our strategic interest—preventing the domination of Europe by the Soviet Union—went along well with the principles of promoting democracy and freedom in Eastern Europe. Now that the Cold War is over, we have a divorce between two sides of our brain. One half is thinking strategically; the other, in terms of humanitarian goals.

Neier: I don't agree that our interests and principles necessarily conflict. In many cases, they still coincide.

Hitt: Give me a principle that coincides with our national interest.

Neier: Halting genocide, for one. Genocide is probably the greatest crime in the human lexicon. And in Bosnia, for instance, our principle of preventing genocidal conduct converges with our interest in order and stability.

Elshtain: We have another interest in halting genocide: for us to do nothing in the face of activities that violate so fundamentally the principles that we stand for erodes our credibility in the international arena.

Hitt: So as president, I should state to the world that genocide is a crime of such magnitude that America is ready to commit blood and treasure to prevent it?

Elshtain: Force isn't the only answer. Often all one can do is say: That's unacceptable. And sometimes intervention can do more harm than good. But you don't want to have a case-by-case foreign policy if it means that you'll ignore genocide over here but not over there. There have to be some standards.

Frank McCloskey: I agree. Halting genocide has to be stated as an absolute principle. That being said, we cannot commit American lives to every instance of genocide. We have to look at each situation, especially in those places where we have leverage. For example, we can't send troops into Tibet and stop Chinese genocide there. But we could have—and should have—taken a more aggressive stance in the Balkans.

Holmes: But that's precisely the problem with elevating any humanitarian principle to a foreign-policy goal: as soon as you state it, you have to start issuing exceptions. In foreign policy, you have to abandon the world of pure moral ideas, where consistency is effortless, for the practical world of international relations, where hypocrisy comes easy. The difference between what we say and what we do is that the former is unlimited and the latter is not.

Neier: There *is* a value in saying that the United States will strive mightily to stop the commission of genocide. But precisely what we should do in trying to carry that out depends on the situation.

McCloskey: Exactly. We state opposition to genocide as an absolute principle. Then we look to our resources, ability, power, and leverage. Sure, there's a political component in all this. We cannot say we are going to intervene everywhere, but neither can we say we won't intervene anywhere. That's not hypocrisy. It's reality. . . .

Marshall: Who defines a nation's interest? My problem with foreign-policy realists is that they arrogate to themselves the ability to divine the nation's true interests. But the national interest is a complex calculation, done by the American people, of values and costs, not an abstract and theoretical truth. If the American people want to intervene on humanitarian grounds, a president would be hard-pressed not to listen. I disagree with Kim; I don't think there has to be a solid substratum of interests on which to base each policy. If the American people think that we should intervene to prevent mass slaughter in Bosnia, fine. That's a worthy and enlightened impulse. But in each case, we have to calibrate the costs.

Holmes: The problem with that formulation is that our foreign policy ends up being defined by television. Let me give you an example. In Angola, a half-million people have been killed in war since the fall of 1992. That's an incredible human tragedy. But we're not talking about Angola like we're talking about Bosnia. Why is that? Is the suffering of an Angolan less acute than the suffering of a Bosnian? What about Tajikistan? There's a terrible war going on there. More than 30,000 people were killed in 1992 alone. It's absolutely brutal. But CNN [Cable News Network] can't get its cameras in, and therefore it's not on our global radar screen. To me, a policy defined by what people see on TV is the least moral position there is. If morality is not applied consistently, it becomes mere posturing.

> ***"Precisely what [America] should do in trying to [stop genocide] depends on the situation."***

Setting Priorities

Hitt: In my role as president, I want to address the country about my new-found commitment to foreign policy and to define what our national interest is.

What do I say are the interests and principles of American foreign policy?

Holmes: First, the prevention of the proliferation of weapons of mass destruction. Second, assistance to Russian democracy. Third, the promotion of a free international trading system. I can keep going down the list.

Hitt: So we'll defend democracy in Russia but not in, say, Haiti?

Holmes: I am setting priorities. Haiti's on the list. It's just down around number ten.

Anderson: What I find curious, Kim, is that I can't really see any difference between your listing of priorities and what Will has said.

Marshall: That's not true: I don't rule out intervention for humanitarian reasons, if that's what the American people decide to do. I don't insist on some narrowly defined national interest as a criterion. In fact, I think this choice between interests and principles is a false one. I also suspect I am more sanguine than Kim about the possibility of advancing U.S. interests through multilateral means and the prospect of reviving collective-security agreements.

Holmes: The other difference between Will and me is that I worry every time the president is asked what we stand for, because the first word out of his mouth—and I'm sure it makes Will happy—is "democracy."

"[Some experts believe] that 'democracy' is a bit of language we use to speak about something else—call it 'interests.'"

Hitt: Well, forty years of containment taught him to say that.

Holmes: Then we have a hangover, don't we? It's time to start talking differently.

Marshall: Kim, two hundred years of American history taught him to say that word.

Holmes: Not true. Democracy was not the key issue of the American Revolution. Liberty was.

Anderson: This is interesting. You admit that "democracy" is a bit of language we use to speak about something else—call it "interests." But Will, too, uses it to signify a deeper set of convictions that is really more about capitalism and consumption. His foreign policy is built upon the good of expressing oneself through the purchase of consumer goods that, it is hoped, promote peace by promoting universal consumer values.

Elshtain: That's "enlargement" for you. It's too murky.

Anderson: But, Jean, it's not murky for people like Will. It's pure Clintonism: foreign policy as a sort of therapy. The City on the Hill goes out into the world not to make it a better place, or even a safer one, but to feel good about itself. That's why this administration is so happy with symbolic actions in places like Bosnia—the war-crimes tribunal, for example. Symbols let it feel just as good as *real* action, which inevitably produces ambiguous results, and hence anxiety.

Marshall: The collapse of Communism left liberal democracy standing as the only credible theory for organizing politics—or economies, for that matter. We didn't create this situation. The Eastern European revolts were indigenous. People are suddenly deciding on their own that political and economic freedom are going to lead to a better life—whether they're inspired by material aspirations or a desire not to have their human rights trampled. Add to that the fact that a liberal world order would be less likely to dissolve into cataclysmic violence, and it's clearly in our interest to construct the new order on liberal, democratic principles.

"The fact is, democracy is not the new organizing order."

Elshtain: I get nervous, Will, when I hear talk of a liberal world order.

Holmes: No kidding. The fact is, democracy is not the new organizing order. Mr. President, if I were your secretary of state, I'd tell you that in deciding our foreign policy for a certain country, the question is not whether that country is democratic but whether it has a pro-Western foreign policy. In Asia, you have countries that are pro-Western but not necessarily democratic. I was just in China, and it's clear that in the next ten or fifteen years the People's Republic will evolve into an authoritarian mix of capitalism and socialism. It's not going to be democratic. It's going to be increasingly capitalist.

Elshtain: Talk of a homogeneous liberal world order strikes me as another nostrum along the lines of enlarging free markets. It pushes a universalism of the sort we should stay away from. We should acknowledge that there exist certain minimal standards beneath which our concern kicks in, but there is a big difference between situations in which people are being systematically slaughtered, populations transported, or victims sent to death camps, and cultural practices we don't agree with, such as women wearing a chador or undergoing clitoridectomy—practices that women in these societies often support and enforce.

Holmes: Let us not forget that we intervened against Adolf Hitler not because of the Holocaust but because he invaded France.

Neier: Yes, but the lesson of that war was the need for international institutions to ensure that a holocaust did not occur again. We created these institutions and adopted in their name a variety of agreements. We have been moving in a certain direction. Now, though, these international institutions are frayed, and we have a definite national interest in making them work.

Anderson: The reason they are frayed is precisely because of the imperial overreach that comes with imagining that the United Nations will enforce some kind of a pax romana.

Defining the World Community

Holmes: Am I the only one at the table who doesn't really know what the "world community" is? I know there are United Nations declarations. But I defy anyone to state even the lowest common denominator.

Anderson: It's worse than that. Communities are defined by setting themselves apart from other communities around them. There won't be a "world community" until the day the Vulcans arrive in our skies and invite us to join the United Federation of Planets. Only then will we know our common elements as a "world community."

Neier: In the past, empires were mechanisms for maintaining a certain degree of order. At this moment, we have no empires. But we do have international institutions created to promote just such an order, and we have a definite national interest in making them work.

Elshtain: In a lot of what gets said nowadays, one can hear a certain nostalgia for empire. We want it to be a nice empire, a benevolent empire, maybe even—I hate to saddle you with this, Will—a liberal world order. But there are ways to promote Aryeh's or Will's notion of order without these nostalgic longings for a supranational power.

Creating a Liberal World Order

Marshall: If you want to build a consensus for internationalism, you must ground your foreign policy in the sentiments of the public. You're going to have to tell people that we're trying to create the world we would all like to live in, which is a world that is liberal in the sense that there are norms and values that are transcendent. We don't want everything to look like the United States. But there's no reason why you can't have national distinctiveness within an increasingly liberal and democratic framework. The end of the Cold War means that our democratic convictions and our interests are more likely to converge than ever. The record of this century is that democracies don't go to war with each other. They are less likely to sponsor terrorism, flout human rights, and violate nonproliferation treaties. Aiding Russia's transition to democracy—which is Clinton's true foreign-policy success—is not just an expression of our moral values, it's an urgent security imperative.

> ***"If promoting democracy produces a pro-Western foreign policy, then we [America] should do it."***

Holmes: If promoting democracy produces a pro-Western foreign policy, then we should do it. But there are many countries in Asia and the Middle East where promoting democracy is *not* a good idea right now.

Neier: So we shouldn't promote democracy in Indonesia, or Singapore, or Malaysia, or China?

Holmes: Or Saudi Arabia.

Neier: So you're saying that America's foreign policy should be: If you're pro-Western, you're entitled to be as authoritarian and abusive as you want?

Hitt: Kim, can you imagine a situation in which you'd recommend a humanitarian policy that would conflict with a national interest?

Holmes: Probably not. If you want me to support some political group in Kuwait or Saudi Arabia that happens to be the latest cause célèbre of Amnesty

International, I would not cut all ties to that regime, as we did with the shah [of Iran], just because of human-rights concerns. Those countries are allies of ours that have, for us, a larger strategic purpose.

McCloskey: Kim, you don't favor democracy in Saudi Arabia, but you listed "democracy in Russia" as your second most important goal. Boris Yeltsin has shelled his own parliament, rounded up people, and suspended the press. Is your goal there really democracy, or is it merely to accelerate capitalism?

Holmes: It depends on what kind of foreign policy Russia has. It just so happened that Yeltsin's enemies in parliament were anti-Western. If Yeltsin creates some kind of Pinochet solution [Pinochet led the military junta that ruled Chile between 1973 and 1988], where he becomes increasingly authoritarian but pro-market and continues a pro-Western foreign policy, then we should continue to support him. See, if we just give our allies a democracy test, we'll wind up hypocrites, and in Yeltsin's case we'll wind up criticizing the only pro-Western Russian leader there is.

McCloskey: Wait a minute. Democracy is *not* going to be a priority, but relations with the West and accelerated capitalism are? That seems strange to me.

Holmes: I'm saying that the promotion of a pro-Western foreign policy is the ultimate priority. If promoting democratic and reform elements inside Russia happens to be the way for us to reach that goal, then that's what we should do.

The United Nations Should Intervene to Save Failing States

by Gerald B. Helman and Steven R. Ratner

About the authors: *Gerald B. Helman, retired from the U.S. Department of State, served as U.S. ambassador to the United Nations in Geneva, Switzerland. Steven R. Ratner, an international relations fellow at the Council on Foreign Relations, works for the U.S. Department of State Office of the Legal Adviser.*

From Haiti in the Western Hemisphere to the remnants of Yugoslavia in Europe, from Somalia, Sudan, and Liberia in Africa to Cambodia in Southeast Asia, a disturbing new phenomenon is emerging: the failed nation-state, utterly incapable of sustaining itself as a member of the international community. Civil strife, government breakdown, and economic privation are creating more and more modern *debellatios*, the term used in describing the destroyed German state after World War II. As those states descend into violence and anarchy—imperiling their own citizens and threatening their neighbors through refugee flows, political instability, and random warfare—it is becoming clear that something must be done. The massive abuses of human rights—including that most basic of rights, the right to life—are distressing enough, but the need to help those states is made more critical by the evidence that their problems tend to spread. Although alleviating the developing world's suffering has long been a major task, saving failed states will prove a new—and in many ways different—challenge.

The Right of Self-Determination

The current collapse has its roots in the vast proliferation of nation-states, especially in Africa and Asia, since the end of World War II. When the United Nations Charter [U.N.] was signed in 1945, it had fifty signatories. Since that time, membership has more than tripled, reflecting the momentous transforma-

From Gerald B. Helman and Steven R. Ratner, "Saving Failed States." Reproduced with permission from *Foreign Policy* 89 (Winter 1992/93).

tion of the pre-war colonial world to a globe composed of independent states. During that period, now nearing its conclusion following the independence of Namibia in 1990, the U.N. and its member states made the "self-determination of peoples"—a right enshrined in the U.N. Charter—a primary goal.

Self-determination, in fact, was given more attention than long-term survivability. All agreed that the new states needed economic assistance, and the U.N. encouraged institutions like the World Bank and the United Nations Development Programme (UNDP) to help them. But fundamental to the notion of decolonization was the idea that peoples could best govern themselves when free from the shackles, or even the influences, of foreigners. The idea, then, that states could fail—that they could be simply unable to function as independent entities—was anathema to the raison d'être of decolonization and offensive to the notion of self-determination. New states might be poor, it was thought, but they would hold their own by virtue of being independent.

Cold War Foreign Aid

While it lasted, the Cold War prolonged the viability of some of the newly independent and other Third World states. Countries with seriously underdeveloped economies and governments received hefty infusions of aid from their former colonial masters as well as from the two superpowers. The systemic corruption that characterized many of the new states did not stop the superpowers from sending foreign aid as they sought to buttress a potential ally in the Cold War. Thus the Philippines, South Vietnam, Zaire, and post-1977 Somalia profited immensely from U.S. aid, while Afghanistan, Cuba, post-1974 Ethiopia, and several of the front-line African states benefited from Soviet aid. Granted, most of the foreign aid recipients were not wholly dependent on it. Many—most countries of the Association of Southeast Asian Nations, for example—have become thriving independent states. But clearly foreign aid was critical in sustaining a number of states, based on their real or imagined strategic significance in the Cold War.

Over time, however, the hurdles faced by some young countries have proven overwhelming, and the assistance cuts that began in the late 1980s brought home the full weight of their shortcomings. In states like Somalia, Sudan, and Zaire, discredited regimes are being challenged by powerful insurgencies. The resulting civil strife is disrupting essential governmental services, destroying food supplies and distribution networks, and bringing economies to a virtual standstill; corrupt and criminal public officials only exacerbate the human misery. In Somalia and Sudan, natural disasters have compounded the suffering, killing large portions of the populations and forcing many others to migrate to already over-

"The U.N. and its member states made the 'self-determination of peoples'. . . a primary goal."

crowded urban areas or to refugee centers abroad. In Cambodia, twenty years of conflict have left the country in ruins, littered with land mines, and still suffering from the Khmer Rouge's genocidal rule. Afghanistan's civil war appears stuck in a stalemate and the country may not be able to hold together. Of course, most states that have suffered economic hardships have not faced governmental collapse. Most governments have been able to muddle through, although they have been heavily burdened by a stagnant standard of living.

Third World countries are not the only ones that could fail. The disintegration of the Soviet Union and Yugoslavia has created almost twenty new states, most of which have no tradition of statehood or practice in self-government. One hopes that most will succeed, but lack of experience in government, weak civic institutions, limited economic prospects, and ethnic strife will inevitably reduce some to helplessness—a condition in which Bosnia, with its civil war, found itself. The world's changing political, economic, and cultural configurations are testing the unity—and the borders—of many other countries. It is impossible to be certain that the political boundaries created under colonialism will, in the end, prove sustainable.

Thus, there are three groups of states whose survival is threatened: First, there are the failed states like Bosnia, Cambodia, Liberia, and Somalia, a small group whose governmental structures have been overwhelmed by circumstances. Second, there are the failing states like Ethiopia, Georgia, and Zaire, where collapse is not imminent but could occur within several years. And third, there are some newly independent states in the territories formerly known as Yugoslavia and the Soviet Union, whose viability is difficult to assess. All three groups merit close attention, and all three will require innovative policies. . . .

"The world's changing political, economic, and cultural configurations are testing the unity—and the borders—of many . . . countries."

Preventing Conflict

In his landmark June 1992 report, *An Agenda for Peace*, Secretary-General Boutros Boutros-Ghali set forth the concept of "post-conflict peace-building" as a new priority for the United Nations. Boutros-Ghali argued forcefully for "action to identify and support structures which will tend to strengthen and solidify peace in order to avoid a relapse into conflict." To prevent future conflict, the international community must create a new political, economic, and social environment for states riven by war. That would include strengthening governmental institutions, protecting human rights, pursuing bilateral cooperation projects, and encouraging demilitarization. Existing U.N. agencies would provide most of the assistance, requiring member states to increase their financial contributions.

Boutros-Ghali largely sought to base his case for assistance on the responsibility of the United Nations under its Charter to "maintain international peace and security." Certainly the argument is a strong one. The demise of a state is often marked by violence and widespread human rights violations that affect other states. Civil strife, the breakdown of food and health systems, and economic collapse force refugees to flee to adjacent countries. Neighboring states may also be burdened with illicit arms traffic, solidarity activities by related ethnic groups, and armed bands seeking to establish a safe haven. As is evident in the Balkans, there is a tangible risk that such conflicts will spill over into other countries.

"The demise of a state is often marked by violence and widespread human rights violations that affect other states."

The need to safeguard international peace and security has already prompted specific U.N. action aimed, at least partly, at rescuing failing states through direct involvement in their internal affairs. The massive U.N. plan to restore peace to Cambodia—with civil administration, peacekeeping, and supervised elections—is meant not only to rebuild Cambodia internally, but to eliminate a great source of regional tension in Southeast Asia. In Central America, too, the United Nations has used nation building as a means of preserving the peace. Its close monitoring of elections in Nicaragua and of the democratization programs in El Salvador has shown the U.N.'s willingness to become involved in the domestic affairs of its members in order to preserve international peace and security. Any future U.N. effort in the Balkans—moving from its peacekeeping and humanitarian assistance programs to creating a long-term peace on the ground—will likely be done under the same rubric.

Traditional Sovereignty

The U.N.'s responsibility for international peace and security is not, however, a sufficient basis for its action to resurrect all failed or failing states. Not all failing states pose true dangers to the peace. Haiti's tragedy has been borne by the Haitians themselves, and Liberia's disintegration only minimally imperils international security, apart from the modest impact of refugee flows from both states on neighbors. In such cases, U.N. members are more reluctant to support multilateral involvement.

That reluctance has both legal and political origins. From a legal standpoint, Article 2(7) of the U.N. Charter states that the organization is not authorized under the Charter to intervene "in matters which are essentially within the domestic jurisdiction of any state," except when the Security Council is enforcing its will under Chapter VII (the same part relied upon for sanctions against Iraq, Libya, and Serbia). The United Nations, then, is explicitly not authorized to interfere in purely domestic issues except to support Security Council resolutions, or with the consent of the concerned state.

More important, deeply rooted political obstacles have tended to prevent extensive U.N. direction of a country's internal matters and even stifled debate about the appropriateness of such involvement. Those barriers stem from the talisman of "sovereignty." That ill-defined and amorphous notion of international law has been used to denote everything from a state's political independence—its separate existence as a political unit on the world scene—the more extreme view that all the internal affairs of a state are beyond the scrutiny of the international community. The states that achieved independence after 1945 attach great—almost exaggerated—importance to the concept of sovereignty. Those countries, organized regionally or as the Group of 77 (now numbering over 120 countries), are quick to resist perceived threats to sovereignty—whether as humanitarian assistance or U.N. peacekeeping in civil conflicts such as the one in Bosnia. They view an unqualified doctrine of sovereignty as a protection against the predatory designs of stronger states.

Many states, especially China in recent years, have sought to hide behind "sovereignty" to shield themselves from international criticism of their abysmal human rights records. Their position endures despite the emerging consensus—codified in the Charter, the Universal Declaration of Human Rights, and numerous U.N. conventions, and institutionalized through the U.N. Human Rights Commission—that human rights are of international concern and that the world community has a right and a duty to promote the basic human dignity of persons in all countries. Sovereignty has been invoked to block international involvement in other issues as well, like pollution, public health, and narcotics.

Exceptions to Absolute Sovereignty

But the tide is slowly changing, or, as Boutros-Ghali has put it, perhaps the tide was never as far out as some proponents of sovereignty would have it. In his June 1992 report, he observed that "the time of absolute and exclusive sovereignty . . . has passed; its theory was never matched by reality." He called for "a balance between the needs of good internal governance and the requirements of an ever more interdependent world." That the theory was never matched by reality is well documented, especially in ways that the world community has aided states in distress.

> ***"Deeply rooted political obstacles have tended to prevent extensive U.N. direction of a country's internal matters."***

Many economic assistance programs, for example, require the recipient state to undertake policies of a wholly domestic nature. Such "conditionality" is widely accepted, despite the occasional objection from target states. Some conditions relate to the use of the money, such as ensuring that it is spent on a specific project. Others link aid to the recipient's policies on other matters, such as human rights practices, expropriation policy, or, more recently, democratization efforts. The International Monetary Fund (IMF) mandates recipients of credit to enter into detailed agreements that require the country to reform, and perhaps even restructure, its economy. The IMF sets targets for inflation, money supply, and foreign exchange reserves, and the recipient has little choice but to comply if it wants to retain access to IMF credit and bank loans. It is therefore unpersuasive to contend that absolute sovereignty—in the sense of full freedom over domestic policy—is undiminished when countries choose to accept such conditioned international assistance.

Also, humanitarian assistance has often been delivered regardless of whether host governments have given formal assent to all the operations. When the U.N. High Commissioner for Refugees (UNHCR) is given authority to enter a country to care for refugees, it normally works with the host government to accomplish its purpose. The International Committee for the Red Cross, in exchange for its vow of secrecy, is granted access to persons in prisons and can conduct other humanitarian activities, such as exchanges of prisoners in countries experiencing civil strife. Even when governments have officially denied permission—as in Afghanistan, Ethiopia, and Sudan during the 1980s—humanitarian entities have deliberately found ways to circumvent official policy. The United Nations itself, in a June 1992 General Assembly resolution on humanitarian involvement, set forth a somewhat remarkable principle governing such efforts. It noted that humanitarian assistance "*should* [not "shall"] be provided with the consent of the affected *country* [not "state" or "government"] and *in principle* on the basis of an appeal by the affected country" (italics added).

"The traditional view of sovereignty has so decayed that all should recognize the appropriateness of U.N. measures inside member states."

In a similar fashion, the problems of the environment overwhelm traditional concepts of national sovereignty. The effects of desertification, global warming, destruction of the ozone layer, and acid rain know no national boundaries. Solutions to such problems will require international regimes that constrain domestic activities, like the emission of ozone-depleting gases.

The long-term acceptance of limitations on absolute sovereignty, the emerging views expressed by the world community regarding the propriety and legality of humanitarian assistance to countries in distress, and member states' increased willingness to entrust more authority to the U.N. all point to new alternatives for responding to the phenomenon of failed states. The international community should now be prepared to consider a novel, expansive—and desperately needed—effort by the U.N. to undertake nation-saving responsibilities.

United Nations Conservatorship

The conceptual basis for the effort should lie in the idea of conservatorship. In domestic systems when the polity confronts persons who are utterly incapable of functioning on their own, the law often provides some regime whereby the community itself manages the affairs of the victim. Forms of guardianship or trusteeship are a common response to broken families, serious mental or physical illness, or economic destitution. The hapless individual is placed under the responsibility of a trustee or guardian, who is charged to look out for the best interests of that person. In a commercial context, bankruptcy codes accomplish a similar purpose, providing a transitional period under which those unable to conduct business relations are given a second chance at economic viability.

> ***"The United Nations should . . . foster democratic institutions and help build elements of a civil society."***

It is time that the United Nations considers such a response to the plight of failed states. The undertaking would flow logically from its historical efforts in non-self-governing territories as well as from the tradition of conditioning aid and credits on certain behavior. Limiting the U.N.'s conservatorship role to the formal Trust Territories (of which only the tiny islands of Palau remain) is much like limiting legal guardianship to minors, or bankruptcy to new companies. Such a qualification stems from an incorrect premise—that only territories not yet fully independent require U.N. protection and oversight—and fails to promote the central Charter values: human rights for all and stability in international relations. The Charter also entrusts the United Nations with achieving "international cooperation in solving international problems of an economic, social, cultural, or humanitarian character, and in promoting and encouraging respect for human rights." Conservatorship would fulfill that goal.

The traditional view of sovereignty has so decayed that all should recognize the appropriateness of U.N. measures inside member states to save them from self-destruction. At the same time, though, the United Nations cannot simply begin to involve itself in the affairs of member states as if they were suddenly part of the trusteeship system. The irreducible minimum of sovereignty requires some form of consent from the host state. Whether that consent must be a formal invitation or simply the absence of opposition would seem to depend upon the circumstances. The only exception to the principle ought to be rare situations involving major violations of human rights or the prospect of regional conflict where warring factions oppose an international presence. Cambodia under the Khmer Rouge might well have merited such an extraordinary form of forcible conservatorship, to prevent completion of the "auto-genocide" the Khmer Rouge started.

Models for U.N. Trusteeship

Three models for a U.N. guardianship role are suggested here: governance assistance, delegation of governmental authority, and direct U.N. trusteeship. Each builds upon multilateral assistance efforts of the past. Each seeks to seize the moment offered by newly evolving conceptions of sovereignty.

Where the target state still maintains some type of minimal governmental structure—where the state is failing, but not yet failed—the U.N. should provide aid through what is best described as "governance assistance." That alternative assumes the existence of a regime that is both effective to some degree—in that it maintains some control over the instruments of state power—and internationally recognized (even if not democratically chosen). Examples of such states might include Georgia, Zaire, and possibly a handful of other states in Africa and Asia. They have experienced economic breakdown or political unrest but not complete civil destruction. The governance assistance would build upon existing technical assistance programs but be far more expansive. Instead of merely offering advice or training, the U.N. would assign personnel to work directly with governmental officials on the country's most pressing needs. U.N. personnel would help administer the state, although the final decision-making authority would remain with the government. Conditions for providing such assistance and intervention might include not only economic change, but modification of the political structure and process where those have a bearing on the health of the state.

> ***"The U.N. Charter should provide a mechanism for direct international trusteeship."***

The technical training of the sort now funded by the UNDP would of course continue. But because the goal of conservatorship is to enable the state to get on its feet again, the aid should be directed at those sectors least equipped to respond to the country's needs, whether they be law enforcement, the military, transportation, or health services. The United Nations should also foster democratic institutions and help build elements of a civil society. Thus, it might help draft a constitution, organize free elections, or encourage nongovernmental Organizations (NGOs) that are working to strengthen civic institutions, including political parties and judicial systems. NGOs have performed such functions in Eastern Europe and in the states of the former Soviet Union. Obviously, the U.N. will have an even more delicate task when the incumbent government is corrupt; the line between reforming it and undermining it may be thin, and close coordination with nongovernmental actors will be needed to ensure that the overall interests of the country are paramount.

Delegation of Authority to the U.N.

For those states that have already failed, a second, more intrusive form of conservatorship would be appropriate. Here, the state could actually delegate certain governmental functions to the U.N. That process is already underway, at least in theory, in Cambodia, which clearly qualifies as a failed state: Twenty years of civil war, invasions, outside arms supplies, gross violations of human rights, massive dislocations of its population, and destruction of its infrastructure have rendered the country incapable of governing itself. When peace efforts aimed at a reconciliation of four warring factions met with no success, the five permanent members of the Security Council developed a formula, ultimately endorsed by those factions, for a U.N. operation: the United Nations Transitional Authority in Cambodia (UNTAC). It exercised oversight over the country until the [May 1993] elections. The unparalleled authority given to the U.N. included aspects of civil administration. It controlled five ministries, supervised others, had access to all documents, could issue binding directives and replace personnel, all to create a neutral environment for elections.

"Placing member states, many would argue, under intrusive U.N. supervision would undermine basic notions of sovereignty and violate the "sovereign equality" of members."

UNTAC's broad powers were fully consistent with Cambodia's status as an independent state because its authority was delegated to it by the warring factions. The Cambodians agreed to create a Supreme National Council (SNC), composed of representatives of the four factions and acting as the "unique . . . source of authority" and embodiment of Cambodian sovereignty. Under the 1991 Paris Agreements, the SNC delegated to the United Nations all the authority needed to ensure that the accords would be successfully implemented. However, the United Nations was required to follow the instructions of the SNC when that body adopted positions unanimously or when Prince Norodom Sihanouk, the country's hereditary monarch and the president of the SNC, chose to speak on its behalf and its views were consistent, in the U.N.'s opinion, with the agreements. That arrangement ensured that Cambodia retained its "sovereignty." At the same time, the U.N.'s role certainly meant that Cambodia lacked full freedom to manage its internal affairs.

The Willingness of the International Community

Whether the reality of the Cambodia experience will match the promise of the Paris Agreements remain to be seen, but the "Cambodia model" has the advantage that it is fully consistent with the Charter while allowing for an extensive U.N. role. It also preserves a modicum of authority for local elites by requiring the U.N. to consider fully their advice when they can all agree. Moreover, if the country actually has a government of some kind that can delegate authority, the conservatorship need not create anything like a Supreme National Council. The Cambodian precedent may well represent the limit to which the international community is willing to consider guardianship for member states. It may also prove the best model for solving Bosnia's woes. If a committee authoritatively representing Croats, Muslims, and Serbs—and their militias—could agree to delegate certain functions to the U.N., pending elections, then there might be a way through Bosnia's seemingly intractable ethnic conflict.

Finally, there is the most radical option: direct U.N. trusteeship. . . . If the forces in a country cannot agree upon the basic components of a political settlement—such as free and fair elections—and accept administration by an impartial outside authority pending elections, then the U.N. Charter should provide a mechanism for direct international trusteeship. Although no state should be the unwilling object of a U.N. trusteeship, states could voluntarily relinquish control over their internal and external affairs for a defined period. The trusteeship plan would go further than the Cambodia model; local authorities wold turn over power to the United Nations and follow its orders, rather than retaining a veto.

In general, the United Nations would act as the administering authority, although a group of states might also perform that function, such as the European Community with respect to Bosnia. In any case, the U.N. and the affected state would negotiate a trusteeship agreement, which would contain the essential elements upon which the state authorities could agree. . . .

Objections

Any of the three types of conservatorship outlined above—and especially formal trusteeships—are bound to bring objections. Placing member states, many would argue, under intrusive U.N. supervision would undermine basic notions of sovereignty and violate the "sovereign equality" of members enshrined in Article 2(1). On a more practical level, the U.N. has never itself administered a territory, except for the brief experience in Irian Jaya in 1962–63; administering trusteeships may prove beyond its capacity and will certainly prove costly.

Those arguments are not decisive. Sovereignty, even as touted by many developing states, is consistent with the idea of conservatorships because the purpose of conservatorship is to enable the state to resume responsibility for itself. Failed states are self-governing only in the narrowest sense. Though not under the control of a colonial power, they hardly govern themselves. It seems appropriate to modernize and reorient U.N. programs to cover the "newly non-self-governing territories." The entire Cambodia operation, for example, is organized toward permitting the Cambodian people to exercise their self-determination, the same goal the Charter posits for the trusteeship system. Thus, U.N. assistance—whether in the form of intrusive oversight or outright trusteeship—furthers sovereignty in the long run. Moreover, notions of sovereignty are changing. The world community's responsibility to promote human rights in failed states suggests that the old notions of sovereignty should not block conservatorships. Such arrangements would advance popular sovereignty in the long run.

"The world community's responsibility to promote human rights . . . suggests that the old notions of sovereignty should not block conservatorships."

Finally, with respect to the U.N.'s lack of experience, its supervision of Namibian independence and conduct of ever more complex peacekeeping functions in Central America and the former Yugoslavia bode well for its ability to adapt to the more complex demands of conservatorship. The results of the Cambodia operation will also prove important. Clearly, though, performing those conservatorship tasks will require significant new resources.

The United Nations Should Foster Self-Government in Africa

by Paul Johnson

About the author: *Paul Johnson is an historian and is the author of* Modern Times: The World from the Twenties to the Eighties.

We are witnessing today a revival of colonialism, albeit in a new form. It is a trend that should be encouraged, it seems to me, on practical as well as moral grounds. There simply is no alternative in nations where governments have crumbled and the most basic conditions for civilized life have disappeared, as is now the case in a great many third-world countries.

The New Colonialism

Third-world governments have long sought military assistance from the advanced powers to put down internal rebellions. But a historic line was crossed when American marines landed in Somalia [in November 1992]—without any request, because no government existed. The intervention, made with the approval of the United Nations Security Council, was a humanitarian attempt to supply some kind of protection for life and property in a country that had shown it could not govern itself. The old-style United Nations approach, of sending officials to hold talks with the opposing factions, was visibly demonstrated to have failed when an angry Somali mob threw rubbish at the walls of the United Nations compound, thinking that the Secretary General, Boutros Boutros-Ghali, was within.

Nor is Somalia the only instance in which the international community is being obliged to take on a semi-colonial role. On March 31 [1993] the Security Council voted, without dissent (China abstained) for direct military intervention in the internal affairs of the former Yugoslavia. This decision indicated, among other things, that the new colonialism is not just about white men running the

Paul Johnson, "Colonialism's Back—and Not a Moment Too Soon," *The New York Times Magazine*, April 18, 1993.

affairs of nonwhite countries but can involve intervention in Europe—or anywhere else.

But it is obvious that Africa, where normal government is breaking down in a score or more states, is the most likely theater for such action. The appeals for help come not so much from Africa's political elites, who are anxious to cling to the trappings of power, as from ordinary desperate citizens, who carry the burden of misrule. Recently in Liberia, where rival bands of heavily armed thugs have been struggling for mastery, a humble inhabitant of the capital, Monrovia, named after the fifth president of the United States, approached a marine guarding the United States Embassy and said, "For God's sake come and govern us!"

The Roots of Trusteeship

The grass-roots origin of the appeal for the return of colonialism puts the whole phenomenon in a different perspective. The present generation, even in the former colonial powers, has been brought up to consider any form of colonialism as inherently evil, a gross form of oppression practiced by technologically superior powers on weaker races. That, of course, is not how its practitioners, throughout history, saw it.

The Greeks, who invented colonialism, founded city-colonies to spread their civilization. The Romans, who inherited the Greek empire, did the same. Most of the people thus colonized welcomed this form of rule and lamented the destruction of the Roman Empire in the fifth century A.D. as a catastrophe.

From the Renaissance through to the early years of the twentieth century, first the European powers and then Russia and the United States competed for colonies, and all believed they were bestowing civilization on those less fortunate. By the early twentieth century, however, colonialism was operating under growing restrictions imposed by liberal opinion.

Indeed, by the end of the First World War, when Woodrow Wilson insured the triumph of self-determination throughout Europe, colonialism was manifestly on the moral defensive. Hence, the Versailles treaty, instead of carving up the former colonies of Germany and Turkey among the victorious powers, created trusteeships. These were territories not yet considered fit for self-government but mandated by the League of Nations to various civilized powers to be prepared for independence. Britain got Iraq, Jordan, Palestine and Tanganyika (now Tanzania); France got Syria and Lebanon; and the United States and Japan were awarded various Pacific territories.

"For God's sake come and govern us!"

"Trusteeship" was a notion derived from English common law, in which a child was made a ward of the court until attaining the age of twenty-one. It had first been applied to a territory in 1899, when Britain, with Egypt, created the

Anglo-Egyptian Sudan, known as a condominium, the aim being to train cadres who would eventually lead it to independence. This British notion that there was no such thing as a colony in perpetuity, but that all territories would become independent when they were ready for it, was already implicit in British administration throughout its Asian and African empire, and had been put into force in its so-called White Dominions of South Africa, Canada, Australia and New Zealand.

Hostility to Colonialism

From Versailles onward, then, there was a growing assumption that all colonies would eventually be freed. Hostility to colonialism increased throughout the Second World War, fueled by American high-mindedness and by the ideological beliefs of the Soviet regime, where Lenin's anticolonial tract *Imperialism* was part of the canon.

These new moral forces, and the physical impact of the Second World War, which weakened the old European colonial powers, especially Britain, brought about the age of decolonization. There was a paradox in this process. Colonies had never been better administered than during their last phase. Britain had set increasingly high standards. Ghana and Nigeria, for example, were meticulously prepared for their freedom. Morocco was admirably ruled by France in the person of Marshal Lyautey, who gave it a superb infrastructure of roads and ports. The Congo, originally looted by Belgium, got a model trustee-type administration in the 1950s.

> ***"By the end of the First World War . . . colonialism was manifestly on the moral defensive."***

But at precisely the time when colonies were deriving the maximum benefit from European rule, the decision was taken to liberate them forthwith. Many experienced colonial administrators were appalled at the way in which the gradualist approach to self-rule was abruptly abandoned. But in the rush, their voices went unheeded. There are fashions in geopolitics as well as in clothes, and instant decolonization was one. By the mid-1960s it was virtually all over.

Then came the reckoning, borne not indeed by the colonial powers themselves, which on balance benefited financially from surrendering their "white man's burden" (as Rudyard Kipling called it), but by their former subjects. In Africa, the instability that began immediately after the Belgian Congo was decolonized in 1960 has since continued throughout most of the continent. Not everyone has suffered. Three categories have flourished: the professional politicians, the army officers and the less scrupulous businessmen. But most ordinary Africans have done badly, as a result of the collapse of constitutional government and the rule of law, as well as civil and tribal conflicts, invasion, corruption and man-made famines.

In the Congo, now [since October 1971] Zaire, average real incomes are now a fraction of what they were in the early 1960s, and this is probably true of a number of countries, though in present conditions statistics are worthless. Some of the smaller states have drifted out of the international economy almost altogether. Certain states, like Chad and Mauritania, have known nothing but internal warfare for a generation—a Hobbesian nightmare in which life is "nasty, brutish and short." The record of Angola and Mozambique is not much better.

"Colonies had never been better administered than during their last phase."

Particularly sad has been the ruin of territories that once were advancing rapidly under colonialism. The Anglo-Egyptian Sudan, the most notable of them, has been the victim of a prolonged civil war, of the famine it inevitably produced and of systematic harassment of the Christian south by the Muslim north. Uganda, another tribute to colonialism, suffered the atrocious tyranny of Idi Amin, and is still impoverished and lawless. Tanzania, a successful mandate, has gone slowly downhill under a quasi-socialist regime, despite having received more financial aid per capita than any other third-world country. There are numerous others: the Central African Republic, Nigeria, Algeria, Liberia, the Horn of Africa.

From Aid to Intervention

Western experts who had backed the rapid transfer of power argued that Africa, in particular, was going through a difficult transition, and that patience—plus assistance of all kinds—was imperative. That view is now discredited. During the 1980s it came to be recognized that government-to-government aid usually served only to keep in power unsuccessful, unpopular and often vicious regimes.

As for patience, the historical record shows it served nobody. By the early 1990s, two of the world's most chronically unstable and poorest black states were Haiti and Liberia, which had been governing themselves for 200 and 150 years respectively. In both, ordinary citizens, who had no security for property or even life, clamored for Western intervention.

During the 1980s, old-style aid was largely discontinued. Western governments underwrote specific, approved projects, and supervised the spending. At the same time, huge quantities of money and goods were distributed by international charities. But both methods, while an improvement on the old, in many cases ran into the insuperable problem of government breakdown, which meant that aid supplies were commandeered and looted or sold on the black market by tribal factions and brigands. By the early 1990s, some international agencies were beginning openly to argue that, in crisis situations, like the famines in East Africa, a Western military presence was essential to supplement a largely nonexistent government.

Recall, however, that it was United Nations theory and practice to deploy troops at the request of a legitimate government. But what was to be done in places like Haiti, where there was no legitimate government, or Somalia, where there was no government at all? Were the United Nations and the West to stand idly by?

During the 1970s the answer would almost certainly have been yes. But in the 1980s geopolitical fashion once more began to change, as Western powers showed a renewed willingness to use force in what they believed to be right. The new fashion was set by Margaret Thatcher's Britain in 1982, when it reversed the aggression in the Falklands. Thus emboldened, President Reagan intervened to reverse an extremist coup in Grenada, and both powers led a mighty coalition of states, including many in the third world, to reverse the Iraqi occupation of Kuwait in 1990.

The decision of the United States, with United Nations authority, to send marines into Somalia marked a new turning point. Here there could be no question of invitation from the local government, since no such body existed and the whole purpose of the landing was to insure aid supplies got to where they were needed, and to protect them, and aid workers, from the armed bands that divided the country between themselves. But such armed intervention, by its very nature, is bound to prove unsatisfactory, and the American effort has already run into difficulties.

Revive Trusteeship

French and Belgian forces used in "rescue missions" in central Africa have met exactly the same problem. They can restore order for a time, and in limited areas, but they cannot tackle the source of the disorder, which is political and requires a political solution. The moment they pull out, the disorders reappear.

It is worth remembering that the original Dutch, Portuguese and British traders who came to the African coasts in the early modern period, with the aim of doing business and with no intention of settling, faced exactly the same problem. They could not trade without stability, and to get stability they had to impose it. So they built little forts, which became bigger and eventually turned into the nucleus of colonies. European colonialism in its origins was to some extent a reluctant and involuntary process.

> ***"Government breakdown . . . meant that aid supplies were commandeered and looted or sold on the black market by tribal factions and brigands."***

Happily, the civilized powers need not get stuck in the old colonial quagmire, because they have the example of the trusteeship system before them. The Security Council could commit a territory where authority has irretrievably broken down to one or more trustees. These would be empowered not merely to impose order by force but to assume political functions. They would in effect be possessed of sovereign powers.

Their mandate would usually be of limited duration—5, 10, 20 years, for example—and subject to supervision by the Security Council; and their ultimate object would be to take constitutional measures to insure a return to effective self-government with all deliberate speed. I stress "effective" because we must not repeat the mistakes of the 1960s. The trustees should not plan to withdraw until they are reasonably certain that the return to independence will be successful this time. So the mandate may last 50 years, or 100.

"The moment ['rescue missions' in Central Africa] pull out, the disorders reappear."

Reviving trusteeship means reversing the conventional wisdom of the last half-century, which laid down that all peoples are ready for independence and that any difficulties they encounter are the result of distortions created by colonialism itself. But this philosophy is false, as painful events have repeatedly demonstrated. Africa's problems—and the problems of some states outside Africa—are not created by colonialism or demographics or natural disasters or shortage of credit. Most of the horrors, including famine, are created by government: bad, incompetent and corrupt government, usually all three together, or by no government at all.

Not Fit to Govern

For more than thirty years the international community has been treating symptoms, not causes. The basic cause is obvious but is never publicly admitted: some states are not yet fit to govern themselves. Their continued existence, and the violence and human degradation they breed, is a threat to the stability of their neighbors as well as an affront to our consciences. There is a moral issue here: the civilized world has a mission to go out to these desperate places and govern.

By "civilized world" we ought eventually to include among potential trustees not only Germany and Japan, which will soon be eligible for permanent membership in the Security Council, but countries like Singapore, which have proved themselves models of public administration. Russia, China and India will eventually play their part—one way to educate them in the global responsibilities that their size and numbers oblige them to assume. There must be several models of trusteeship, ranging from the provision of basic government where none exists to the setting up of internal security networks and mandatory economic management.

If done firmly and confidently, such state-building will prove popular. It is important, therefore, that the first pilot projects should be carefully chosen, and its trustees experienced. Somalia is an obvious choice. So is Liberia and perhaps Haiti. Zaire, where the crumbling Mobutu [Sese Seko] tyranny will be followed by anarchy, is another candidate, as are Angola and Mozambique.

Making a start will not be easy because it means scrapping the easy assumptions of decades. Once again, the already overburdened United States will have to take the major responsibility, though it can count on staunch support from Britain and, in this case, from France. Labor and expense will be needed, as well as brains, leadership and infinite patience. The only satisfaction will be the unspoken gratitude of millions of misgoverned or ungoverned people who will find in this altruistic revival of colonialism the only way out of their present intractable miseries.

The United States Should Protect New Democracies

by Morton H. Halperin

About the author: *Morton H. Halperin, former Washington director of the American Civil Liberties Union and a senior associate of the Carnegie Endowment for International Peace, was nominated but not confirmed for the position of assistant secretary of defense for democracy and peacekeeping by President Bill Clinton in 1993.*

With the collapse of the Soviet Union and the discrediting of communism as a rival model, more and more people are coming to view constitutional democracy as the only legitimate form of government. Around the globe, people are seeking to establish constitutional democracies. Many newly democratic governments are turning to the international community for support, and the international community is beginning to respond. The new democracies face internal and external enemies who oppose progress toward constitutional democracy that undermines entrenched personal, institutional, and financial interests.

Guarantee Democracy

The United States should take the lead in promoting the trend toward democracy. Democratic governments are more peaceful and less given to provoking war or inciting violence. States that are constitutional democracies are less likely to go to war with the United States or other democracies, and are more likely to support limits on weapons trade, encourage peaceful resolution of disputes, and foster free trade. Thus, when a people attempts to hold free elections and establish a constitutional democracy, the United States and the international community should not only assist but should "guarantee" the result. Those measures should be institutionalized in organizations like the United Nations and the Organization of American States (OAS), which would be responsible

Abridged from Morton H. Halperin, "Guaranteeing Democracy." Reproduced with permission from *Foreign Policy* 91 (Summer 1993). Copyright 1993 by the Carnegie Endowment for International Peace.

for carrying out missions to ensure the success of constitutional democracy.

The international community should establish a process that parallels the provision of the U.S. Constitution under which the federal government should be obliged to guarantee to each state what was in 1789 called a "republican" form of government. Although the Founding Fathers wrote the Guarantee Clause of the Constitution for the American federal government of the eighteenth century, the same principle has become valid for the international community of the twentieth century. Peace, security, and the establishment of a true world order require that all states, including the United States, work toward that goal by seeking to preserve democracy where it is being established. We are now at a historic crossroads; the opportunity to take a giant step toward universal constitutional democracy is here and should be seized.

> ***"The United States should take the lead in promoting the trend toward democracy."***

There is no reason why American foreign policy should not reflect American values. Americans prefer to see other countries enjoy the same liberties they do. That desire is especially strong when other peoples show that they too want to decide their fate by democratic means—as the Soviet people did in August 1991 [when popular opposition defeated an attempted coup by hard-line Communist Party members]. Further, if Americans saw that U.S. policymakers were promoting democracy around the globe, they would be more likely to support American policy with financial commitments and military action when necessary to accomplish those foreign policy objectives.

Democratic Rights

That is not to argue that the United States or the international community should try to impose constitutional democracy on those with different views. Our efforts ought to focus on situations in which a people aspire to constitutional democracy and request global support.

The essential elements of constitutional democracy derive from Western ideals. But they have become enshrined in agreements and resolutions that have garnered broad support from the international community in the post-Cold War era. Those tenets include free elections, the right of political dissent, limits on arbitrary police power, and an independent judiciary with the power to protect those rights. They find expression in the two key international documents laying out the basic rights of persons: the Universal Declaration of Human Rights, adopted by the U.N. General Assembly in 1948, and the International Covenant on Civil and Political Rights.

The cornerstone of democratic governance is the right to conduct free and fair elections. The Universal Declaration of Human Rights states that "the will of the people shall be the basis of the authority of government; this shall be expressed in periodic and genuine elections which shall be by universal and equal suffrage, and shall be held by secret vote."

More recently, the General Assembly adopted a resolution establishing procedures to authorize the monitoring and certification of "genuine elections" when requested by member states. U.N. supervision of elections is crucial to the trend toward constitutional democracy because in order to be considered "free and genuine," elections must meet certain criteria.

In addition to universal franchise, elections should be open to multiple parties, use a secret ballot, and be free of fraud or intimidation. The winning party should be able to form a government capable of fulfilling its mandate. It should also be willing to relinquish power if subsequent election results require it. An elected government should be forbidden to alter basic constitutional provisions in an effort to seize extra-constitutional powers or stop new elections.

The growing importance of elections as the only way of validating governance is clear: More than 110 governments are now legally committed to permitting open, multiparty, secret-ballot elections with universal franchise. Many have made that commitment within the last several years.

Minority Rights

The final essential element of constitutional democracy—respect for minority rights—was buried as an international legal concern during the Cold War in order to discourage claims for self-determination and to encourage assimilation of minority groups. The end of the Cold War, however, has changed the political climate. States are more willing to adhere to documents that protect minority rights, albeit within the confines of noninterference. A working group of the U.N. Sub-Commission on Prevention of Discrimination and Protection of Minorities has prepared a draft Declaration on the Rights of Minorities. The draft affirms protection of minority rights as elemental to stability within multi-ethnic states.

"U.N. supervision of elections is crucial to the trend toward constitutional democracy."

The Conference on Security and Cooperation in Europe (CSCE) also renewed its interest in minority rights at its June 1990 Conference on the Human Dimension in Copenhagen. Further, the Charter of Paris for a New Europe, signed by all CSCE members in 1990, declared that "the rights of persons belonging to national minorities must be fully respected as part of universal human rights."

When a meeting of experts on national minority problems convened in Geneva in 1991 under CSCE auspices, it linked minority protections to constitutional democracy and called for the elimination of noninterference principles for that particular issue:

> Issues concerning national minorities, as well as compliance with international obligations and commitments concerning the rights of persons belonging to them, are matters of legitimate international concern and consequently do not constitute exclusively an internal affair of the respective state.

Thus, an international consensus is emerging not just about words like "democracy" and "free elections," but about their real operational meaning and the minimal requirements of a constitutional democracy: free elections, right of political dissent, rule of law, and protection of minority rights, all enforced by an independent judiciary.

The United Nations' Role

The notion that the international community should guarantee those rights in specific situations is gaining strength, too. Though an "international guarantee clause" has not yet been articulated . . . the international community is moving in that direction. . . .

The United Nations, no longer a prisoner of Cold War politics, has also become more active in advocating democracy. The General Assembly in 1991 passed a resolution entitled "Enhancing the effectiveness of the principle of periodic and genuine elections." The resolution was prompted by frequent demands from member countries for monitoring elections and certifying the results. It also endorsed the secretary-general's view that a senior official be assigned to coordinate and ensure fair consideration of any such requests.

However, the U.N.'s commitment to constitutional democracy goes beyond resolutions. In particular, two recent U.N. missions represent the most forceful and persistent efforts to implement the principles of constitutional democracy. The peace processes in Cambodia and El Salvador were designed specifically to establish constitutional democracy in those war-torn countries. The extensive deployment of both peacekeeping "blue helmets" and human rights monitors and administrators is evidence of the U.N.'s recognition of its obligation to guarantee not just "peace" but also constitutional democracy. It is a model for action under an international guarantee clause.

Peace in Cambodia

The Cambodian peace process is the most ambitious the United Nations has ever undertaken. Signed in Paris in October 1991, the accord established the United Nations Transitional Authority in Cambodia (UNTAC), the umbrella organization for peacekeeping and administration until the first elections, scheduled for May 1993, could be held. UNTAC used blue helmets [U.N. forces] to police the country, protect the right of all political parties to campaign for election, ensure freedom of speech and the press, and conduct and certify elections.

"Protection of minority rights [is] elemental to stability within multi-ethnic states."

The Paris accord's most striking feature is that all factions to the conflict signed on to cooperate with the United Nations in rebuilding the political infrastructure in Cambodia. The Khmer Rouge's subsequent violations of the accord notwithstanding, all the Cambodian factions agreed to create "a system of liberal democracy, on the basis of pluralism," which is in essence a constitutional democracy. The Paris accord cites all the elements necessary for a constitutional democracy: periodic and genuine elections; freedom of assembly and association including that for political parties; due process and equality before the law; and an independent judiciary. Further, the agreement clearly makes it both a right and an obligation for outside contracting powers to guarantee human rights should abuses occur. In the event of violations, the powers agreed to consult immediately and to take appropriate steps. Specifically, "they will call upon the United Nations" to take steps to prevent human rights violations.

"The U.N.'s commitment to constitutional democracy goes beyond resolutions."

The peace accord undercuts the argument that constitutional democracy is a Western notion, not applicable beyond Europe and perhaps the Western Hemisphere. Though many would argue that the Cambodians would not accept the principles of constitutional democracy, all the parties at the negotiating table explicitly agreed to a peace plan that requires them to eventually establish a constitutional democracy. The factions could have negotiated some kind of power-sharing arrangement instead, but they went further. The Cambodia accord is, in essence, a contractual obligation between external powers and internal factions.

[The U.N. operation was withdrawn in September 1993] though the strident Khmer Rouge were refusing to cooperate with the international mandate to lay down their arms and accept a cease-fire. While the outcome of the accord hung in the balance, the international commitment to work to establish constitutional democracy in Cambodia remained solid, although its willingness to use major force to enforce that objective is not clear.

Peace in El Salvador

The U.N.-sponsored peace process in El Salvador is similar in many respects to that in Cambodia. The National Commission for the Consolidation of Peace (COPAZ) operated parallel to the U.N.'s Observer Mission in El Salvador [until elections were held in March/April 1994]. COPAZ, like the Cambodian Supreme National Council, comprised representatives from all interested parties: the National Assembly, the leftist Farabundo Martí National Liberation Front (FMLN), and the military. Significantly, the passage of Security Council Resolution 693 in 1991, which created the Salvadoran observer operation, was a landmark for the United Nations; it was the first time the organization had constructed a mission with three component divisions—human rights, military, and police—to verify a peace settlement by parties to an internal conflict.

With difficulties, the Salvadoran peace process has progressed. Most important for the international community, both the government and the FMLN have pledged formally to cooperate in establishing a constitutional democracy. They have agreed to reform the electoral system and the judiciary as well as establish the Office of the National Counsel for the Defence of Human Rights, which will direct special attention to the parties' observance of the rights to life, integrity, and security of the person, due process of law, personal liberty, and freedom of expression and association—rights outlined in the 1990 San José Agreement on Human Rights and enforced by the U.N. observers. Regrettably, no outside power explicitly guaranteed the outcome of the peace process, but Mexico, Spain, the United States, and Venezuela all have actively pushed it forward.

Intervention Rules

Democratization has an undeniable momentum in countries around the world today. Within multinational organizations a parallel movement toward international guarantees to protect budding constitutional democracies is also gaining force. Those trends are strongly in the American interest. The next step for U.S. policy is to actively support, even push, the development of such trends. First, the United States must unequivocally declare its willingness to help fledgling democracies persevere against internal and external enemies. Still, that commitment cannot be unqualified; the United States should offer such guarantees only upon the request of a state and should not try to impose its will or its own version of government on people who do not ask for assistance. For its commitment to democracy to be credible, the United States must also make it clear that any assistance to a government, economic or otherwise, will be withdrawn if the process of democratization is interrupted.

"It [is] both a right and an obligation for outside contracting powers to guarantee human rights should abuses occur."

Second, the United States should explicitly surrender the right to intervene unilaterally in the internal affairs of other countries by overt military means or by covert operations. Such self-restraint would bar interventions like those in Grenada and Panama, unless the United States first gained the explicit consent of the international community acting through the Security Council or a regional organization. The United States would, however, retain the right granted under Article 51 of the U.N. Charter to act unilaterally if necessary to meet threats to international peace and security involving aggression across borders (such as those in Kuwait and in Bosnia-Herzegovina).

Third, the United States should work closely with other powers—including the permanent members of the Security Council, Germany, Japan, and Mexico—to develop norms and procedures for international guarantees to support constitutional democracy. We need a consensus on when to offer such guarantees, how to determine if there is a disruption of the democratic process, and how the international community should decide on steps to counter the disruption. For example, the United States and other guarantors might respond following requests from a country's political factions that wish to craft a peace plan, or after requests by a government to the U.N. or a regional organization to monitor or conduct elections. The international community should also respond when a group struggling for self-determination seeks international recognition. The United States should consider recognition and provide assistance only if the group makes a firm commitment to constitutional democracy.

An International Guarantee Clause

In all such cases, the United States, the United Nations, and regional organizations should insist on a guarantee clause by which they ensure the maintenance of constitutional democracy. An international guarantee clause will be credible only if key countries, including the United States, commit to using force if necessary to restore or establish constitutional democracy. Force should be employed only after nonviolent actions, including condemnation and isolation through economic boycotts and blockades, have been tried.

An international guarantee clause would also require standard procedures for authorizing intervention including any combination of the following: a U.N. Security Council resolution, a resolution of a regional organization, or the consensus of a group of guaranteeing powers designated in an agreement with a particular country. The next step would involve establishing in the country a monitoring presence of indefinite duration with broad rights of access, as happened in El Salvador. Though it could be argued that an open-ended presence is not politically or financially feasible, the lack of such a presence would be much more costly. Breaches of democracy can initiate mass migrations, internal violence, or a further collapse of democracy in an unstable neighboring country. . . . Then, if requested, a permanent or open-ended presence of an international police force ought to be provided to keep the peace and to prevent police abuse or even a military coup.

Those who find the idea of an international guarantee clause utopian should be reminded that a Southerner at the time of the American Constitutional Convention might have had the same reaction to the U.S. Guarantee Clause. The two-century-old promise to defend a republican form of government within each state, and thus to ensure peace and stability among the states of the union, has become a model for the international community today. In fact, the pursuit of American values, if done with pragmatism and respect for the opinions of humankind, can combine the best of American idealism and realism to yield a position that is truly in the national interest. Today, the effort to guarantee democracy, at least to people who have it and want to keep it, is just such a policy. Americans should strive for no less.

The West Is Responsible for Peace and Democracy in Africa

by Jennifer Parmelee

About the author: *Jennifer Parmelee is a* Washington Post *special correspondent based in Ethiopia.*

Before April 1994, those outsiders who could pinpoint Rwanda on a map might know it as "the Switzerland of Africa," a tiny republic of rolling green hills where mountain gorillas cavorted with anthropologist Dian Fossey. But then, for one ephemeral and terrible moment, Rwanda was thrust in our faces in images that screamed of blood and terror.

Fifteen Minutes of Infamy

At first, the world was riveted in horror to scenes of carnage: Women and children were hacked to pieces by machete-wielding gangsters who reveled in the gore; the heads and limbs of victims were sorted and piled neatly, a bone-chilling order in the midst of chaos that harked back to the Holocaust; the leaders on all sides of the conflict boomed away at each other with their big guns, while panicked foreigners scrambled to flee the country.

At a certain point, however, the eyes of the world closed, the cameras clicked off, the capacity to absorb such a living nightmare shut down. Ironically, Rwanda's fifteen minutes of infamy—which confirmed the cliches in the minds of many foreigners that Africa is doomed to an eternal hell of ethnic violence—may consign it to an even deeper oblivion.

The camera lens of international attention is restless and clinical; Sarajevo and South Africa beckon. Another day dawns, so does another story, another crisis. The world, it seems, would like to forget what happened to Rwanda. The U.N. Security Council's decision on April 21, 1994, to pare down its operation in Rwanda to a skeletal staff is a blunt expression of the international commu-

Jennifer Parmelee, "Closing Our Eyes to Rwanda," *The Washington Post National Weekly Edition*, May 2-8, 1994, ©1994 The Washington Post. Reprinted by permission.

nity's sense of powerlessness and unwillingness to intervene further.

There are explanations for this, some logical, none "fair" to the thousands left to the slaughter—and perhaps all of them balanced out by compelling reasons why the world should in fact do everything it can to help.

Like many African countries after the Cold War, Rwanda suffers from the near-total absence of any perceived Western "interest": the country has no oil or other essential commodity, no strategic value and—as of the latest frantic evacuations—virtually no Westerners living there.

A Daily Diet of Disaster

Secondly, the international community—taxed by an unprecedented number of apparently intractable conflicts clamoring for outside help—is stumped in Rwanda's case. U.N. officials puzzle out loud about just how their "mandate" can be applied to the mess that is Rwanda. Thirdly, the appetite for foreign news in the West is diminishing, especially from parts of the world that seem to dish up a daily diet of disaster. That Rwanda, like so many other African conflicts, is not, in the memorable words of U.N. Secretary-General Boutros Boutros-Ghali, "a white man's war," certainly plays into it.

What else can explain why on a single day in February 1994, the bombing of a Sarajevo market, claiming about 60 lives, was prime-time news, while the mortaring of the town of Quito Angola, in which a minimum of 350 black Africans were killed and hundreds maimed, was virtually ignored? Well over 100,000 men, women and children, by conservative estimates, were butchered in fall 1993 in Burundi, which shares a similar pattern of tribal hatred and pogroms with its neighbor Rwanda. But the world hardly shrugged.

> ***"The camera lens of international attention is restless."***

In Somalia, it took tens of thousands of deaths to finally crack open Western consciousness in 1992; it played big on the screens so long as the American and other Western troops were there. In March, when the last of the U.S. troops left, reporters joked that they were writing the "obit" on the Somalia story. They were right.

Beyond Comprehension and Compassion

Contributing to the apparent eagerness to turn away from Rwanda is that this exceedingly bloody conflagration, for most of us, defies comprehension, explanation and thus to a large degree, compassion.

It is not as if Africans have any monopoly on armed madness (look at Afghanistan or Washington, D.C.), ethnic strife (Yugoslavia or Los Angeles) or disregard for human rights (China). There is a grim universal truth at work in Rwanda. As British author Nigel Barley once wrote: "It is one of the more depressing discoveries of the anthropologist that almost all peoples loathe, fear and despise the people next door."

Rwanda, however, somehow has gone way off the charts of international "norms" in times of conflict. It's a plunge deep, deep into the heart of darkness, bringing back images from the worst days of genocide in Cambodia. There is no ideology or religious zeal at work—just raw hatred. Nor can the destructive passions that erupted be defined in purely political terms, nor as the simple result of population pressure in a country that counts about 500 people per square mile.

> ***"Almost all peoples loathe, fear and despise the people next door."***

Terry Leonard, a reporter for the Associated Press who has covered a raft of modern war zones from Sarajevo to Somalia, was shocked and shaken by what he saw in Rwanda. Like the rest of us, he has struggled to put it in some sort of context.

But what context?

Leonard says that although tens of thousands have died in former Yugoslavia over the past year, more than 20,000 were believed killed in a single week in Rwanda. The International Red Cross lost 30 of its Rwandan workers in the same slender time frame, the worst single loss in its 75-year history.

Virtually every journalist in Rwanda had witnessed plenty of human cruelty. Yet most of us still drew a distinction—however fine it might seem—between the act of standing back and shooting a fellow human with a gun and that of standing over a child and hacking him or her to pieces, blood spurting all over you, then sorting the body parts into tidy heaps.

To many of us, "explaining" such brutality comes very close to forgiving.

"I've seen a lot of terrible things in Sarajevo and Somalia, but nothing like what I saw in Rwanda. It was extra-planetary," Leonard told me, recalling the bodies "stacked like cord-wood" at checkpoints manned by young, glassy-eyed, alcohol-breathing thugs who shoved live grenades under his nose.

"How do you find a frame of reference?"

The Constant Reporting of the Exceptional

Some analysts say that reporting the bad news from Rwanda without a frame of reference reinforces all the negative stereotypes that flow out of the Third World.

Peter Adamson, co-founder of Britain's *New Internationalist* magazine and author of UNICEF's annual "State of the World's Children Report," says there are few reports about positive developments in the Third World to counter the emotional and distressing images of catastrophe—what he calls "the constant reporting of the exceptional."

"The hallucination it [reporting] creates is of an oasis of affluence surrounded by an ever-growing, ever-threatening desert of hopelessness and despair," Adamson wrote in the *Independent* last summer. "From this comes an oasis mentality, tinged with guilt and anxiety, and an irksome sense of obligation. . . .

"We are willing to give when the manifestations of poverty are thrust before us; but we wish, for the most part, that the poor world would disappear from our consciousness, like a coin into the darkness of the collecting box."

Wishing them away won't do the trick, however. Africa will not disappear into the darkness of the coin box. Responsibility has a way of coming home to roost, and the West has got its share in Africa.

The Western Push for Democracy

In the case of Rwanda and its twin state, Burundi—for they are inextricably linked—the West had pushed hard for multi-party democracy. But, as with many other African countries, the emphasis on the ballot box was not matched by adequate action on reconfiguring the armed forces, perhaps democracy's biggest enemy on the continent.

In the summer of 1993, Burundi voted in its first-ever president from the Hutu ethnic majority, breaking the hammerlock on power held by the minority Tutsi elite since independence in 1963. Melchior Ndadaye lasted just 100 days before he was cut down by the Tutsi-dominated army, his dismembered body a grim echo of democratic progress. The inter-ethnic bloodbath that followed claimed between 30,000 and 50,000 lives, according to human rights groups.

In Rwanda, much as in Angola before it, the two warring sides had committed themselves in August 1993 to a power-sharing arrangement that included integration of the mostly Tutsi rebels into the Hutu-dominated national army. Unfortunately, as with Angola, they didn't work fast enough. Longtime President Juvenal Habyarimana, as well as a host of top government officials working hard toward inter-ethnic reconciliation, were the first to be cut down.

The Arms Race in Africa

There's another compelling moral factor in the case of Rwanda and much of the Third World: arms. Although much of the slaughter in Rwanda has been carried out with "everyday" weapons like machetes and clubs, the introduction of large amounts of more sophisticated heavy weapons has broadened the scope of the killing.

> ***"Responsibility has a way of coming home to roost, and the West has got its share in Africa."***

Ever since the two superpowers stopped their arms race, the affluent arms-dealing countries have been compensating for lost markets by dumping as many arms as they can on the Third World. The Rwanda Patriotic Front rebels are reportedly armed by Uganda (denied by the Ugandan government). But the biggest suppliers of arms to the Rwandan government are from the West.

The Arms Project of Human Rights Watch in January 1994 released a report that identified France as the major military backer of the government of Rwanda—with details on arming, training and combat assistance to its army. The report states that, despite France's denials, the French military's activities were "tantamount to direct participation in the war."

"'Blood was in the air for months.' But still, the arms kept flowing."

In spite of the alleged armistice, inter-ethnic tensions had been building up a long time before the cataclysm. This tension was evident to almost everyone who lived in Rwanda. As one Belgian diplomat puts it: "Blood was in the air for months." But still, the arms kept flowing.

One of Human Rights Watch's chief consultants on the report said a large European arms shipment to Rwanda on January 26, 1994, had been confiscated by U.N. peacekeepers because it violated the terms of the peace accord. U.N. officials in Kigali confirmed the shipment, saying, "We managed to convince the government that it was not appropriate to a situation of peace."

How the World Can Help

Human Rights Watch says one way the world can help is to push hard for a cease-fire, and try to help protect the innocent civilians the best it can. The U.N. is apparently trying hard on the former, but on the latter seems paralyzed in the face of the all-encompassing terror on the streets. As the top U.N. commander, Brig. Gen. Romeo Dallaire, put it: "We have trouble getting safely to the airport. How can we protect all the civilians?"

If the virulent ethnic cleansing and military battles continued, he added, "We [the U.N.] might as well reduce to a skeleton staff with a briefcase and a flak jacket."

Dallaire's words, addressed to journalists in Kigali in April 1994, have proved prophetic. The U.N. "peacekeeping force" was slashed to about 270 individuals, hardly adequate to keep guard over the more than 20,000 civilians the U.N. put under its "protection" in Kigali.

Journalists too feel powerless to help in a meaningful way. As outsiders, we can almost always leave somebody else's mess behind. Yet it was unspeakably painful to walk out of the Hotel des Mille Collines, where a volatile mixture of Tutsi civilians and Hutu army officers seemed ready to explode at any minute. Even as we headed out to the airport, gangs of young men, armed with machetes and automatic weapons, were circling the surrounding streets, seemingly waiting to close in for the kill.

Men, women and children gathered in the lobby, some begging with tears streaming down their faces to go too. One clear-eyed young man, who seemed to accept their lot in the new world order, was philosophical. "You can't help us," he said, "but you can tell the world that we are here."

Economic Sanctions Can Be Effective

by Ivan Eland

About the author: *Ivan Eland is a national security affairs analyst with the Congressional Budget Office.*

When one nation imposes sanctions on another, it often does so because it has few other policy options. The target nation usually has committed an unacceptable act and pressure is building—particularly in a democratic state—to "do something." As the pressure becomes more intense, the government of the sanctioning nation feels an acute need to respond.

The Goals of Sanctions

The sanctioning government may also feel pressure from the international community to punish the target nation, to uphold international norms, to demonstrate solidarity with allied nations or with internal opposition in the target nation, or to deter worse behavior by demonstrating the will to escalate to a stronger response.

The sanctioning nation wants to take an action stronger than a diplomatic response, but less drastic than covert action or military intervention. Nations have limited ways of influencing the behavior of other nations. Because sanctions occupy the middle ground between diplomatic and paramilitary or military action, they are often selected as the means to put pressure on a target nation.

Since sanctions have both instrumental and symbolic goals, it is not easy to analyze the effectiveness of any particular action. For example, it is commonly supposed that the grain embargo that President Jimmy Carter imposed against the Soviet Union after it invaded Afghanistan [in December 1979] was a failure—after all, the Soviets had not withdrawn their forces by the time Ronald Reagan lifted the embargo [in 1982]. In addition, many analysts point out that the sanctions had very little economic effect because the Soviet Union was able to replace U.S. grain with that of its competitors. But this perception of failure derives from the belief that compliance with the instrumental goal is the sole criterion for success.

At the time, Carter indicated that he was using sanctions to demonstrate U.S. resolve and to deter the Soviets from further aggression in more strategic areas such as Iran, Pakistan, and the Persian Gulf. While it is difficult to determine whether the Soviets intended to take further military action against these other nations, or whether U.S. sanctions deterred them from doing so, given the strategic nature of the Near East and the level of U.S. concern about the invasion, the sanctions could be viewed as a vital symbolic response.

> ***"Sanctions occupy the middle ground between diplomatic and paramilitary or military action."***

Even when policy-makers state publicly that their goal is to make the target retreat from objectionable behavior, they may not really believe that sanctions alone will achieve this objective. They may overstate what sanctions can do in order to sell the use of sanctions domestically or to stake out a strong bargaining position vis-à-vis the target nation. Policy-makers may in fact believe they will only achieve symbolic goals. Sanctions have a much greater chance of accomplishing symbolic goals than more grandiose objectives like getting the target nation to retreat from aggression or changing its system of government. Therefore, despite the inflated rhetoric of policy-makers at the time they impose sanctions, analysts should be realistic about what the measures can accomplish and they should look beyond public statements to explore policy-makers' more realistic goals.

Symbolic goals should not be dismissed as insignificant, however. In an anarchic and chaotic international environment, symbolic signaling is vital. Nations watch the behavior of other countries carefully for subtle clues about their intentions and resolve. The sanctions levied by the League of Nations against Italy, after Benito Mussolini invaded Ethiopia in 1935, show just how powerful sanctions can be—particularly when they send the wrong message.

A dispute arose between two of the League's principal nations imposing sanctions. Britain favored strong measures, but France—because it felt it must cultivate Mussolini as an ally against Adolf Hitler's Germany—favored milder steps. The resulting embargo, omitting key items such as oil, coal, and steel, sent a signal that lacked the depth of disapproval that had been intended. According to Albert Speer, a former high-level Nazi official, Hitler interpreted the dispute as showing that Britain and France were too irresolute to stop his further territorial ambitions.

Ineffective Sanctions

Sometimes the goals of sanctions will vary over time. When sanctions were first imposed against Iraq [in 1990], they were ostensibly designed to compel

Saddam Hussein to withdraw from Kuwait and impede the Iraqi army's readiness for war. Later, the sanctions were justified as an incentive to make Iraq comply with U.N. resolutions ending the Gulf War, which called for routine U.N. inspections of Iraqi weapons facilities and the destruction of Iraq's weapons-manufacturing capabilities. Later, the Bush administration added that sanctions would not be removed until Hussein was ousted from power, although the Clinton administration seemed to be backing away from this latter requirement.

Compliance is a difficult objective to achieve with sanctions, as the Iraqi case bears out. Iraq endured the most universal, comprehensive sanctions in modern history, which were enforced by a tight naval blockade and had a severe effect on that country's economy. Yet the sanctions failed to achieve their goals.

The results in the Iraqi case would seem to validate the pessimistic conclusions of Johan Galtung, who argued that sanctions with severe economic effects could be rendered ineffective by non-economic factors. Galtung coined the term "rally-around-the-flag effect"—arguing that leaders in target nations use the economic pain caused by foreign nations to rally their populations around their cause. Rather than causing political disintegration in the target state, Galtung said, sanctions actually foster political cohesion.

It can be further argued that target regimes that control the media and suppress political opposition can generate even larger rally-around-the-flag effects. This is especially true if the target regime can blame all its economic problems on hostile foreign powers. Fidel Castro has apparently been able to rally Cubans in the wake of the tightened U.S. sanctions against Cuba called for in the 1992 Torricelli-Graham measures [Cuban Democracy Act].

"Symbolic goals should not be dismissed as insignificant."

Thus, Galtung showed that the political success of sanctions is not closely associated with the amount of economic damage they cause. If that is true—if even strong sanctions can be negated by the political cohesion they engender in the target nation—can economically weak effects ever "succeed" politically? Sanctions against South Africa demonstrate that they can.

Selective Use of Sanctions

To use a military analogy, severe comprehensive sanctions with severe economic effects are the equivalent of war by attrition; that is, trying to win a war by materially crippling the opponent. In contrast, more restrained, selective sanctions with the all-important threat of more can be compared with maneuver warfare. In maneuver warfare, the objective is to destroy, by well-timed attacks in key places, the opponent's will to fight. Instead of incurring heavy losses by grinding down the entire opposing army, shattering the opponent's confidence holds friendly casualties to a minimum and shocks the opponent into surrender.

In war and with economic sanctions, the goal should be to induce the termination of unacceptable activities, not to destroy the opponent's society. In fact, trying to destroy the target society may cause the opponent to fight harder. For example, the saturation bombing of Germany toward the end of World War II that was designed, among other things, to crush the German will to fight, may have actually strengthened the resolve of the German population. Galtung would probably agree that the psychology of war is similar to the psychology of economic sanctions.

"With economic sanctions, the goal should be to induce the termination of unacceptable activities, not to destroy the opponent's society."

In the case of South Africa [from 1986 to 1994], sanctions by governments (national, state, and local) and private businesses and groups—on selected imports, exports, and financial transactions—were the equivalent of maneuver warfare. Reduced lending and investment and the threat of more sanctions chilled business confidence and induced a long-term drag on the South African economy.

The measures also isolated South Africa politically, making it an international pariah. South African whites, who consider themselves European, were startled when shunned by the West. The South African case also shows that sanctions need not be economically devastating to achieve their desired psychological effect—banning sports-crazy South Africa from international sporting events had a particularly potent negative impact on the psyche of South African whites.

Selectively imposed sanctions gave South Africa a taste of the economic pain that comprehensive sanctions could have brought, but they did not induce a severe rally-around-the-flag effect against foreign meddling that often accompanies severe measures. Some rallying did occur as conservative whites reacted to foreign pressure, but the absence of severe economic hardship mitigated this effect. Wrenching economic dislocation would have forced the business community into an alliance with the South African government, and opposition would have been muted. Severe sanctions would have disproportionately hurt both the white and black opposition, the latter being the group that sanctions were supposed to help.

The Fifth Column Effect

In most cases, a target government can direct the pain of severe sanctions away from its supporters to its opponents—in many cases the poorest sectors of society. Iraq's Saddam Hussein was able to channel the hardships of sanctions away from the security forces that keep him in power. In Haiti, the poor suffered greatly while the rich were less affected by the sanctions employed against the military junta that overthrew the Aristide government in 1991.

In sum, economic sanctions will rarely result in compliance unless a strong political opposition within the target nation is allied with the sanctioning nation and puts domestic pressure on the target government (the "fifth column effect"). As illustrated by the case of South Africa, the fifth column effect is strongest and the rally-around-the-flag effect is weakest when selective sanctions are imposed but more are threatened. The political benefits of imposing graduated sanctions override their major disadvantage—allowing the target nation time to adjust its economy. This is good news for sanctioning nations because domestic economic costs often make the imposition of severe comprehensive sanctions unlikely. Furthermore, when comprehensive measures are imposed rapidly (the ideal case according to conventional wisdom), even the political opposition in the target nation may become allied with its government for economic survival, thus creating an insurmountable rallying effect.

Sanctions imposed by a friendly nation—a nation with well-developed political, economic, and cultural relations with the target nation—will have a greater chance of inducing compliance than measures initiated by an adversary. The target nation's cost of non-compliance—the disruption of close ties—is greater when a friendly nation imposes sanctions. Western sanctions contributed to the South African government's movement toward political reform because that country obtained 80 percent of its trade and all of its capital from six Western nations with which it had extensive political and cultural ties.

The same close ties that make sanctions on friendly nations more likely to be effective, however, can also make them less likely to be imposed. Disrupting ties with friendly nations has greater costs than disrupting them with adversaries.

Multilateral Sanctions

Sanctions do not need to be multilateral to have positive political effects. In 1933, the British government imposed import sanctions and successfully achieved the release of its citizens held in Russia. In 1989, India imposed sanctions on Nepal, a traditional buffer against its adversary, China, because of a pro-China tilt in Nepal's foreign policy. The sanctions reversed the tilt.

Multilateral sanctions, however, can have enhanced political effects, but not necessarily because of their greater economic pressure. Despite the recent examples of severe multilateral sanctions against Iraq and Serbia, which are rarities, it is usually difficult to get many countries to agree to impose harsh, comprehensive measures because of their economic interests. It is easier to win multilateral support for selective sanctions. As more nations impose selective sanctions on the target, the psychological threat of future measures and the potential economic damage caused by this threat are made more credible. Also, the more nations that impose sanctions, the greater political legitimacy the effort has and the greater the international ostracism and isolation the target experiences.

> ***"The target nation's cost of non-compliance . . . is greater when a friendly nation imposes sanctions."***

But particular care is needed when seeking multilateral support. Failure to get adequate multilateral cooperation can send a message of weakness rather than a signal of resolve. For example, in the wake of martial law in Poland in 1981, the Western alliance disagreed on an embargo on equipment to be used in constructing a Soviet natural gas pipeline. The dispute made the alliance seem divided instead of sending Moscow an unambiguous signal of protest against the crackdown. As noted before, the quibbling between Britain and France in the League of Nations over the severity of sanctions to be imposed on Mussolini for his invasion of Ethiopia led Hitler to believe that these countries would lack the resolve to stop his expansion in Europe.

Being Realistic

Except in rare cases, the goal of sanctions should not be to destroy the target nation's economy, but to have the maximum political effect by putting maximum psychological pressure on its political leaders and populace. (The sole exception to this might be illustrated by the case of Serbia and Montenegro, when the target state's behavior is so objectionable that severe sanctions are the only punishment suitable to uphold international norms. Sanctioning nations, however, should hold no delusions that strangling the target nation's economy will improve its behavior by compelling compliance with their wishes.)

To put maximum psychological pressure on a target nation, selective sanctions should be targeted at vulnerable sectors of the target's economy. If the target nation feels pain in these sectors, its political leaders may tend to overestimate the effects of whatever additional measures are being threatened, either implicitly or explicitly. The threat of future measures may have more psychological effect on the target than their actual implementation because of the many alternative paths of trade and finance—both legal and illegal—that become apparent to the target after imposition. But even if the goal of sanctions is symbolic (for example, to deter, to demonstrate resolve or disapproval, or to show support for allies or the political opposition in the target nation), selected sanctions should at least have a demonstrable economic effect on critical sectors of the economy. Sanctions that are too weak will cause the target nation to dismiss the threat of future measures.

The sanctioning state or states should aim for the type of economic effect that raises the cost of commerce for the target nation, slows its economic growth, and makes credible the threat of future measures. Unless a tight military blockade that completely seals off all of the target nation's borders is instituted (a rare exception), limited economic effects are the most that sanctions can hope to achieve.

In sum, selective sanctions with the threat of more severe measures will have the greatest psychological effect on the target nation and the most chance to induce the target to comply with the sanctioning nation's wishes. Because obtaining compliance is difficult, however, sanctions may have more success in achieving important symbolic goals.

Promotion of Western-Style Democracy Has Encouraged Violence

by Aryeh Neier

About the author: *Aryeh Neier is president of the Open Society Fund and Open Society Institute, which provide scholarships and grants to students in Eastern Europe and South Africa. His "Watching Rights" column appears regularly in the* Nation.

When I visited India [in 1990], two disputes dominated the news there. One involved demonstrations and riots by students opposing a plan by the government of then–Prime Minister V.P. Singh to set aside a certain proportion of government jobs for the disadvantaged—"scheduled castes" (untouchables), "scheduled tribes" and "other backward classes." Over a period of several weeks some 160 young men and women, apparently members of higher castes who feared that their own employment opportunities would be diminished, tried to burn themselves to death in protest.

Majorities Oppressing Minorities

The other controversy concerned the campaign by a militant Hindu political group, the Bhartiya Janata Party (B.J.P.), to tear down a mosque in Ayodhya, Uttar Pradesh, built by the sixteenth-century Mogul emperor Babar. They were determined to build a Hindu temple in its place, to mark the site that they believe is the birthplace of the epic hero Lord Rama.

Two governments later, the job reservations plan is still being disputed. As for the mosque, it was torn down on December 6 [1992] by a mob of Hindu militants incited by the B.J.P. A number of those who helped dismantle it were killed by falling debris. The action set off violence in several other countries as well.

In both of these episodes members of a majority behaved as though they were a persecuted minority that had no recourse but violent protest. In the case of the self-immolators, they were willing to pay with their lives to end what they considered to be an injustice.

The phenomenon of majorities oppressing minorities in the belief that such oppression is a necessary defense of their own rights is one of the remarkable developments of our time. Probably the most extreme example is the appalling conduct of Serbian forces in Bosnia and Herzegovina. Having persuaded themselves that they are threatened with a continuation of the kind of violence that they suffered for several centuries—from their defeat at the battle of Kosovo in 1389 through World War II, when hundreds of thousands of Serbs were murdered by the Nazi puppet states in Croatia and other parts of the former Yugoslavia—they apparently consider that they are now struggling for survival. They attribute collective guilt to their victims, though hardly any of those now bleeding at the hands of the Serbs took part in the earlier offenses. The great majority were not yet born when the Serbs were being massacred; in the case of the Bosnian Muslims, the main injustices that the Serbs seem intent on avenging took place more than half a millennium ago.

"The belief that . . . oppression is a necessary defense of [majority] rights is one of the remarkable developments of our time."

Portrayed As Victims

A similar approach is evident in some of the rhetoric of Islamic fundamentalists, who portray themselves as victims while demonstrating extreme intolerance of deviations from the orthodoxy that they prescribe. Israel's [December 1992] summary deportation of more than 400 alleged members of Hamas, of course, provides grounds for the sense of persecution among Islamic fundamentalists. Yet fundamentalists have justified everything from assaults on college women in Western dress in Algeria, to assassinations of human rights advocates in Egypt, to systematic forcible displacement of the Nuba in Sudan in a manner that threatens their survival as a people.

The racism and xenophobia sweeping through Western Europe follow the same pattern, as does resentment by white males in the United States against affirmative action practices that open doors to employment and education for women and minorities. Even here, many members of dominant sectors of society have come to think of themselves as victims and justify their responses, which thus far have fortunately been much less violent than in other parts of the world, on the ground that they are being persecuted.

Ironically, one of the factors that has contributed to this worldwide phenomenon is the manner in which the U.S. government has championed the human rights cause internationally. Particularly during the past decade, the United States has been a vigorous proponent of democracy as an alternative to another universal (but worn out) ideology, communism. Unfortunately, the idea of democracy has not been very well explained.

Characteristics of Democracy

In much of the world today, democracy is understood principally as the right of the majority to prevail. This idea is manifested in the rapid spread of movements for self-determination by peoples who define themselves along ethnic-linguistic or religious lines, insisting on their right to their own states in regions where they constitute majorities. Such other essential characteristics of democracy as the right of each person to count equally, respect for the rights of minorities and the subordination even of majorities and their representatives to the rule of law have not taken root in the same way. Indeed, they were often not significant components of the message that the U.S. government was disseminating in its espousal of democracy.

During the [1992] presidential campaign, George Bush bragged about the worldwide turn to democracy and claimed credit for his administration and that of his predecessor. In debate Bill Clinton chose not to challenge him on this point. Now it is Clinton's turn to take charge of foreign policy. Some of the neoconservatives who abandoned Bush and attached themselves to Clinton's campaign, and who now wish to reap the benefits of their support, are trying to make certain that he continues along the Reagan/Bush path. They want the United States to purport to promote human rights internationally by promoting democracy. Very likely, some are not even aware that the version of democracy they have advocated, which has lacked an emphasis on minority rights, has helped to create the world epidemic of ethnic and religious nationalism. It has been a disastrous course, as Clinton should become aware, contributing to the besetting evil of our time: the global proliferation of communal violence.

> ***"Democracy is understood principally as the right of the majority to prevail."***

Intervention Should Not Be Used to Solve Regional Conflicts

by Barbara Conry

About the author: *Barbara Conry is a foreign policy analyst at the Cato Institute.*

The threat of tensions' escalating into superpower confrontations helped stifle regional conflicts for many years, but age-old disputes across the globe have exploded since the end of the Cold War, and regional conflicts are on the rise. The "World Military and Social Expenditures" report counted an unprecedented 29 "major" wars in 1992. ("Major" meant a war that involved one or more governments and killed at least 1,000 people in the year.) An informal *Time* magazine study a number of years ago revealed that approximately 20 wars were likely to be under way at any given time, but a [February 7] 1993 *New York Times* study identified 48 wars in progress (defined as two organized sides fighting and causing casualties). Although such precise numbers are not often cited, there is widespread agreement that regional conflicts, driven by religion, nationalism, and political and economic disputes, are rising dramatically and will continue to do so.

American Desire to Intervene

"Regional conflict" is difficult to define precisely, and experts use the term in a variety of ways. For the purpose of this analysis, the term will mean an armed upheaval, either cross-border or internecine, that affects a limited area but has little direct impact on the security of the rest of the world. The definition is necessarily broad, applicable to wars between established sovereign states, such as the Iran-Iraq conflict in the 1980s; internal strife in the absence of a functioning government, as in Somalia; a dispute between a sovereign government and an armed group within its borders, as in Sudan; or a conflict that involves both

Abridged from Barbara Conry, "The Futility of U.S. Intervention in Regional Conflicts," *Cato Institute Policy Analysis*, May 19, 1994. Reprinted by permission of the Cato Institute, Washington, D.C.

sovereign states and external nonstate parties, as in the former Yugoslavia.

In the age of mass communication, the entire world often witnesses the human tragedy associated with regional wars. Americans who are accustomed to basic human rights, relative stability, and freedom are often moved by distressing media images of remote war-torn regions. Those tragedies inspire in many Americans a sincere desire—even a sense that it is the duty of the United States—to alleviate the suffering. There is also widespread conviction that we have the means to do so. Since the American triumph in the Cold War and the successful expulsion of the world's fourth largest army [Iraq's] from Kuwait with so few allied casualties, Americans and foreigners alike have tended to assume that the U.S. military is capable of managing regional conflagrations whenever it chooses to do so.

"In most cases regional conflicts cannot be helped—and may well be exacerbated—by the intervention of outside parties."

In reality, U.S. military intervention is generally not a viable solution to regional conflicts and should not be undertaken except in the rare instances in which American national security is at stake. In most cases regional conflicts cannot be helped—and may well be exacerbated—by the intervention of outside parties. U.S. intervention can be especially counterproductive, since it often intensifies smaller, less powerful countries' (the very nations most likely to be involved in regional conflicts) fears of America's hegemonic intentions. Militarily, too, the United States is ill suited to suppress regional conflicts, in which warring forces frequently rely on guerrilla warfare, street fighting, and other tactics that are not easily met by America's high-tech war machine. Retired British diplomat Jonathan Clarke has pointed out that

> America's adversaries know full well that they are uncompetitive on a "First World" battlefield. Their response, like that of the Massachusetts Minuteman confronting that British Redcoat, is to lower the threshold of war to prevent the full range of American advanced weaponry and electronic wizardry from operating. The result is that Americans enter today's messy Third World battles not as odds-on favorites but on level terms.

Indeed, it was precisely that type of warfare that prevented the United States from achieving its objectives in both Vietnam and Somalia—proving that the most powerful military in the world is far from invincible.

Not only does inappropriate military intervention fail to reconcile regional conflicts, it also has negative consequences for the United States. There can be significant political costs, ranging from diminished American credibility, as the result of an unsuccessful mission, to resentment on the part of foreign governments and populations of Washington's meddling in their affairs. More serious, injudicious military intervention can create threats to national security where none previously existed, stoking the fires of anti-Americanism, jeopardizing the lives of U.S. troops, and ultimately undermining our ability to protect vital national interests in the event of a direct threat. . . .

Idealism in Intervention

In the absence of a clear and defensible strategic rationale for intervention in regional conflicts, a smattering of idealistic justifications has emerged. In the past, idealism sometimes served as a fig leaf for more mundane motives. During the Gulf War, for instance, President Bush invoked such notions as the preservation of the new world order, protection of sovereignty, and a stance against "naked aggression" to obscure the harsher truth that he was deploying U.S. troops primarily to protect economic interests—American access to gulf oil. The idealistic arguments were essential to gain the support of those who are uncomfortable with the notion of war for self-interest yet accept war as a tragic but necessary sacrifice for the sake of altruistic objectives. For some people, humanitarian reasons or the advancement of various moral principles are in themselves adequate justification for U.S. military involvement in regional wars.

Democracy, human rights, national self-determination, and humanitarian assistance are among the most common rationales for military intervention where no threat to national security exists. All are admirable ideals. Yet military interventions based on such ideals are even more problematic than those that are at least rhetorically rooted in national security, and intervention is usually an ineffective way to advance ideals. If anything, coercion tends to make a mockery of the very principle it was intended to defend. As Paul W. Schroeder of the United States Institute of Peace argued in the *Washington Quarterly*, "The more the lesson desired is inflicted by external armed force, the less the experience of defeat and failure is likely to be internalized in a useful way and lead to the kind of durable change desired."

"If anything, coercion tends to make a mockery of the very principle it was intended to defend."

Military intervention for reasons unrelated to American security also forces the United States to embrace inherently hypocritical policies. Because it is impossible for the United States to intervene in every instance in which American principles are offended, the necessary selection process inevitably gives priority to some conflicts while marginalizing others. As Robert Oakley, President Clinton's special envoy to Somalia, said, "The international community is not disposed to deploying 20, 40, 60,000 military forces each time there is an internal crisis in a failed state." To take action in some cases and not others does not make for consistent policy.

If the United States were to declare genocide in Bosnia sufficient grounds for American military intervention, for example, it would be blatantly hypocritical to ignore the (clearer and considerably more severe) genocide in Sudan. Similarly capricious was Washington's determination that the breakdown of the Somali government merited American intervention, while officials ignored the crisis in Rwanda after the apparent assassination of President Habyarimana on April 6, 1994 (100,000 were said to have been killed in the first two weeks of fighting alone) except to evacuate Americans from the area. Likewise, demands that U.S. troops protect democracy in Haiti are incongruous in light of Washington's quiet indifference toward the suspension of democracy in Algeria when Muslim extremists were poised to win elections in 1992. The inconsistency and hypocrisy of those policies are evidence of the weakness of intervention on the basis of nebulous principles.

A History of Failure

The United States should also avoid military intervention in regional conflicts because, in the vast majority of cases, it does not work. In fact, it usually aggravates the situation. Even if a consensus were to develop that global stability or any other objective should be pursued by all viable means, military intervention would remain an unwise course in most cases. It rarely achieves its purpose and often has the perverse effect of obstructing, rather than advancing, what it seeks to achieve. (American peacekeepers in Lebanon in 1983, for example, were an aggravating rather than a stabilizing force.) Intervention usually harms American interests as well. The most compelling arguments against American intervention are its ineffectiveness and the harm it causes all parties involved.

The ability of military action to achieve political objectives in the modern era is very limited. "Beware of the facile assumption that wars are fightable and winnable again. Beware of the illusion that there is a military solution to every geopolitical problem," warns journalist Theo Sommer. Many deeply rooted political and economic problems are impervious to military solutions.

Lack of Endurance

Intervening powers are at a disadvantage because their stake in the outcome is usually far smaller than that of the primary combatants. In the former Yugoslavia, for example, Bosnian Muslims, Croats, and Serbs are fighting out of nationalism, which they perceive as closely related to their very existence as states (or as distinct cultures). Nationalism in that case is an ideal for which many people are prepared to kill and die. Outside parties that become involved for essentially altruistic reasons are not prepared to fight with the same intensity or endurance. Altruism and nationalism simply do not inspire equal determination.

> ***"The ability of military action to achieve political objectives in the modern era is very limited."***

Moreover, the American public is renowned for its unwillingness to sustain heavy casualties in remote regional wars. American support for military action abroad tends to decline dramatically at the prospect of an extended occupation that will entail significant U.S. casualties. The erosion of public support usually leads to the erosion of congressional support, resulting in serious divisions within the government that is supposed to be directing the intervention. With leadership divided, there is little chance for success. The military, already operating under handicaps inherent to intervention, is virtually assured of failure. As political scientist Richard Falk has commented, "It is not that intervention can *never* work but that it will almost never succeed unless a costly, prolonged occupation is an ingredient of the commitment."

"The American public is renowned for its unwillingness to sustain heavy casualties in remote regional wars."

The failure of interventionism is not merely a post–Cold War phenomenon. During the Cold War it may have been easier to "sell" an intervention because Soviet influence in a regional conflict was always a potential, if indirect, threat to American security. Nevertheless, in the instances in which Washington deemed the threat sufficient to warrant intervention, the track record was poor. The pinnacle of failed Cold War intervention—at immense cost to the United States—may have been Vietnam, but it certainly was not the only failure. In Korea there were 137,000 American casualties in a war that ended in stalemate; there were a number of other, smaller but equally ineffectual interventions in conflicts in Africa and Central America during the Cold War as well. In all instances Americans bore significant human and economic costs, yet their sacrifices brought no lasting substantive gain and made little sense, even when rivalry with the Soviet Union was a factor. Similar sacrifices would make even less sense today in the absence of a superpower challenger.

The Vietnam disaster greatly diminished Washington's enthusiasm for military involvement overseas. Ronald Reagan tentatively resumed foreign adventurism, most notably by sending U.S. Marines to Beirut, Lebanon, as "impartial" peacekeepers in the Lebanese civil war. American interests in the outcome of the Lebanese war were remote at best, and Reagan's foray into the conflict was unproductive. The costs, however, were great—especially to the 241 Marines killed in their barracks by a suicide bomber, who clearly did not consider American involvement impartial.

The Impossibility of Impartiality

Indeed, U.S. involvement was not impartial. The presence of U.S. troops strengthened the position of the Christian-dominated regime of President Amin Geymayel at the expense of the other factions. The Lebanon debacle underscores a larger problem. It is exceedingly difficult for any outside party, acting alone or in concert with others, to remain impartial during an armed conflict, no matter how sincere the intention. That point was painfully proven once again in

Mogadishu [Somalia] ten years after Beirut.

When President Bush sent U.S. troops to Somalia in 1992, he cited a humanitarian reason: to feed the starving Somali population. Civil order had broken down, and warring factions were using starvation as a weapon against innocent people. Despite the simple and narrow focus of the mission, the United States eventually found itself party to the civil war. Under the auspices of the United Nations, American troops were engaged for several months in a manhunt for "warlord" Mohammad Farah Aideed, culminating in a ferocious firefight on October 3, 1993, that cost the lives of 18 Army Rangers. The search for Aideed was futile and, in the end, abandoned. In an ironic twist of events, a U.S. military plane carried "political leader" Aideed to a peace conference in Ethiopia only weeks after U.S. troops gave up their search.

Nothing substantial was accomplished. While it is true that Somalis were no longer starving, the worst of the famine was over before American troops arrived. According to many sources, some regions of Somalia were actually producing an agricultural surplus at the time the United States intervened. "Mission creep" transformed the objective from easing starvation to "nation building," and no substantive progress was made toward that goal. Street fighting diminished for a time, but even before the American withdrawal in March 1994 it began to resume. Again, the costs have been tremendous: American, UN, and Somali lives; scarce economic resources ($1.3 billion for the United States alone); and American credibility were all squandered in the unsuccessful mission. . . .

> ***"It is exceedingly difficult for any outside party . . . to remain impartial during an armed conflict."***

Yankee Go Home

Another cost of military intervention is a rise in anti-American sentiment, which was evident throughout the Cold War in Africa and Latin America and more recently in Somalia. When U.S. Marines made their dramatic landing in Mogadishu in December 1992, the Somalis greeted them with cheers. Less than a year later, on October 3, 1993, 18 Americans died in a single day at the hands of Somalis. Hatred of the United States was unmistakable, particularly in the gruesome and widely published photograph of smiling Somalis dragging the corpse of an American soldier through the streets. Despite the apparent goodwill at the beginning of the mission, American involvement was violently resented once the United States became part of the war.

Similar ill will greeted U.S. soldiers when they attempted to land in Haiti as part of a UN force assisting the implementation of the Governors Island accord. Given the long history of U.S. interference in Haitian domestic affairs, the resistance should not have been surprising. The United States has meddled so much there—American troops occupied Haiti for nearly twenty years beginning in 1915, and Washington has frequently granted or withheld financial assistance in crude attempts to influence Haiti's domestic affairs—that UN secretary-general Boutros Boutros-Ghali initially rejected American participation in the peacekeeping force. Only after President Clinton threatened to withdraw American support for the agreement did the United Nations reluctantly accept a U.S. contingent. Faced with violent opposition to the American presence, which occurred soon after the massacre of U.S. troops in Mogadishu, the Clinton administration ordered the ships not to land. (The most powerful country in the world's lack of will to confront opposition described as a few hundred "thugs" also did significant damage to American credibility.)

Anti-Americanism in Haiti and Somalia should not be dismissed lightly. The Pentagon has identified north-south conflict—the "haves" vs. the "have-nots"—as a serious future problem for the United States. In a study entitled "Terrorism Futures," religious, ethnic, and regional conflicts were cited as probable sources of terrorism in the next decade. At the beginning of the study in late 1991, researchers anticipated that religious extremism would be the gravest threat. The unexpected conclusion, though, was that an "us vs. them" mentality would be a more alarming threat, pitting "fanatics from impoverished countries" against wealthier nations.

In view of the likelihood that the Third World, or the south, will be the site of many future conflicts, American intervention could provide the impetus for an era of divisive north-south confrontation. An interventionist policy could also make the United States a high-priority target for terrorists and other disgruntled factions. The flaring of hostility toward American military personnel in Somalia may be an omen of that danger.

Creating New Problems

Interventionism also jeopardizes U.S. vital interests in other ways. The most obvious threat is to the lives of American soldiers sent into the conflict. Once troops have been deployed, it becomes a vital interest to ensure their security. If they are in danger or if troops have been taken hostage, the United States has a responsibility to protect them. It was for that reason that President Clinton announced March 31, 1994, as the date for withdrawal from Somalia and, at the same time, took what appeared to be the contradictory action of sending several thousand additional troops to Mogadishu. To guarantee the security of the troops already there, additional forces had to be deployed. The intervention had created a threat to U.S. interests where there had previously been none.

"[One] cost of military intervention is a rise in anti-American sentiment."

Other, more abstract, threats arise from interventionism as well. The argument has been made that American credibility, like American soldiers, constitutes a vital interest that must be protected at all costs. Owen Harries, editor of the *National Interest*, made this argument with reference to American interests in Bosnia:

> At the beginning of the Bosnian crisis there was, in my opinion, no significant American interest at stake. . . . But that was then. In the meantime, the Clinton administration has managed to create a serious national interest in Bosnia where none before existed: an interest, that is, in the preservation of this country's prestige and credibility.

Harries goes on to say that American credibility is not merely a matter of national self-respect or patriotism. It is a vital interest with implications for national security. "For the greater one's prestige, the less necessary it is to resort to force and other forms of coercion in order for one's will to be effective—and vice versa," he says.

Intervention in regional wars is a distraction and a drain on resources. Diverting time, money, and manpower from areas that have a significant impact on national security to peripheral nonsecurity interests is never desirable. But in the event of a crisis that affects U.S. vital interests, it is downright dangerous. It is difficult for the United States to be well prepared to protect national security when its military resources are diffused all over the globe and are configured to participate in nebulous peacekeeping or peace enforcement operations.

Unnecessary interventions also waste another very important and readily depleted resource: public support for U.S. military operations. Failed military missions engender tremendous public skepticism about future operations. Although that caution may serve a useful purpose in keeping troops out of other regional conflicts, it may be dangerous in the event of a genuine threat to national security. The American people's support is essential to the success of military operations. Lack of public support when vital interests are at stake could weaken American resolve—and therefore jeopardize our ability—to protect those interests. . . .

The United States should avoid regional intervention except in cases in which there is a direct and substantial threat to national security or American vital interests. No matter how superficially appealing the rationale, military intervention in regional conflicts generally does not work and often creates threats to U.S. security where none previously existed. In this era of proliferating regional wars, the United States must resist the impulse to intervene. To do otherwise is to invite further tragedy, increasing the suffering not only of the combatants but of the American people as well.

The United States Must Cease Its Imperialist Interventions

by *Revolutionary Worker*

About the author: Revolutionary Worker *is a publication of the Revolutionary Communist Party, USA.*

Between June 1993 and March 1994, fighting flared between U.S. invaders and Somali people who hate them. Hundreds of Somalis died as U.S. helicopter gunships raked neighborhoods with machine-gun fire and missiles.

Urgent Truths

This clash illustrates some basic ABCs about the world today: The intervention of U.S troops cannot improve the conditions of the masses of people in the world. The U.S. rulers are *imperialists*. Even when military actions are packaged as "pure humanitarianism," the rulers of the United States have sent their soldiers to fight for profit and domination.

These are truths that urgently need to be learned and spread.

Under both George Bush and Bill Clinton, the United States has threatened to intervene in the Balkan wars. They have sent planes to control the skies. They have prevented the Bosnian Moslems from getting arms. They have threatened to bomb the Serbs. And more recently, they have actually *inserted* U.S. troops into the nearby republic of Macedonia.

And the U.S. fleet is circling Haiti like a pack of sharks—insisting that *Washington* knows best how to calm the anger of the people and that *Washington* decides who rules Haiti.

U.S. actions in Somalia, the Balkans, and Haiti have met almost no forceful, organized mass resistance to these actions *within the borders of the United States*. Far too many people have accepted the logic of the U.S. government itself: that as the "sole superpower," it now has the right (and even the duty!) to

"The Bloody Truth About the New U.S. Colonialism and Why the People Must Oppose U.S. Invasions," *Revolutionary Worker*, November 7, 1993. Reprinted with permission. Subheadings and title have been changed and pulled quotes added by Greenhaven editors.

directly dictate across the planet. Far too many people have allowed themselves to believe that the U.S. troops "may do some good."

These illusions need to be broken down using some basic science—the revolutionary science of Marxism-Leninism-Maoism (called MLM, for short).

A History of Interventions

Throughout its history, the United States has *always* claimed that it was "helping" the people whenever it invaded and conquered. When the U.S. invaded southern Vietnam in 1965 to prop up a brutal pro-U.S. dictatorship there, they claimed it was to "protect democracy." When George Bush sent an invasion force to seize the Persian Gulf and directly control its oil, he *claimed* it was to protect Kuwaiti people from occupation. The reason for such deceit is simple: The class interests of the U.S. rulers are different from the interests of the people of the world, *including* the masses of people *within* the borders of the United States.

Imagine if the U.S. ruling class announced their *true* motives. Imagine if Clinton said: "Our need to exploit people throughout the Western Hemisphere means we must impose a regime in Haiti that is both strictly loyal to U.S. interests *and* better able to contain the Haitian people." If they did this they would meet much more resistance, both within Haiti and the United States itself.

These days, the United States insists that people in many spots of the world cannot resolve their problems without "U.S. help." They say U.S. troops (and so-called "aid") are needed to solve the many problems people face across the planet. They say that when U.S. troops land they are "peace-keepers," or "humanitarians" or "helping to restore democracy." People should not be fooled by this old, old game.

During the 1800s, when European colonialists seized colonies in Africa, Asia, and Latin America, they insisted they were doing this to "help inferior races" who were supposedly incapable of governing (or "civilizing") themselves. This lie was called "shouldering the white man's burden." In reality, they were brutally robbing these countries and enriching themselves.

"Far too many people have allowed themselves to believe that the U.S. troops 'may do some good.'"

In 1898 the United States capitalists invaded Puerto Rico, Cuba and the Philippines—just when the people of these countries were freeing themselves from Spain's domination. The United States claimed its troops were helping their "little brown brothers" and defending U.S. lives and property. Within a few years, hundreds of thousands had died in these island nations, as the U.S. troops carried out a war of mass murder to suppress the bitter resistance—a century of exploitation followed.

When troops land, it is necessary to analyze the *class* interests they serve. For example, when the U.S. rulers claim they are carrying out "nation-building" in countries like Haiti and Somalia, they have really sent their armed forces and political agents into those nations to build up *pro-U.S. states.*

What kind of states are these? States (armies, police, ministries, etc.) that serve the interests of the class that rules the United States: states that are "stable" enough to control the masses of people and create a "favorable environment" for U.S. profit-making. They want obedient states that allow U.S. banks and corporations to exploit their countries.

"This lie [justifying 19th-century European colonialism] was called 'shouldering the white man's burden.'"

A U.S.-imposed "order" can't help the people. In the world today, the basic *cause* of the people's suffering is the current world structure of capitalism—and that is *precisely* what the United States is trying to strengthen.

If U.S. guns succeed in stabilizing countries and regions, those same guns will then guarantee that the economies are linked to U.S. profit-making. They will raise up local ruling class forces to serve U.S. interests—and the United States will train local armed forces to suppress the people. They will defend reactionary property relations where a small handful have a right to own the land and factories—and enrich themselves on the labor of millions. If they build an "infrastructure" of roads and railroads, it will connect the mines and plantations with harbors, so U.S. corporations can cart off the wealth of the country. They compel agricultural countries to produce cash crops for the world market, while they make the people dependent on U.S. grain imports for their daily food.

Because the class interests of the U.S. rulers are fundamentally *opposed* to the interests of the people of the world, U.S. troops *cannot* serve or help the people. And this does not change if they are blessed by a U.S.-dominated United Nations.

In Somalia, for example, the United States has preferred to operate as commander of a "multinational force" because this allows them to send troops from nations like Pakistan out to do the dirtiest work of killing Somalis and patrolling the capital city. But such a "multinational" cover (so popular among Democrats) doesn't change the class nature of the U.S. troops, or the oppressiveness of the world order they are fighting to shore up.

Imperialism Is Not a Policy

A vampire does not sit around each sunset deciding whether or not to go seek warm blood. Bloodsucking is not a "policy" he can adopt or reject depending on his mood. He has no choice: Bloodsucking is in his very nature. The same thing applies to the U.S. ruling class. Imperialism is not a "policy" that they sit down and debate. They have no choice: their daily functioning and survival *depends* on dominating whole nations and exploiting *billions* of people. To survive, they must enforce that exploitation using armed force. Global capitalist bloodsucking is in the very nature of their system.

As Chairman [of the Revolutionary Communist Party Bob] Avakian says: "Imperialist war is precisely the outgrowth of imperialist economics and imperialist politics." Some people think that U.S. forces *could* possibly "play a constructive role"—if they are guided by "the right policies." A liberal Democrat with anti-war credentials sits in the White House—and people think that maybe, he *might* use the U.S. armed forces to help the people of the world.

This is wrong. The basic class interests of the U.S. government don't change when some new administration comes in. *Whoever* sits in the White House seeks to promote the "national security interests" of the United States. And those interests are defined by the international profit interests.

Foreign Policy, a magazine for ruling class debates, summed up that the U.S. approach over most of this century has been to use "preponderant American power" to "foster a world environment in which the American system can survive and flourish." They added: "Underpinning U.S. world order strategy is the belief that America must maintain what is in essence a military protectorate in economically critical regions to ensure that America's vital trade and financial relations will not be disrupted by political upheaval." *Humanitarianism* doesn't appear in these inner-bourgeois discussions!

"U.S. troops* cannot *serve or help the people."

Imperialism is the name for today's worldwide *capitalist system*. Chairman Avakian writes: "Why do we call them imperialists? Because they exploit people all over the world. They have developed an empire and they will do anything to try and preserve it. It is the same people robbing and exploiting, degrading and humiliating us every day that are doing the same thing, and want to do more of it, to people all around the world. That's why we call it *imperialism*, because that's what it is."

Don't Rely on Big Oppressors

Clinton will not be "pressured" into adopting a "non-imperialist" foreign policy—this is as absurd as asking a vampire to become a vegetarian. It was the liberal Democrats Kennedy and Johnson who invaded Vietnam in the 1960s. The *original* liberal Democrat, Franklin Roosevelt, was hailed as "The Emperor of Haiti" for overseeing the 1915 U.S. conquest of that country. And who can miss that Clinton has followed his predecessors' aggressive policies closely: staging his own bombings of Iraq, his own naval blockade of Haiti and his own deepening of the U.S. occupation of Somalia!

MLM shows that the only way to end imperialism is to make revolution—to organize the people, defeat those who defend the system and move on to radically transform human economics, politics, social relations and culture.

Some people say: "Maybe revolution is the *ultimate* solution to oppression, but that has little practical significance. There is no revolutionary army ready to go save the Bosnian women from rape—the only force capable of intervening is the U.S. military and its North Atlantic Treaty Organization (NATO) allies. It is sterile and dogmatic to oppose U.S. intervention simply because of abstract principles."

Sometimes such people point out that some political and military forces the United States is threatening in Iraq, Somalia, Haiti and Serbia are *themselves* oppressors of the people. "It is hard for us to get worked up over the United States attacking such forces. How does it hurt," such people say, "if the United States knocks them down a peg?"

"Global capitalist blood-sucking is in the very nature of [the U.S. ruling class's] system."

This logic considers it "realistic" to rely on big oppressors in order to defeat small oppressors. And it assumes that the masses of people fundamentally *can't* organize themselves and can't liberate themselves—so that any talk of revolution is just fantasy.

The same logic is used by government agents who insist that the people in the inner city must support police in order to help "fight crime." The result of this logic is to support the *strengthening* of the world's *most powerful* reactionary armed forces—and create new obstacles to the liberation of the people.

There are progressive people who watch the suffering of people in Bosnia and are filled with rage that there is not an army of righteous revolutionary warriors on the scene. However, it does no good to spread the lie that the U.S. Marines can solve people's problems, even in the short run!

Every means must be used to speed up the creation of *revolutionary* forces throughout the world—so people can defeat their tormentors. . . .

As Chairman Avakian says: "If you want to be emancipated, you're going to have to fight for your emancipation. If we want to be free, we're gonna have to free ourselves, and nobody else can do it for us."

U.S. Bullying

The United States has long preferred to dominate countries *by building up* loyal local forces to do its dirty work. It is true that forces like Saddam Hussein, Haiti's General Cedras, and Somalia's General Aidid are themselves oppressors of the people—in fact, all of these forces have received arms, money and training from the United States. But big gangsters like the United States have no right to bully small and medium-sized gangsters!

The fact that the United States has repeated conflicts with reactionary forces it has *itself* promoted and armed—like Panama's Noriega or Iraq's Saddam Hussein—is a sign of deep crisis within the U.S. empire. One way the United States has tried to deal with this is to "make an example" in one place—to better enforce its control in other places. For example, the United States says it "can't allow" Haiti's military to defy them because it would encourage such defiance in even more strategic parts of the empire.

The stand of oppressed and progressive people must be to uphold the right of dominated and oppressed nations to settle their own affairs—this is especially true, of course, when genuine revolutionary movements are leading the oppressed people. But this is also true *even when the forces confronting the imperialist power are themselves reactionary.* MLM calls this "the right of nations to self-determination."

The United States is acting to strengthen its ability to impose domination over people throughout the world. And oppressed and progressive people have every reason to oppose this.

Monsters with Soft Clay Feet

Look at how uncertain the United States is about intervening militarily these days! Even as they crow that they are "the world's only superpower shaping a New World Order," they are shaken when Somali militias down three helicopters and inflict a few dozen casualties. They hesitate when the Haitian military threatens to defy them. Arguments break out *within* the U.S. ruling class itself. They nervously debate which is more dangerous for them: to intervene and risk getting "bogged down"—or to stay out and risk "looking weak and impotent."

> ***"This logic [of interventionism] considers it 'realistic' to rely on big oppressors in order to defeat small oppressors."***

All this shows tremendous *internal* weaknesses of the United States that people need to understand. The U.S. rulers hesitate over each military adventure because they know their actions are *against* the interests of the people. They fear that if victory does not come to them quickly, they will be "bogged down" and people will rise up against them—including within the United States. And they fear that various imperialist *rivals,* like Germany, Japan and perhaps Russia once again, will take advantage of any setback the United States suffers.

Lenin described imperialist powers as giant monsters with feet made out of soft clay: They look and act powerful, but their support starts to crumble when they try to make their move. Lenin meant that their society is weak because of the antagonistic class conflict between the oppressors and the oppressed.

Chairman Avakian writes: "This system is enmeshed in crisis and they're scrambling to try to keep it together and can't do it. They're like a juggler that's losing his grip, they might throw one or two more up, but each time it's clearer and clearer that the whole thing is going to come crashing down."

Such weakness of the imperialists shows that it is *not at all* "impractical" or "sterile" to talk about organizing the masses to end oppression! Revolution is alive and growing on the planet today—most forcefully represented by the People's War in Peru, which is itself confronting the plots of U.S. imperialism.

The United States is committing great crimes around the world right now—and they are certain to attempt even greater crimes in the future. The very fact that the imperialists *fear* resistance confirms that it is completely wrong for people here, *within* the belly of the beast, to stand passive when these gangsters send their troops or to mutter that "maybe they can do some good."

The opposite is needed. Every crime of the U.S. imperialists must be exposed. Every military move they make to strengthen their position must be opposed. Every difficulty they face must be seized. Militant resistance must hound them at every step—to weaken them, to arouse and organize the masses of people.

Such resistance is an important contribution people within the United States can make to the liberation struggles of the world. It is our internationalist duty to our brothers and sisters. And such struggle will also help create the conditions for revolution here—when we can perform our *ultimate* duty and rid the world of U.S. imperialism forever.

There are people who believe we should "give the U.S. government a chance" to see if they can change their nature. Chairman Avakian says: "Let's give them not just a few months or a few years. Let's give them a long time—say maybe 200 or 300 years . . . Okay . . . TIME'S UP!"

Economic Sanctions Are Not Effective

by Gary Hufbauer

About the author: *Gary Hufbauer is a fellow of the Institute for International Economics and is coauthor of* Economic Sanctions Reconsidered.

Editors Note: In September 1991, the Haitian military overthrew Haiti's first democratically elected president, Jean-Bertrand Aristide, and took control of the country. In June 1993, the United Nations imposed economic sanctions on Haiti in an attempt to weaken the military's hold. In September 1994, under the threat of an imminent invasion by U.S. forces, the military leaders stepped down and allowed Aristide to return to power.

Economic sanctions against Haiti are now in place [as of June 1994], aimed at allowing only food, medicine and cooking gas to enter that country. Sanctions against North Korea, too, are being seriously discussed: They were endorsed by both Rep. Newt Gingrich (R., Ga.) and Sen. Bill Bradley (D., N.J.), and may be voted on by the United Nations Security Council. The question is: Do sanctions work?

Cheap Foreign Policy

With my colleagues Kimberly Elliott and Jeffrey Schott, I have studied economic sanctions and their effectiveness. It was our conclusion that sanctions work only under certain circumstances, less common today than in the past. Sometimes they are asked to achieve impossible goals. Most important, governments often try to use economic sanctions as a means of conducting foreign policy on the cheap. Not only are "cheap" sanctions likely to be ineffective, but the costs of sanctions are very real, especially to the poor and powerless in target countries.

Sanctions seldom change the policies of large, powerful countries, no matter how brilliantly implemented. For example, U.S. sanctions did not influence So-

Gary Hufbauer, "The Futility of Sanctions," *The Wall Street Journal*, June 1, 1994. Reprinted with permission of *The Wall Street Journal*,

viet policy in Afghanistan or Poland. Nor did the Soviet Union fare any better in changing Chinese ways by cutting off credits and technical assistance to China in the 1960s. U.S. sanctions against China following the Tiananmen Square massacre were similarly ineffective. (In fact, President Clinton's decision [in May 1994] to renew China's most-favored-nation status demonstrates the weakness of sanctions in changing important policies of major countries.)

Midsized countries can also thwart sanctions, when local dictators are able to quell dissent with a powerful military and divert pain to citizens with no influence. It is true that, in Iraq, sanctions have helped to achieve the modest goal of coercing Saddam Hussein's cooperation with the United Nations concerning Iraq's weapons of mass destruction. But as long as Mr. Hussein is able to insulate himself and key supporters from the drastic economic impact of sanctions, he will make no concessions that threaten his political or physical survival.

Even a small country can escape the punitive effects of sanctions if they are not enforced. In Haiti, they have been undermined by the porousness of the border with the Dominican Republic, whose president, Joaquin Balaguer, has long stated that he cannot control smuggling from his country. Even as new, more stringent, measures took effect, ships loaded with embargoed fuel lined up in the Haitian port of Jacmel, having made the short trip from the Dominican Republic. And of course smuggling in the interior, across the border, will be very hard to stop. Mr. Balaguer has said he will step up efforts to enforce the sanctions. But whether such efforts will be effective is an open question. In any case, the Haitian junta has gained invaluable time to stockpile essential commodities.

Era of Effectiveness

Have sanctions always been so ineffective? In fact, the United States had considerable success with them from the end of World War II through the early 1970s. In this period, economic sanctions contributed to the achievement of U.S. foreign policy goals in 18 of 35 cases we studied.

For example, in 1956, the United States successfully pressured France and Britain to withdraw their troops from Egypt when those countries intervened following Gamal Abdel Nasser's nationalization of the Suez Canal. The United States also used sanctions to encourage the Netherlands to recognize Indonesian independence in 1949–50 and to settle claims over expropriated American-owned property in Sri Lanka (then Ceylon) and Brazil in the early 1960s.

> ***"Even a small country can escape the punitive effects of sanctions if they are not enforced."***

By the 1970s, however, U.S. economic leverage was waning. Europe and Japan had recovered from the devastation of World War II and many developing countries were rapidly industrializing. With the global economy becoming increasingly open, there were more suppliers of goods, technology and finance, and many alternative markets. Countries targeted by American sanctions had choices—and they used them.

The most spectacular failures came in the 1980s, with Jimmy Carter's ill-fated grain embargo and Ronald Reagan's gas pipeline sanctions, which bothered America's European allies far more than the Soviet Union. More modest U.S. sanctions against military dictators in Latin America and elsewhere largely failed to improve human rights, while export controls on nuclear fuels and technology did little to slow potential proliferation in South Asia or Latin America. Overall, our research finds that sanctions failed to contribute to U.S. foreign policy objectives in 38 of 46 episodes between 1973 and 1990.

International Cooperation in Sanctions

The question for the future is whether the members of the United Nations, acting together, can replicate the leverage that the United States enjoyed early in the postwar period and once again make economic sanctions a reasonably useful foreign policy tool.

Obviously, international cooperation increases the leverage that sanctioners can bring to bear against a target, but it does not ensure the physical capability to enforce sanctions, or the political will to do so. Multilateral sanctions against South Africa contributed modestly to ending apartheid, but even there the political will took years to develop.

Similarly, in theory U.N. sanctions against Serbia and Montenegro cover all trade and most financial flows, but they were not imposed in the former Yugoslavia for nearly a year after fighting broke out. Even then, member states did little to control smuggling along the Danube for several months. Two years later, extensive smuggling continues.

By contrast, comprehensive U.N. sanctions were imposed less than a week after Iraq's invasion of Kuwait. Within a month the Security Council approved the use of naval forces to enforce the sanctions. Within two months, the council had added an air embargo and authorized secondary boycotts of countries violating the resolutions. In addition, the United States took the lead both in recycling short-term windfall profits gained by Saudi Arabia and other oil producers and in encouraging Japan and Germany to provide grants and low-cost loans to countries hurt by higher oil prices and lost trade. Nearly all these backup mechanisms—and the political will that made them possible—are missing in both the Serbian and Haitian cases.

If the sanctioning country or coalition is not prepared to bear the political and economic costs necessary to make sanctions effective, then the economic losses and human suffering caused by sanctions are wasted. In Haiti, the administration has been unwilling to bear those costs. That leaves the poor Haitians to bear the burden of an inept sanctions policy.

Chapter 3

What Role Should the United Nations Play in Interventions?

United Nations Interventions: An Overview

by Lucia Mouat

About the author: *Lucia Mouat reports on the United Nations for the* Christian Science Monitor *newspaper.*

As the United Nations sends more lightly armed peacekeepers into civil wars to protect civilians and get relief supplies through, the world body is encountering a new set of practical and institutional problems.

New Challenges

With 70,000 peacekeepers deployed in 17 missions around the world [as of June 1994] (such operations cost an estimated $3.2 billion in 1993), the challenges are mounting:

- The job is getting more complicated and dangerous. Convoys often are pilfered, delayed, or blocked. In the absence of lasting cease-fires, relief workers sometimes are shot at, kidnapped, or killed. In the early months of 1994, peacekeepers have been killed at the rate of about one a week.
- Warring factions tend to see the aid as a weapon and UN peacekeepers as partial to one side or the other and in the way. Bosnian Serbs have accused the UN peacekeeping forces, for example, of backing the Bosnian Muslims with firepower and logistical support. As France prepared [in June 1994] to send troops to Rwanda under UN approval until a larger contingent of peacekeepers arrived, the rebels denounced the intervention as an attempt to affect the situation on the ground.

  "In classical warfare, the whole purpose of the siege is to starve the people out, so the way we intervene . . . is actually changing the dynamics of war rules and behavior," says Colin Keating, ambassador to the UN from New Zealand. "Anything you do is seen as helping one side or the other, so it's

Lucia Mouat, "The Trouble with Being the World's Fire Brigade," *The Christian Science Monitor*, June 22, 1994. Reprinted with the author's permission.

going to be dangerous."

- As the risks and costs have increased, UN member nations have become more reluctant to offer troops unless they perceive their national interest as directly involved. Only the political pressure of widespread public disgust at the massacres in Rwanda, for instance, forced the UN Security Council in May 1994 to reverse an earlier decision and raise troop levels there. But the UN continues to have difficulty coming up with the troops to fill the mandate.

UN peacekeepers will never be any match in numbers for fighting forces in such conflicts. One hope, says UN Secretary-General Boutros Boutros-Ghali, is that the very presence of UN forces, no matter how limited, can help to keep a war situation from deteriorating further.

Aid agencies and analysts are divided on the need for peacekeeper protection and whether such help should be more forceful. Shellshocked aid workers on the scene usually welcome the help more than their office chiefs back home do.

"I believe that if you have humanitarian assistance in these conflict areas, you must have some kind of military protection," says Rita Hauser, board chairwoman of the International Peace Academy. "[But] before you use force, you have to know why you're using it and under what terms and conditions."

UN Credibility Damaged

The UN's frequent lack of success in brokering the passage of aid convoys in Bosnia-Herzegovina and Somalia has damaged UN credibility, diplomats and analysts say. Even having the technical authority to force the aid through appears to make little difference. But more assertive action can make UN troops the targets, and commanders often sense that the collective political will on the Council is not strong enough to support a more aggressive stance.

New Zealand has proposed that attacks against UN peacekeepers and civilian staff become a universal offense, as the world community has done with airline hijacking, now punishable anywhere in the world. The General Assembly expects to take up the proposal soon.

Beyond the practical physical problems faced by UN troops in their new role, some analysts say that deeper structural contradictions among UN agencies and goals also need to be faced.

> ***"Warring factions tend to see the aid as a weapon and UN peacekeepers as partial to one side or the other."***

The new UN role in protecting aid must never become a substitute for taking more significant political or military action to resolve the conflict, insists Thomas G. Weiss, an expert on peacekeeping at Brown University, Providence, R.I.

Some analysts argue, for instance, that it was largely the British and French threat to withdraw their humanitarian peacekeepers in Bosnia that prompted US,

Russian, and Western European officials to work more closely on a Bosnian accord and agree on what points of pressure to apply on the warring parties.

Yet one Western diplomat cautions that there is an important difference between pressuring warring factions to settle disputes and imposing a solution. He says most diplomats on the Security Council agree that no peace is durable unless the warring parties choose the terms and willingly sign on. Yet Council diplomats struggle regularly with where the proper UN role lies on the spectrum.

Peter Hansen, UN undersecretary-general for humanitarian affairs, agrees that relief efforts are no substitute for political action, but says aid efforts must not be politicized. He says the UN is still moving in "uncharted waters" in giving aid convoys military protection, and that UN tactics need constant review.

Problems Studied

Many of these problems have been under study since 1989 in a special Humanitarianism and War Project conducted by Brown University and the Refugee Policy Project in Washington and funded by dozens of private aid groups and UN agencies.

Researchers have concluded from in-depth field studies in a wide variety of civil conflicts that (1) UN humanitarian efforts lack a concerted and effective strategy for dealing with obstinate warring parties, and (2) many Council humanitarian efforts amount to "half measures" that substitute for tougher political decisions. Aid recipients often told project researchers, for instance, that they knew they were being fed to compensate for the failure of UN member governments to agree on what other steps to take.

"The new UN role in protecting aid must never become a substitute for taking more significant political or military action."

"If the international community isn't prepared to address what's producing the conflict that's causing emergency starvation, then humanitarian intervention can actually be counterproductive and fuel, rather than ease, the conflict," insists project co-director Larry Minear.

He says UN troops in Somalia, for example, provoked the Somalis and actually contributed to instability rather than restoring it. "However well-meaning and assertive," he says, "humanitarian initiatives are not really solutions to these complex problems that create suffering."

Project researchers also conclude that the UN needs to clarify differences in its political, military, and humanitarian functions in order to ease tensions and make UN aid efforts more effective. In its most recent report on the former Yugoslavia, the project cites the apparent contrast between the UN policy of economic sanctions on Serbia and Montenegro and UN-led relief efforts to ease the suffering of civilians there. The same contrast is apparent in Haiti.

"There's a real structural contradiction in trying to do humanitarian programs in a sanctions environment," Mr. Minear says. "We think the contradictions in the UN system need to be better understood."

> ***"Humanitarian initiatives are not really solutions to these complex problems that create suffering."***

The Humanitarianism and War Project recommends that the UN automatically authorize standard humanitarian exemptions to sanctions programs.

Yet one purpose of sanctions is to encourage hard-pressed civilians to pressure their governments to change policies. Refining sanctions, says one European diplomat, can undercut the Security Council's political aims.

The Humanitarianism and War Project stands firmly behind the concept of humanitarian aid for everyone in need.

"The heartbreak and failures in Bosnia and Somalia have made us forget that humanitarian intervention, while not easy, can be done," says Brown's Dr. Weiss.

He views UN efforts to help the Kurds in northern Iraq, backed by the allied coalition's threat of airstrikes over the no-fly zone there, as a successful example. "Military power was used in an appropriate way, and, most importantly, there was an overall political strategy," he says.

"Stay the Course"

Weiss argues that if the UN decides to intervene on humanitarian grounds in any war, it must be willing to "stay the course," and "do the job right." Noting that the US announced its departure from Somalia even before its troops arrived, he says a key danger lies in assuming that any operation will be a "quick fix," failing to take such often-necessary steps as disarmament and the rebuilding of civil institutions.

Project researchers say more creative diplomacy early on can help to prevent some conflicts, but that tough choices for humanitarian intervention still lie ahead.

"I think there are limits not only to international resources but to international political resolve," Minear says. "One has to develop a much more discriminating array of reactions and responses."

Mr. Boutros-Ghali agrees that the UN's reactive capacity needs thorough review. Yet he says the changes will have to take place while the UN keeps on trying to prevent and resolve conflicts. It is like flying a plane while redesigning and repairing it, he says.

The United Nations Should Be the World's Policeman

by Lincoln P. Bloomfield

About the author: *Lincoln P. Bloomfield, formerly a U.S. State Department and National Security Council official, is professor emeritus of political science at the Massachusetts Institute of Technology, in Cambridge.*

In the five years from 1945 to 1950 a monumental victory was won over tyranny, a major new challenge loomed, the democracies responded with strategies for the long haul, and a whole set of international institutions was set in motion to perform important pieces of the world's business.

The New World Order

In the five years from 1989 to 1994 a monumental victory was won over tyranny, new challenges loomed, the United Nations (UN) began to cope with them, the democracies were overcome in varying measure by self-absorption, moral flabbiness, and military vacillation, and the prospects were shaken for the kind of reformed international security regime their interests dictate.

How could that happen? What kind of international security system is realistically possible? What should be the U.S. role in such a regime?

Reversing Iraq's assault on Kuwait in 1991 seemed to jump-start the process of collective security. But cross-border aggression was not the main challenge of the 1990s. Instead, the volcano of change spewed forth what [Czech president] Václav Havel called "a lava of post-communist surprises," generating a panorama of turbulence and strategic ambiguity as multinational states broke up, and other states simply broke. For leftover conflicts UN peacekeeping was the method of choice to monitor cease-fires and help with transitions in old cold war battlefields from Angola and Mozambique to El Salvador and Nicaragua, along with older trouble spots like the Western Sahara, Namibia, Suez, southern

Abridged from *The Washington Quarterly*, vol. 17, no. 3 (Summer 1994), Lincoln P. Bloomfield, "The Premature Burial of Global Law and Order," by permission of The MIT Press, Cambridge, Mass., and the Center for Strategic and International Studies.

Lebanon, and Cyprus.

But the trickiest of the new threats arose not among states and their surrogates, but from mayhem within state borders. Renewed anarchy in Cambodia, man-made starvation in Somalia, mugging of newly won democracy in Haiti, and slow-motion genocide in Bosnia all violated not so much the "law" as the underlying moral order. It was behavior that article 2 (7) of the UN Charter bars the organization from touching because it is "essentially within the domestic jurisdiction of any state." Those new cases would also not have passed the cold war test of "strategic threat." But with the fear of superpower escalation gone, and with a potent assist from worldwide TV coverage, they powerfully assailed the conscience of the nations. Waiting in the wings were equally hairy scenarios of tribal warfare in Russia's "Near Abroad" [former Soviet republics] and in some "states-but-not-nations" like Burundi, along with human rights outrages in Sudan, Myanmar, Iran, Syria, the People's Republic of China—you name it.

> ***"The trickiest of the new threats arose not among states and their surrogates, but from mayhem within state borders."***

The New Era of Humanitarian Intervention

Working within a drastically altered strategic landscape, a born-again UN Security Council began a chapter of law-in-the-making with novel interventionary doctrines to deal with famine-producing anarchy, ethnic cleansing, and the deliberate creation of refugees. It was not exactly "peacekeeping" as in Cyprus, and certainly not "collective security" as in the Persian Gulf. It was an unprecedented "policing" function carrying such provisional labels as "peacemaking," "humanitarian enforcement," and "second-generation operations," led by a United States committed to a stance of "assertive multilateralism." The UN Charter's criterion of "threats to the maintenance of international peace and security" became stretched beyond recognition. But despite all the ambiguities, the early 1990s looked like an open moment for the liberal internationalists' dream of a system of global law and order, and one equipped with a heart. The moment was brief.

The new era of multilateral intervention for humanitarian purposes began fairly successfully in Iraq after the defeated regime turned savagely on its disaffected Kurdish population in the North [in April 1992]. In response to public outrage, the victorious coalition moved inside Iraqi territory and established protected aid channels to "Kurdistan," although not in the South where the regime was busily crushing Shi'ite dissidence. Successive UN resolutions mandated destruction of long-range ballistic missiles and weapons of mass destruction, along with unprecedentedly intrusive monitoring of missile testing and other sites. When Baghdad boggled at monitoring, UN threats backed by U.S. bombing of selected targets alternated with promises to unfreeze badly needed

Iraqi oil revenues, and in February 1994 the International Atomic Energy Agency (IAEA) reported that all declared stocks of weapons-grade material had been shipped out. But compliance by Baghdad came only after credible threats of punishment. Indeed, these events also raise the question of whether an offending power has to be militarily defeated before the community will *enforce* its norms against intolerable national behavior.

Three Cases from Hell

Three other UN "peace-enforcement" operations did not pose that particular question but for other reasons brought the trend to a screeching halt. In Somalia, where anarchy was generating mass starvation, the UN was shamed into action by Secretary General Boutros Boutros-Ghali, and the Security Council for the first time launched a peacekeeping operation not requested by the "host government" (in this case there was no government at all). Humanitarian aid was authorized with a mandate to create "a secure environment" for its delivery. The primarily U.S. force used both diplomacy and military presence to stem the famine, but the UN mission became controversial when it actually used force to create the required environment. Willingness to back up a humanitarian operation with force if necessary may turn out to be the price of humanitarian intervention by the international community. But the reaction of risk-averse Americans to casualties fewer than New York experiences in a slow week suggests that the use of force, even to carry out a unanimously agreed mission, had better remain as a last resort, particularly if the situation on the ground gets murky—as it invariably does.

> ***"Compliance by Baghdad came only after credible threats of punishment."***

In splintered former Yugoslavia, the UN undertook another humanitarian mission of aid to refugees, in an environment in which Serb authorities escalated their noxious policy of "ethnic cleansing" to uproot and terrorize Bosnian Muslims. The Security Council authorized use of "all means necessary" to protect aid. But Britain and France, which had put a modest number of noncombatant peacekeepers on the ground, balked at facing down those blocking aid. In May 1993 the Council established six "safe havens" for embattled Muslim populations and authorized force to protect, not the people, but the peacekeepers. But once more the available enforcers of the community's rules were unwilling to stand up for their own norms.

It was only after a particularly murderous—and televised—mortaring of a Sarajevo market crowd that the North Atlantic Treaty Organization (NATO) finally stirred itself into a credible posture and Serb guns were pulled back. Nothing could more clearly illustrate both the "CNN effect" and the painful truth that bullies respond only to believable threats. But it was disgracefully late in coming and useless to the thousands already left dead and the hundreds of thousands left homeless.

In Haiti the issue was restoration of democratic rule in the face of official thuggery. To do so required at least a believable show of force. But a United States once burned wanted none of that and executed a humiliating retreat, leaving the Security Council incapable of enforcing its own decisions. . . .

In diplomacy as in war, success has 100 fathers but defeat—or even plain bad luck—is an orphan. In Bosnia a European Union suffering from tired blood and historical amnesia for far too long turned away from its responsibilities, and Washington—regrettably but in my view correctly—declined to act alone. In Somalia and Haiti humanitarian intervention was overtaken by a bloody endgame between claimants for power. In all three cases the Security Council and secretary general made some questionable judgments, and the responsible powers blinked when it came to taking casualties. Just when the international community had begun to act like one, its staying power and seriousness of purpose were suddenly in serious question. . . .

Is There Really an "International Community"?

Discussions of multilateralism assume the existence of an "international community," but some challenge that concept as a figment of the liberal imagination. In a little-remarked assertion in a much-discussed article Samuel Huntington stated that "the very phrase 'the world community' has become the euphemistic collective noun . . . to give global legitimacy to actions reflecting the interests of the United States and other Western powers." Is he right? How different from a genuine community is today's international society?

According to political theory, a viable community rests on a minimum consensus of community-held values. It is endowed with core powers of taxation and policing, which depend on a relative monopoly of force. People generally accept rules because of a shared sense of commonality, whether ethnic, linguistic, religious, or ideological. They also benefit from a governance system that protects them from physical threats. People know what "compliance" and "enforcement" mean in familiar local settings. They know the cost of breaking the rules and consider believable the probability of enforcement action, whether by cops on the beat, sheriffs, tax collectors, or armies.

> ***"Is international society today capable of behaving like a real rather than a rhetorical community . . . ? The answer is 'No—but.'"***

Government works because there is a presumptive self-interest in abiding by the rules and a known penalty for noncompliance. Is international society today capable of behaving like a real rather than a rhetorical community, armed with enforceable "law and order" rules complete with credible incentives to comply and disincentives to misbehavior? The answer is "No—but."

When it comes to bottom-line law and order, the limiting realities are the world's infinite variety, decentralized power centers, fragmentary structures, and primary reliance on self-help with only a contingent possibility of community "police" assistance when threatened. The combined logic of economic interdependence, technology, and weaponry tells us that peace, security, and prosperity all require strengthened forms of "international governance." But international society is still a bit like 1930s China, equipped with a "constitution" and functioning central apparatus, but with real power monopolized by provincial warlords, some benign and cooperative with the center, some decidedly not. The UN may simulate a government; but it cannot really act like one. World society is a partial and imperfect community when it comes to gut qualities of sovereignty, legitimacy, and power. Its characteristics all fall short of the definition of true community.

Areas of International Cooperation

But does that really mean that all recent actions in the international system can be explained by U.S. pressure? Hardly. Enormous majorities in the UN voted to condemn the Iranian seizure of the U.S. embassy in 1979. Why? Because states of every religion and ethnic background have a deep interest in keeping inviolate the global diplomatic nexus. Large majorities condemned the Soviet invasion of Afghanistan in 1979 and the Iraqi invasion of Kuwait in 1991. Why? Because virtually all agree on the primordial rule of interstate relations that forbids invading, trashing, and obliterating the identity of a neighboring state. [As of Summer 1994] thousands of troops from 57 non-Western countries help to staff 18 current UN operations in the field. Why? Because they decided their national interests are served by that kind of community policing.

"There are unmistakable signs that some broad common values and interests are cutting across 'civilizations.'"

At the UN Conference on Environment and Development in Rio de Janeiro in 1992 the great majority—opposed, incidentally, by the United States—voted goals and policies reflecting the conclusions of cross-cultural environmentalists. And over 140 states have voluntarily signed the Nuclear Non-Proliferation Treaty (NPT). Why? Because sensible people have noticed the twin realities of environmental interdependence and the unusability of nuclear weapons.

Even in the most neuralgic [painful] sector, UN human rights bodies have recently distanced themselves from their ideological and cultural biases and now publicize violations in Muslim, Orthodox, Christian, Slav, Turkic, Jewish, and secular societies—including the United States. One reason has been Western pressure to apply what are arguably universal values. But equally influential is the revolution in mass communication that informs people about common standards of civility.

The evidence is obviously mixed, and several things are going on at once. But there are unmistakable signs that some broad common values and interests are cutting across "civilizations." It is this evidence of commonality that constitutes the foundation of a minimal "world community" for limited but crucial common purposes. To turn Marx on his head, the basic global *structure* is composed of states and significant nongovernments, powerfully driven by their cultures. Common problems none can handle alone constitute the agenda of the *superstructure* of agencies of international cooperation and coordination. The global architecture is, so to speak, split-level, and one level is not going to replace the other.

> ***"A more coherent international system will feature compliance procedures that resemble a process of* law enforcement."**

So is there a genuine "world community"? Not really. Should we act as though it exists on matters of common concern? Of course. The goal is certainly not world government, which even if practical could become world tyranny. But the system already functions effectively in the sectors where states agree to pool sovereignty without actually saying so. Indeed, the UN's critics do not challenge (or even seem to know about) the networks that already monitor and to a degree regulate global trade, telecommunications, mail, health, air travel, weather forecasting, nuclear power, and refugee flows.

Improving Compliance with UN Rules

Most of the powers of governance will continue to be "reserved" to the member states on the model of the U.S. Constitution, and we should not become distracted by theological arguments about sovereignty. The vexing question as we grope our way toward the next stage of history is how to achieve improved compliance with the limited but crucial rules agreed upon by the larger community.

Here, of course, is the central dilemma of the "international community." In a true community the actions required to cope with violations of its rules add up to a graduated continuum of responses—a kind of updated "escalation ladder," based on the principle that the earlier one achieves compliance, the cheaper and less hair-raising the level of policing required. But in a world of sovereign states the center has no independent power, national interests change, today's terrorists and war criminals can become tomorrow's rulers, the UN inherits conflicts after they have got out of hand, ground rules are imprecise, aggression has never been universally defined, threats to peace are subjectively assessed, and ethnic cleansing and making refugees of one's own people are not adequately on the lawbooks.

This is not to say that nothing can be done now to improve matters. UN supporters have proposed new varieties of stand-by forces, whether old-fashioned peacekeeping units in blue berets, peacemaking/peace-building protectors in flak jackets, or even a standing 10,000-man "UN Legion." The end of the Cold War also revived discussion of the never-implemented article 43 agreements under which the great powers would make major forces available to the Security Council. Secretary General Boutros-Ghali's *Agenda for Peace* is a major, if premature, statement of both doctrine and plans for what he terms "peace enforcement."

Some practical operational processes can also be reformed, such as headquarters operations, which need to be more efficient, and the UN information system, which is improved but still needs to be more autonomous and to have backup from national intelligence (as it reportedly had in Iraq from the U.S. Central Intelligence Agency and Britain's MI5). It is at least theoretically possible that such improved readiness would make it easier to respond to calls for UN intervention. . . .

A Process of Law Enforcement

The times are not propitious for upgrading the enforcement of international "law and order" beyond some useful but modest procedural fixes, but the issue is of course far more political than it is technical. Action is always subject to veto by the permanent members of the Security Council, and Russian and Chinese cooperation cannot be taken for granted in perpetuity. Nevertheless, conditions may return that make progress again possible, and it is useful to have a defined goal in mind as a target for discussion and planning. The following sketches a modestly reformed process that falls short of what happens in cohesive communities, but goes beyond what most people consider feasible today.

A more coherent international system will feature compliance procedures that resemble a process of *law enforcement*. It will look less like a traditional binary choice between war or peace and more like a step process that mimics domestic *policing*. Violations of agreed rules will take many forms along a broad continuum, matched by a continuum of community responses.

A state-backed bomb-thrower or electronic terrorist represents the lowest end of the law-breaking spectrum. Next come violations involving limited nuclear, chemical, biological, or missilery development, all potentially reversible. A more serious challenge comes from a pair of countries threatening or sporadically skirmishing against each other. And a major threshold is crossed when organized, uniformed military forces engage in "small wars." A similar threshold is crossed with an internal "small war" when civil strife afflicts the global conscience or imperils regional stability. At the extreme end lie the wars of conquest of other peoples' countries.

> ***"If diplomacy and peacekeeping fail, a well-armed blue-bereted 'posse' would use whatever force is required."***

A step process of "community responses" begins with article 33 of the Charter, which enjoins states to settle disputes themselves before unloading them on the UN. Early-stage responses are exemplified by the diplomat with the briefcase and the observer with the binoculars and electronic sensors. At the next step up, failure to halt illicit work on weapons would bring a kind of SWAT team of technicians such as IAEA inspectors accompanied by UN guards in civvies (as in Iraq today) armed with state-of-the-art nonlethal weapons. If fighting breaks out but can be halted, the truce would, as now, be monitored by nationally contributed, nonfighting, peacekeeping units—a low-cost trip wire, primarily symbolic but respected because the sides want to be separated, whatever their rhetoric.

"The real danger is not U.S. domination but its withdrawal from the game."

Coercive enforcement starts with article 41 economic and communications sanctions. For the first 40 years international sanctions were applied only twice—on Rhodesia (ineffectively) and against South Africa (military only, but more effective because observed by the major powers). Recent UN sanctions against Iraq, Haiti, and Serbia were technically effective, those against Libya and Angola less so. But sanctions against Iraq, Haiti, and Serbia devastated the innocent. Sanctions should be targeted primarily on leaders' overseas bank accounts and travel rights, and compensation should be made to third countries that suffer from sanctions the way Turkey did in the Iraq case.

If diplomacy and peacekeeping fail, a well-armed blue-bereted "posse" would use whatever force is required to persuade the sides to separate and get relief supplies to civilians—the still unlabeled "peacekeeping plus" model of armed humanitarian intervention that for so long tragically failed on this count in Bosnia. . . .

U.S. Marshal–Type Peace Officers

The greatest need up to this point on the spectrum is for technical personnel who can monitor, recognize, and if necessary dismantle illicit weaponry and production; for "peace officers" on the lines of U.S. marshals, who can protect both relief operations and UN monitors; and for quick-reaction U.S. National Guard–type units that can be dispatched to protect the protectors—precisely the capabilities that never successfully functioned in the cases from hell.

The final point is the rare instance of coercive military force under article 42—son of Desert Storm [Persian Gulf War], as it were. Overt armed aggression is mercifully rare. But we have learned the hard way that some few situations turn out to be genuinely nonnegotiable, and that doctrinal pacifism can give a green light to aggression and tyranny, whether to a Hitler planning the conquest of Europe, a Saddam Hussein coveting neighboring states, or Serbs and Croats murderously pursuing dreams of expansion. All act in the spirit of Bismarck who, asked if he wanted war, reportedly said "Certainly not, what I want is victory."

If the community leaves matters until this explosive point, it will confront the worst case: having to force compliance with Security Council directives through deployment by powerful states of UN-flagged national ships, tanks, and assault helicopters, whether under article 43 or not. If the aggressor is a nuclear-armed great power, the system will be back where it was at the height of the Cold War. . . .

Inconsistency and Hegemonic Power

Intervention in civil wars and other forms of domestic mayhem is, with the best of motives, going to violate the fourth cardinal rule of diplomacy (never get between a dog and a lamppost), and at best appear inconsistent. The Security Council enforced its no-fly zones in northern Iraq but turned a blind eye until spring 1994 to violations in Serbia; forcibly protected famine relief in Somalia but not Bosnia; defended Kuwait but not Azerbaijan. Burundi was doubtless as deserving as Haiti, but as Boutros Boutros-Ghali said, "The United Nations cannot solve every problem," while Under Secretary General James Jonah acknowledged that Rwanda but not Burundi got peacekeepers and money because "maybe they were first in line." As with the rest of human life, consistency cannot be the major litmus test. It is not cynical but realistic to acknowledge that political triage is the likely prospect, and that the world is fortunate if the large matters—Iraqi aggression, starving children, the ozone layer, nuclear spread—are tackled by the community even while some lesser issues remain unresolved.

> ***"Definitive conclusions drawn from recent events are likely to be misleading."***

Another troublesome reality is the disparity between states' power, money, and influence. Even a modestly reformed international "law and order" system will appear to be dominated by the strong both in making and enforcing rules. There are times—Korea in 1950 and the Gulf in 1990—when the community agrees to meet aggression by naming one country as "executive agent" for the Security Council (the formula used in Korea). If in such extreme circumstances—cross-border aggression or domestic genocide—the system fails to respond, action on behalf of the community could be carried out by what I have dubbed a "coalition of the willing." Both U.S. leadership and coalition surrogates run counter to the principle/fiction of sovereign equality. But only a minority of states are in a position to give leadership based on advanced technology, capital, educated and trained armed forces, and a democratic process that protects the rights of individuals against governmental abuse. Others resent the unique influence of the United States. But the precondition for any enforcement system is the power and logistical reach the United States alone commands.

The real danger is not U.S. domination but its withdrawal from the game. The future could look a lot more dangerous if setbacks and scapegoating in Somalia, Haiti, and Bosnia reversed the recent U.S. turn toward cooperative security, or if premature intervention fatigue allowed new breaches of the "civil peace" to turn into serious security threats. Nothing is more important than to persuade would-be violators that failure to enforce the community's rules in Bosnia, plus erratic behavior in Somalia and Haiti, have not switched on a green light for arson in other tinderboxes.

U.S. Agony Over the Cases from Hell

In the turbulent wake of controversy over the cases from hell, Washington crafted a policy toward UN "peace operations." In part political damage-limitation with the help of rhetorical straw men ("We will never compromise military readiness to support peacekeeping . . . [or transfer] troops into a standing world army . . . the President will never relinquish his constitutional command authority over U.S. troops," etc.), the bottom line is continuity in policy toward selective involvement after "asking tough questions," getting the Pentagon to help pay, and demanding fairer assessments and more efficient management. The United States in fact retains a unique role in providing logistical support. . . . But U.S. domestic agonies over the cases from hell would seem to confirm the wisdom of traditional UN peacekeeping policy under which, except for enforcement, UN policing units on the ground were drawn from countries other than Russia and the United States. The concept of impartial peacekeeping and peacemaking by "neutrals" may still have high political value even if it is no longer clear what they are neutral about, and even though they are backed by great-power logistics, air and sea cover, and Japanese money.

Definitive conclusions drawn from recent events are likely to be misleading. After all, no one predicted the fantastic changes [that have occurred since 1989]. Our age is a hinge of history, and the post–cold war order is a work in progress. Winston Churchill once observed that "The United Nations was set up not to get us to heaven, but only to save us from hell." There is nothing wrong with the basic norms and ground rules contained in the present UN Charter, which provides ample machinery for prevention, deterrence, and enforcement. The fault, pace [contrary to] Shakespeare, is not in our stars but in our leaders and those of us they represent.

Despite setbacks and loss of nerve, the innovative collective measures of the early 1990s could in time become habit-forming, particularly if politicians keep their nerve and eschew [what F.M. Cornforth calls] the "Principle of the Dangerous Precedent," which says that nothing should ever be done for the first time. Once again, as in 1945, the future hinges on the political imagination and moral authority of those in power. Absent those qualities, there is no UN, no law, and no order.

The United Nations Should Keep Peace and Promote Development

by Boutros Boutros-Ghali

About the author: *Boutros Boutros-Ghali of Egypt began a five-year term as secretary general of the United Nations in January 1992.*

A new chapter in the history of the United Nations has begun. With newfound appeal the world organization is being utilized with greater frequency and growing urgency. The machinery of the United Nations, which had often been rendered inoperative by the dynamics of the Cold War, is suddenly at the center of international efforts to deal with unresolved problems of the past decades as well as an emerging array of present and future issues.

Peacekeeping Is a Growth Industry

The new era has brought new credibility to the United Nations. Along with it have come rising expectations that the United Nations will take on larger responsibilities and a greater role in overcoming pervasive and interrelated obstacles to peace and development. Together the international community and the U.N. Secretariat need to seize this extraordinary opportunity to expand, adapt and reinvigorate the work of the United Nations so that the lofty goals as originally envisioned by the charter [of 1945] can begin to be realized.

Peacekeeping is the most prominent U.N. activity. The "blue helmets" on the front lines of conflict on four continents are a symbol of the United Nations' commitment to international peace and security. They come from some sixty-five countries, representing more than 35 percent of the membership.

Peacekeeping is a U.N. invention. It was not specifically defined in the charter but evolved as a noncoercive instrument of conflict control at a time when Cold War constraints prevented the Security Council from taking the more forceful steps permitted by the charter. Thirteen peacekeeping operations were established between 1948 and 1978. Five of them remain in existence [as of 1992] and are between fourteen and forty-four years old.

Peacekeeping has sometimes proved easier than the complementary function of peacemaking. This shows that peacekeeping, by itself, cannot provide the permanent solution to a conflict. Only political negotiation can do that.

The Principles of Peacekeeping

During the Cold War years the basic principles of peacekeeping were gradually established and gained acceptance: the consent of the parties; troops provided by member states serving under the command of the secretary general; minimum use of force; collective financing. It was also learned, often the hard way, that peacekeeping success requires the cooperation of the parties, a clear and practicable mandate, the continuing support of the Security Council and adequate financial arrangements.

The end of the Cold War led to a dramatic expansion in demand for the United Nations' peacekeeping services. Between 1988 and 1992, fourteen new operations were established, five of which completed their mandates and were disbanded. In the first half of 1992 the number of U.N. soldiers and police officers increased fourfold; by the end of the year they exceeded 50,000.

Some of these new operations have been of the traditional, largely military type, deployed to control unresolved conflicts between states. Examples are the military observers who monitored the ceasefire between Iran and Iraq from 1988 to 1991 and those who patrol the demilitarized zone between Iraq and Kuwait.

"Peacekeeping, by itself, cannot provide the permanent solution to a conflict."

But most of the new operations have been set up to help implement negotiated settlements of long-standing conflicts, as in Namibia, Angola, Cambodia, El Salvador and Mozambique. Namibia was a colonial situation but each of the other four has been an internal conflict, albeit with significant external dimensions, within a sovereign member state of the United Nations.

A New Role for Peacekeeping

There is another aspect to the end of the Cold War. The thawing of its frozen political geography has led to the eruption of savage conflicts in, and sometimes between, newly emerging independent states. The former Yugoslavia has become the United Nations' largest peacekeeping commitment ever. Ethnic conflict across political borders and the brutal killing of civilians there are reminiscent of the ordeal that U.N. peacekeeping forces faced in the 1960s in the then Congo [now Zaire]. U.N. forces again are taking an unacceptable level of casualties. It is difficult to avoid wondering whether the conditions yet exist for successful peacekeeping in what was Yugoslavia.

The 1990s have given peacekeeping another new task: the protection of the delivery of humanitarian supplies to civilians caught up in a continuing conflict. This is under way in Bosnia-Herzegovina and Somalia, member states whose institutions have been largely destroyed in a confused and cruel web of civil conflicts. This task tests the established practices of peacekeeping, especially the circumstances in which U.N. soldiers may open fire. Existing rules of engagement allow them to do so if armed persons attempt by force to prevent them from carrying out their orders. This license, used sparingly in the past, may be resorted to more frequently if the United Nations is to assert the Security Council's authority over those who, for personal gain or war objectives, try to rob or destroy humanitarian supplies destined for suffering civilian populations.

Beyond Peacekeeping

All these new modes of peacekeeping have had far-reaching implications for the way in which U.N. operations are organized and conducted.

In internal conflicts, or indeed in interstate conflicts where one or other of the governments is not in a position to exercise full authority over territory nominally under its control, not all the parties are governments. As a result the peacekeepers have had to learn how to deal with a multiplicity of "authorities." The leaders of such groups are often inaccessible and their identity even unknown; chains of command are shadowy; armed persons who offend against agreements signed by their supposed leaders are disowned; discipline is nonexistent or brutal. And everywhere there is an evil and uncontrolled proliferation of arms.

Peacekeeping operations still invariably include military personnel. But now the civilian elements often have an even more important role. This is especially true when the task is to help implement comprehensive and complex settlements, as was or is the case in Namibia, El Salvador, Cambodia and Mozambique. Political action is required to resolve disputes between the parties and persuade them to implement the agreed arrangements. Information programs must explain the United Nations' role and advise the people of the opportunities the settlement gives them. Refugees must be brought home and resettled. Elections must be observed and verified or even, in Cambodia, organized and conducted by the United Nations.

> ***"U. N. forces . . . are taking an unacceptable level of casualties."***

Local police must be monitored to ensure that they carry out their duties in the spirit of the new order and not the old. Respect for human rights must be verified, an especially important task in El Salvador and Cambodia. In the latter country the United Nations also has responsibility for controlling the key parts of the existing administrative structures.

All of these tasks, some of them very intrusive, must be carried out with complete impartiality by civilian peacekeepers. Staff members of the U.N. system, with policy and election observers made available by member states, have risen to these new civilian challenges.

The involvement of such a variety of civilian personnel, alongside their military colleagues, creates a need for tight coordination of all aspects of an operation. As a result it has become normal for the overall direction of a multifaceted peacekeeping operation to be entrusted to a senior civilian official as special representative of the secretary general, to whom the force commander, the police commissioner, the director of elections and other directors report.

"[A variety of] tasks, some of them very intrusive, must be carried out with complete impartiality by civilian peacekeepers."

Responses Must Be Quick

One of the lessons learned during the recent headlong expansion of U.N. peacekeeping is the need to accelerate the deployment of new operations. Under current procedures three or four months can elapse between the Security Council's authorization of a mission and its becoming operational in the field. Action is required on three fronts: finance, personnel and equipment.

On finance, the member states should provide the secretary general with a working capital fund for the start-up of new operations, so that cash is immediately available. They should also revise existing financial procedures so that the secretary general has authority to spend that cash, within reasonable limits, as soon as the new operation is authorized.

The question of personnel is more complicated. Procedures for the transfer of U.N. staff to new operations in the field are being simplified for more rapid reaction. But most peacekeeping personnel (troops, police, election observers) are made available by governments. The answer is not to create a U.N. standing force, which would be impractical and inappropriate, but to extend and make more systematic standby arrangements by which governments commit themselves to hold ready, at an agreed period of notice, specially trained units for peacekeeping service.

A handful of governments already do this. A recent invitation to all member states to volunteer information about what personnel and equipment they would in principle be ready to contribute, if asked, produced disappointing results. I have now decided to take the initiative and put specific proposals to governments, in order to identify with reasonable certainty sources of military and police personnel and equipment that governments would undertake to make available at very short notice. These commitments would constitute building blocks that could be used, when the moment came, to construct peacekeeping operations in various sizes and configurations, ranging from a small group of military observers to a full division, as required.

Allied with this effort will be the provision of more extensive guidance to governments on training troops and police whom they may contribute to the United Nations for peacekeeping duties.

Equipment can cause even greater bottlenecks than personnel. There are two complementary ways in which this problem can be eased. First, member states should make it possible for the United Nations to establish a reserve stock of basic items (vehicles, radios, generators, prefabricated buildings) that are always required for a new peacekeeping operation. Second, member states could agree to hold ready, at various locations around the world, reserves of such equipment. These would remain their property but could be made immediately available to the United Nations when the need arose.

An even more radical development can now be envisaged. It happens all too often that the parties to a conflict sign a ceasefire agreement but then fail to respect it. In such situations it is felt that the United Nations should "do something." This is a reasonable expectation if the United Nations is to be an effective system of collective security. The purpose of peace enforcement units (perhaps they should be called "ceasefire enforcement units") would be to enable the United Nations to deploy troops quickly to enforce a ceasefire by taking coercive action against either party, or both, if they violate it.

> ***"Procedures for the transfer of U.N. staff to new operations in the field are being simplified for more rapid reaction."***

This concept retains many of the features of peacekeeping: the operation would be authorized by the Security Council; the troops would be provided voluntarily by member states; they would be under the command of the secretary general; and they would be impartial between the two sides, taking action only if one or other of them violated the agreed ceasefire. But the concept goes beyond peacekeeping to the extent that the operation would be deployed without the express consent of the two parties (though its basis would be a ceasefire agreement previously reached between them). U.N. troops would be authorized to use force to ensure respect for the ceasefire. They would be trained, armed and equipped accordingly; a very rapid response would be essential.

This is a novel idea that involves some obvious difficulties. But it should be carefully considered by the international community as the next step in the development of the United Nations' capability to take effective action on the ground to maintain international peace and security. . . .

Mounting Development Needs

Political stability is not an end in itself; it is a condition of durable economic and social development and the fulfillment of the human potential. At the same time inseparable links between peace and development need to be acknowledged and understood. The world has seen the deterioration of economic and social conditions give rise to political strife and military conflict. The activities of the United Nations for peace and security should not be carried out at the expense of its responsibilities for development. It is essential that peace and development be pursued in an integrated, mutually supporting way.

"The purpose of peace enforcement units . . . would be to enable the United Nations to deploy troops quickly to enforce a ceasefire."

One can point to a number of situations where the United Nations has kept the peace, or at least prevented conflicts from escalating, but the balance sheet on the development side is less than encouraging. A billion people live on less than one dollar a day; children in many parts of the world are dying unnecessarily of diseases that could easily be cured; women are striving to be both breadwinners and homemakers in situations of intolerable strain; and there are too few jobs. The crisis is deeper than merely another manifestation of the familiar disparity between the developed nations of the North and the developing South.

No such clear-cut pattern offers itself to our eyes today. East European countries and the former Soviet Union are struggling in their transition toward democracy and market-based economies. Even the nations of the Organization for Economic Cooperation and Development are not immune to economic and social ills. Poverty, unemployment, inequity and growing insecurity exist in virtually every part of the globe. Even rich nations are tempted to turn inward to attend to their own agendas. But today there is no longer any such thing as "someone else's problem"; the globalization of economies and communications deepens our interdependence.

The responsibilities of the United Nations in the field of social and economic development are central to the purposes and principles of the charter: first, because the maintenance of international peace and security is inextricably entwined with economic and social progress and stability; and second, because the promotion of social and economic progress is a specific task given to the United Nations by the charter.

The Origins of Third World "Development"

Development policy was significantly shaped by the Cold War and the process of decolonization. When the charter was being framed at San Francisco in 1945, and when most of our current world economic institutions were being created, most of today's states were either colonies, semi-colonies or parts of extensive empires. The notion of "development" was unformed; the concept of the "Third World" had not emerged. The idea that the United Nations should be concerned with economic and social issues sprang from what has been called "welfare internationalism," which evolved in wartime planning for the peace and was a formative influence on the Bretton Woods institutions dating from that period [the International Monetary Fund and the World Bank].

As demands for independence gathered momentum in African and Asian lands, programs of assistance and economic cooperation were initiated by former colonial powers. These were joined by assistance programs established by states with no recent colonial past, such as the Nordic countries. Meanwhile the World Bank was becoming the lead institution in the channeling of multilateral development finance to developing countries.

Provision of development assistance to newly independent nations became part of the foreign policies of the industrialized countries, intricately bound up with the global contest for power and influence. The United States, through its Agency for International Development, became a major provider of development finance and technical assistance in Africa, Asia and Latin America. The Soviet Union was deeply involved with a relatively small number of states considered potentially significant in its ideological sphere, and provided substantial technical support for them. In both cases development assistance was often interwoven with military aid.

Just as the Cold War distorted the vision of collective security set forth in the U.N. Charter, it also impaired cooperation for development. Bilateral foreign aid programs were often an instrument of the Cold War, and remain deeply affected by considerations of political power and national policy. Multilateral development programs, even when managed well and with admirable ethical purpose, derived from ideas and ideologies that proved inadequate at best and in some cases ruinous.

Social Development and Stability

At this time of change in world affairs, when restructuring the institutions of international relations is high on the agenda, there are increasing demands for action in the field of economic and social development. The call for a new unity and clarity of purpose from the United Nations in the field of development—which is now commonly understood to include social and economic development and environmental protection as well—has come from developing and developed countries alike.

Traditionally U.N. social development activities have concentrated on the most vulnerable groups of populations. Increasingly in developing countries efforts at modernization tug at institutions that hold the social fabric together. Declining social cohesion, in turn, can undermine economic progress. The organization is beginning to take a closer look at specific phenomena affecting social cohesion and to view the social and economic dimensions of development in a more integrated way. Issues of demography and cultural, religious, ethnic and linguistic

> ***"It is essential that peace and development be pursued in an integrated, mutually supporting way."***

diversity are so closely related today to prospects for political stability and economic advancement that the involvement of the United Nations in issues of social development is acquiring a qualitatively different nature.

If the process of decolonization is over and the Cold War has ended, and now that there is no "struggle" or bipolar competition to dramatize and distract development efforts, how can the United Nations seek consensus on the need for a fairer, more just, world and focus on the long-standing needs of the poor?

Today a consensus is emerging around a fundamental perception that the unfettered talents of individual human beings are the greatest resource a society can bring to bear on the task of national development. But the troubled state of the global economy indicates that we are still far from achieving universal economic prosperity, social justice and environmental balance. Cooperation for development will require the greatest intellectual effort in the period ahead because, as understood and applied until now, it has not resolved the urgent problem of the development of the planet. The need is comprehensive. Issues once approached separately, or sequentially, now may be seen as essentially indivisible.

The United Nations Should Have Its Own Volunteer Armed Forces

by Brian Urquhart

About the author: *Brian Urquhart, scholar in residence in the International Affairs Program of the Ford Foundation, is a former undersecretary-general of the United Nations.*

The vast expansion of the United Nations' (UN) peace-keeping commitments has sorely tested the UN's ability to intervene in violent local conflicts before they get out of hand, as well as its willingness to place soldiers at risk when they do. Though UN forces have achieved major successes in such places as Namibia, El Salvador, and the Golan Heights, they have faced increasing difficulty elsewhere. In Cambodia, lightly armed peace-keepers are shot at, harassed, and even killed with impunity. In Angola, a tiny contingent of UN monitors has been overwhelmed by a rebel army determined to get its way by force of arms. In Mozambique, it took months for the UN to convince governments to contribute troops to an urgent mission in a situation that did not catch the attention of the Western press and television.

An Idea from the Past

Above all, the tragedy of Bosnia has shown that international organizations are not able to deal effectively, and when necessary forcefully, with violent and single-minded factions in a civil war. The reluctance of governments to commit their troops to combat in a quagmire is understandable. Yet the Bosnian Muslims, among others, have paid a terrible price, and the credibility and relevance of international organizations are dangerously diminished. How can such impotence be prevented in the future? A stillborn idea from the past may suggest an answer.

The first Arab-Israeli war in 1948 was also the first major test of the UN's ability to make its decisions stick. In a speech at Harvard during that tumul-

Brian Urquhart, "For a UN Volunteer Military Force," *The New York Review of Books*, June 10, 1993.

tuous summer, the first secretary-general of the UN, Trygve Lie, proposed the establishment of a "comparatively small UN guard force . . . recruited by the Secretary-General and placed at the disposal of the Security Council." Lie argued that "even a small United Nations force would command respect, for it would have all the authority of the United Nations behind it." The kind of task he had in mind for such a force was to put an end to factional fighting in Jerusalem and to shore up the truce decreed by the Security Council.

"Peace-keeping forces have been unable to impose the Security Council's decisions."

In fact, the UN Charter had originally envisaged something much more ambitious. One of the great innovations of the Charter was the provision, in Article 43, for member nations to make military forces available to the Security Council. It is worth recalling the scale on which action by the Security Council was originally envisaged. The United States estimate of the forces it would supply under Article 43, which was by far the largest, included twenty divisions—over 300,000 troops—a very large naval force, 1,250 bombers and 2,250 fighters. However, by 1948, action along the lines of Article 43 had already been frozen by the cold war and by Soviet insistence that the great powers must make exactly equal contributions.

In Palestine the Arab states had rejected the UN partition decision and had gone to war to suppress the new state of Israel. Trygve Lie regarded this challenge to the UN's authority as a vital test of the organization's effectiveness in dealing with breaches of international peace and security and, faced with the paralysis of the Charter provisions for military forces, he proposed a UN legion. Lie's proposal attracted considerable public attention but no governmental support at all.

Security Council Unanimity Without Force

Forty-five years later, in the milder post–cold war political climate, it may be time to revive Trygve Lie's idea. The Security Council is today able to reach unanimous decisions on most of the important questions that come before it. The Council's problem now is how to make these decisions stick. The technique of peace-keeping without using force has often proved effective in conflicts between states, whether in the Middle East, Cyprus, or Africa. Predictably enough, in chaotic and violent situations within states or former states, peacekeeping forces have been unable to impose the Security Council's decisions on partisan militias and other nongovernmental groups, particularly when they are being manipulated indirectly by governments.

Although international enforcement action was successfully used against Iraq in Operation Desert Storm, the inability of the Security Council to enforce its decisions in less conventional military situations is the most serious setback for the world organization since the end of the cold war. Bosnia provides a particularly poignant example of this failure, but there are, or may well be, others—Angola and Cambodia, for example, and, before the US intervention there, Somalia. There will certainly be future conflicts in which an early display of strength by the Security Council will be needed if later disasters are to be prevented.

At the moment, the Security Council is often reduced to delivering admonitions or demands which have little or no impact on the actual situation. Like the legendary King Canute, it orders the waves to go back with small hope of practical results.

A Capacity for Early Peace Enforcement

Whether or not it is too late to relieve the tragedy of Bosnia, it is essential to give the necessary authority and strength to the Security Council to deal with such situations more effectively in the future. The capacity to deploy credible and effective peace enforcement units, at short notice and at an early stage in a crisis, and with the strength and moral support of the world community behind them, would be a major step in this direction. Clearly, a timely intervention by a relatively small but highly trained force, willing and authorized to take combat risks and representing the will of the international community, could make a decisive difference in the early stages of a crisis.

> ***"A timely intervention by a relatively small but highly trained force . . . could make a decisive difference."***

Retrospective speculation about what might have been done at an early stage in Bosnia may have little value; the problem itself was, and is, uniquely complex. It is possible, however, that a much tougher early reaction to interference with humanitarian aid and to breaches of the cease-fire might have deterred the Serbian forces from their later excesses, particularly if it had been made clear that the small UN force would, if necessary, have had air and other strategic support from member states. In other words, a determined UN peace enforcement force, deployed before the situation had become desperate, and authorized to retaliate, might have provided the basis for a more effective international effort.

At the present time, financial, military, and political obstacles all combine to make such early intervention difficult or impossible. It is by now very clear that few, if any, governments are willing to commit their own troops to a forceful ground role in a situation which does not threaten their own security and which may well prove to be both violent and open-ended. National leaders are naturally reluctant to commit troops to distant operations in which they may sustain more than a few casualties.

A UN Volunteer Force

The new unanimity of the Security Council on important problems, the confused intrastate conflicts now confronting the UN, and the natural reluctance of governments to involve their own forces in violent situations where their own interest and security are not involved—all these point strongly to the need for a highly trained international volunteer force, willing, if necessary, to fight hard to break the cycle of violence at an early stage in low-level but dangerous conflicts, especially ones involving irregular militias and groups. This is not a new idea. In *An Agenda for Peace* Secretary-General Boutros Boutros-Ghali recommended "peace enforcement" units from member states, which would be "available on call and would consist of troops that have volunteered for such service."

An international volunteer force would be under the exclusive authority of the Security Council and under the day-to-day direction of the secretary-general. To function effectively, it would need the full support of members of the United Nations. Such support should include, if necessary, air, naval, and other kinds of military action. The volunteer force would be trained in the techniques of peace-keeping and negotiation as well as in the more bloody business of fighting.

A UN volunteer force would not, of course, take the place of preventive diplomacy, traditional peace-keeping forces, or of large-scale enforcement action under Chapter VII of the Charter, such as Desert Storm. It would not normally be employed against the military forces of states. It would be designed simply to fill a very important gap in the armory of the Security Council, giving it the ability to back up preventive diplomacy with a measure of immediate peace enforcement. As Secretary-General Boutros Boutros-Ghali has recommended in *An Agenda for Peace*, the Security Council should "consider the utilization of peace enforcement units in clearly defined circumstances and with their terms of reference specified in advance."

Raising Troops

There can be little doubt that there would be more than enough volunteers from around the world for an elite peace force of this kind. Thousands of men and women would apply, many of them with extensive military experience. The problem would be to select, organize, and train the best of them, develop a command and support structure, and form them into suitable operational units. All of this would take time, strong leadership and expertise, and, of course, money.

> ***"The Security Council [would have] the ability to back up preventive diplomacy with a measure of immediate peace enforcement."***

Situations in which such a force is urgently needed are likely to develop long before an international, volunteer UN peace force could be ready to take the field. An interim solution would be to recruit such a force from volunteers from national armies, as is suggested in *An Agenda for Peace*. Such volunteers would already be trained and might even make up national subunits in a UN volunteer force. To have volunteers from national armies serving together in such subunits would simplify administration and problems of command. The volunteer status of such troops should go far to relieve governments of inhibiting concerns about casualties and open-ended commitments that now make them unwilling to commit their national forces to such tasks. Volunteers from national armed forces could serve for limited periods with the permission of their national establishments, and could then return to their national armed forces. Meanwhile, the development of a permanent, standing UN volunteer force could go forward.

The Costs of a UN Force

Any number of possible objections can be posed to the idea of a UN volunteer force. Until quite recently I myself, after a long association with UN peace-keeping, would have argued against it. The idea will certainly raise, in some minds at least, the specter of supranationality that has always haunted the idea of a standing UN army. If, however, the force can only be deployed with the authority of the Security Council, the necessary degree of control by member governments is guaranteed. The main difference from peace-keeping will be the role, the volunteer nature, and the immediate availability of the force.

The question of expense inevitably arises. As a rough guide, it has been estimated elsewhere [by John M. Lee, Robert Von Pagenhardt, and Timothy W. Stanley, in *To Unite Our Strength*] that a five-thousand-strong light infantry force would cost about $380 million a year to maintain and equip, if surplus equipment could be obtained below cost from governments. The total cost of peace-keeping operations in 1992 was $1.4 billion, and it was much more in 1993 [$3.2 billion]. The average ratio of expenditure between UN peace-keeping costs and national military outlays is of the order of $1 to $1,000. Units from a highly trained volunteer force might also replace traditional peace-keeping forces in some situations, thus reducing costs for traditional peace-keeping. Most important, the possibility of the UN's intervening convincingly at an *early* stage in a crisis would almost certainly provide, in the long term, for a large reduction in the complication and expense that belated intervention almost invariably entails. The delay in intervening in Somalia, for example, certainly created a much larger disaster, which in turn necessitated a much larger international response.

> ***"The main difference from peace-keeping will be the role, the volunteer nature, and the immediate availability of the force."***

Finally, it may be feared that a UN volunteer force will run the risk of acquiring a "mercenary" image. Outstanding leadership, high standards of recruitment, training, and performance, and dedication to the principles and objectives of the UN should help to address such concerns.

There is one overwhelmingly good reason for creating a UN volunteer force: the conditions of the post–cold war world and the new challenges faced by the

United Nations urgently demand it. The UN was founded nearly fifty years ago primarily as a mechanism for dealing with disputes and conflicts between states. It is now increasingly perceived, and called upon, as an international policeman and world emergency service. The Security Council lacks the capacity for the kind of swift and effective action that could give it the initiative in the early stages of a low-level conflict. Obviously, intensive thought would have to be given to the many problems involved in such an enterprise—selection, training, command, size, location, organization, discipline and loyalty, rules of engagement, legal status, logistical and other support, and, of course, financing. The cooperation of national military establishments would be essential, especially in such matters as air and logistical support.

"[The UN] is now increasingly perceived, and called upon, as an international policeman and world emergency service."

It will take much imaginative effort for a UN volunteer force of this kind to become a working reality. As its experience and reputation grew, however, its need to use force would certainly decrease. Its existence, known effectiveness, and immediate availability would in themselves be a deterrent to low-level violence and would give important support for negotiation and peaceful settlement. It could become a decisively useful part of the machinery of the Security Council.

In 1948 Trygve Lie sadly concluded [in *In the Cause of Peace*] that a UN legion

> would have required a degree of attention and imagination on the part of men in charge of the foreign policies of the principal Member nations that they seemed to be unable to give . . . to projects for strengthening directly the authority and prestige of the United Nations as an institution.

Forty-five years and millions of casualties later, the time has come to summon up that attention and imagination.

The United Nations Should Play a Limited Role in Interventions

by Kim R. Holmes

About the author: *Kim R. Holmes is vice president and director of foreign policy studies at the Heritage Foundation in Washington, D.C.*

For over forty years, the Cold War conflict between the United States and the Soviet Union paralyzed the peacekeeping functions of the United Nations. With few exceptions, the United Nations and other multinational organizations were ineffective in resolving major conflicts because of the zero-sum nature of the Cold War. Now that the Cold War is over, many believe that the United Nations can play a greater role in resolving conflicts and maintaining order in the so-called new world.

New Responsibilities for the United Nations

Glowing in the success of the Persian Gulf War, the United Nations has renewed stature and expanding peacekeeping operations in Cambodia, the former Yugoslavia and elsewhere. At this point, some believe the time has come to further expand the peacekeeping responsibilities of the United Nations. Advocates of this position call for the creation of a standby U.N. army; the expansion of the definitions of security threats to include environmental and humanitarian concerns; the increase of the United Nations' powers to intervene in the internal affairs of states; and the creation of what has been referred to as the New World Order, in which the United Nations (and perhaps other multinational organizations) will be the world's main body for not only keeping the peace, but enforcing it.

To be certain, the passing of the Cold War offers new opportunities to make the United Nations more effective. The success of the United Nations in the Gulf War demonstrates that the organization can be used as an effective vehicle of warmaking against an aggressor. In El Salvador, Angola, Namibia and other

Abridged from Kim R. Holmes, "New World Disorder: A Critique of the United Nations," *Journal of International Affairs*, vol. 46, no. 2 (Winter 1993). Published by permission of the *Journal of International Affairs* and the Trustees of Columbia University in the City of New York.

former Cold War crisis zones, the United Nations has proven to be effective to different degrees in facilitating the establishment of peace and order once a cease-fire has been established.

Yet the millennium for the United Nations and other multinational organizations has not arrived. In all cases of recent U.N. involvement in warmaking or peacekeeping operations, the underlying cause of success was neither the triumph of the multinational ideal in international politics nor was it the birth of a new belief in the ideals of global democracy. Rather, it was the natural and logical consequence of the end of the U.S.-Soviet rivalry, and the general collapse of Soviet support for client states and groups.

As policy makers ponder the wisdom of expanding the United Nations' role in peacekeeping, they should remember one fact: The United Nations remains a mere instrument of nation-states, and its success or failure depends, as always, not mainly on the United Nations itself, but on the degree to which sovereign nation-states believe that international cooperation suits their own national interests. This fact defines both the limitations of and the opportunities for the United Nations as a peacekeeping body. . . .

Redefining State Sovereignty

As the peacekeeping role of the United Nations expands in the post–Cold War era, the definitions of international security and state sovereignty may need to evolve to accommodate the desired capacity of that organization. In the Security Council's 31 January 1993 *Annual Summit Declaration*, definitions of new threats to international security included "non-military sources of instability in the economic, social, humanitarian and ecological fields." Here the United Nations is moving well beyond traditional definitions of international threats involving civil wars or the aggression of states. In fact, some at the United Nations go so far as to see that body as an international police force to protect the environment, avenge human rights abuses, stop humanitarian tragedies and even right perceived social and economic wrongs.

An apt example of this sentiment is contained in the words of former U.N. Under Secretary-General Sir Brian Urquhart, who stated, "It is no longer acceptable that international action is taken only when a situation threatens the interests of the most powerful nations." Believing that the days of state-specific national interests are over for good, Urquhart proposes establishing a U.N. police force deployed to end random violence and perform armed police actions. He concludes, "The unraveling of national sovereignty seems to be a feature of the post–Cold War period." Clearly he views the traditional concept of autonomous states as eroding somewhat with the end of the Cold War.

"The United Nations remains a mere instrument of nation-states."

This disregard for national sovereignty has also surfaced in discussions of the now-expanded U.N. operations in Somalia. Private relief experts, including CARE president Philip Johnston and Bread for the World president David Beckmann, have proposed that the United Nations take over and rule Somalia, claiming the country is in chaos and has no government. Furthermore, the U.S.-led, U.N.-authorized Operation Restore Hope has set the precedent for military intervention based on strictly humanitarian grounds. Further involvement and control, including increased military oversight, is being sought by the United Nations as the United States backs resolutions to enforce humanitarian assistance. The United Nations has begun a new type of operation, unlike the peacekeeping or wars that the Security Council authorized in Korea and the Persian Gulf. This may become a model for similar crises in the future.

"This disregard for national sovereignty has also surfaced in discussions of the now-expanded U.N. operations in Somalia."

Andrew Natsios, Assistant Administrator for the Bureau of Food and Humanitarian Assistance at the U.S. Agency for International Development, has said concerning Somalia, "We may have to redefine sovereignty." Others are saying that the United Nations should establish a trusteeship over the territory to establish law and order and control relief efforts.

During much of the Cold War, the United Nations championed the idea of state sovereignty, primarily because most less-developed countries (LDCs) were sensitive to outside interference in their internal affairs. Whether it be Mexico, Israel or Cuba, most non-Western countries raised the banner of state sovereignty to protect themselves from the unwanted interference of larger states, and the United Nations repeatedly upheld this principle in Security Council resolutions. As the United Nations adopts the principles of global democracy and redefines the notion of state sovereignty, LDCs' ability to restrict international interference will be diminished. The new thinking is that if all U.N. member-states are equal voices in a global democratic order, then LDCs not only have a right to interfere in the internal affairs of other states through the United Nations, but can expect to have their independence restricted as well by that organization. Restrictions of this type are already occurring with the U.N. peacekeeping operation in Cambodia, where the United Nations has taken control of major government ministries. The action in Somalia, though draped in humanitarian concern, points to further disregard and redefinition of state sovereignty by the United Nations.

U.N. Military Independence

The idea of broadening the role of the United Nations in conflict resolution has an influential champion in the current U.N. Secretary-General, Boutros Boutros-Ghali. In *An Agenda for Peace*, Boutros-Ghali states:

> United Nations operations in areas of crisis have generally been established after conflict has occurred. The time has come to plan for circumstances warranting preventive deployment. The Security Council has the authority to take military action to maintain or restore international peace and security. While such action should only be taken when all peaceful means have failed, the option of taking it is essential to the credibility of the United Nations as a guarantor of international security. This will require bringing into being, through negotiations, special agreements . . . whereby member states undertake to make armed forces, assistance and facilities available to the Security Council . . . not only on an ad hoc basis, but on a permanent basis.

Boutros-Ghali's recommendation is tantamount to creating a standing U.N. army. Member-states presumably would turn over troops to the U.N. Military Staff Committee (MSC), which is composed of the military chiefs of staff of the five permanent members of the Security Council—the United States, France, United Kingdom, China and Russia. Although dormant for many years, the MSC, according to the U.N. Charter, is "responsible under the Security Council for any armed forces placed at the disposal of the Security Council."

Boutros-Ghali's proposed U.N. standing army includes force contributions from twenty member-states, each providing 2,000 troops on 48-hour notice. To pay for the program, Boutros-Ghali has suggested an international sales tax on weapons and international air travel providing $50 million for emergency humanitarian purposes and a $1 billion peace endowment.

"The primary concern for any member-state contributing to the proposed U.N. force is an elusive command structure."

The primary concern for any member-state contributing to the proposed U.N. force is an elusive command structure. The MSC's command of a U.N. force would likely alternate periodically between the five permanent members, meaning four-fifths of the time permanent members would not command their own forces. This allows the use of force to be taken out of the hands of those nations that provide and support the forces. Furthermore, non-democratic nations would have the opportunity to participate with and even control democratic forces, thus undermining the will of the people in all democratic nations.

U.N. Peacekeeping Operations

As the United Nations expands its role in resolving conflicts, it is necessary to clarify definitions of its various peacekeeping activities. . . .

Today the term *peacekeeping* applies when the United Nations sends lightly armed soldiers from neutral countries into an area, usually to preserve a cease-fire and provide a buffer zone between warring combatants. Peacekeepers are only allowed to use their weapons in self-defense, and arrive with the consent of all parties. Peacekeeping also involves monitoring elections and ensuring that warring factions adhere to demobilization agreements. A good example of this activity is the U.N. Interim Force in Lebanon (UNIFIL), which was established in 1978 and is still in existence today.

The term peacekeeping has also been used to define what could be more appropriately termed *peace-enforcement*. Peace-enforcement occurs, essentially, when peacekeeping goes awry. If a cease-fire breaks down, a revolt breaks out or the peacekeepers lose the support of one side and become themselves the targets of a warring faction, U.N. peace-enforcers can pacify the aggressor army. U.N. peace-enforcement occurred during the 1960–64 United Nations Operation in the Congo in which 234 U.N. troops were killed as various factions turned against the United Nations. There is the potential for this type of situation to develop in the conflict in the former Yugoslavia if the United Nations were to launch military operations against Serbian-backed forces in Bosnia and Hercegovina. U.N.-authorized Operation Restore Hope in Somalia can also be considered to be peace-enforcement, though it has taken on the additional unprecedented aspect of being strictly humanitarian in purpose and scope.

"In the past, aggression against nations was the only acceptable reason for war."

A third category might be called U.N. *warmaking*, illustrated by the United Nations' endorsement of the use of force in the Korean War and the Persian Gulf War. In obvious contrast to peacekeeping, warmaking exists when the use of force is employed without the consent of all parties. In both instances of this type of warmaking operation, the United States led a coalition against an aggressor nation, using the United Nations essentially to mobilize international support.

The nature of U.N. warmaking may change as the reasons for its undertaking broaden. In the past, aggression against nations was the only acceptable reason for war. Now, however, human rights abuses or humanitarian crises may be defined as sufficient cause for the United Nations to wage war against a country or guerrilla faction. . . .

The Limits of U.N. Peacekeeping

The United Nations is now undoubtedly a more effective peacekeeper, and to some extent peace-maker, than during the Cold War. It served a useful purpose in the Persian Gulf War and in the many peace settlements associated with post–Cold War restructuring. Before expectations are unrealistically elevated, however, the limits of the United Nations in the areas of peacekeeping, peace-enforcement and warmaking should be examined given the organization's successes and failures in those areas. Such an examination may temper the more utopian visions held by those who believe that the world has entered into a new age where state sovereignty, national interest and war are passe. The lessons to follow can be viewed as guiding principles to practical U.N. expansion.

Most important to note is that U.N. peacekeeping has been most effective when its role involved only mediating and observing peace successfully brought about by other parties. This was the case in U.N. operations in Angola, El Salvador and Nicaragua, for example. As the Cold War ended, the warring factions backed by the Soviet Union lost their patron and were forced to give up fighting and accept the democratic process. The United Nations was called in afterwards to help implement agreements already reached by individual states.

Furthermore, the United Nations cannot end conflicts unilaterally, but only when all warring parties call for peace. Once again El Salvador serves as a useful example of this type of peacekeeping. Both the government and the Farabundo Martí National Liberation Front (FMLN) were exhausted by their civil war and so turned to the United Nations as a neutral, third party to negotiate a settlement. When the two parties signed a cease-fire in 1992, they called on the United Nations to verify the settlement and help demobilize the FMLN guerrillas. At no point did the United Nations actually force an agreement on the Salvadoran government or the FMLN. Both sides wanted an end to the war, and the United Nations worked effectively as an objective peace-broker to facilitate the process.

The U.N. Cannot Create Peace

Finally, when warring factions have agreed to a cease-fire only for tactical reasons, the United Nations can guarantee a cease-fire or peace settlement only through the deployment of large numbers of ground troops. The best example of this lesson is Korea, where the United States sent tens of thousands of troops to guarantee the armistice. Since North Korea never completely accepted the terms of the armistice, the Communist North remained a threat to the South. Failing to achieve peace, the United Nations had to retreat from what became a permanent war zone and rely on U.S. troops to deter future attacks by North Korea.

Another example of a U.N. operation failing to enact peace and order due to a misguided peace-enforcement effort was in the Congo from 1960 to 1964. Originally supporting the U.N. operation there, the Soviet Union reversed its policy and opposed the authority of the United Nations. Eventually, the Congo's government dissolved and the warring factions turned on the United Nations. The situation in the Congo proved that in volatile situations, the circumstances of U.N. involvement can change and shatter the consensus that originally led to the United Nations' involvement. When a government turns against the United Nations, as it did in the Congo, the United Nations itself becomes a military target. The United Nations could not create through peace-enforcement what did not already exist: a willingness on the part of the warring parties to negotiate for peace.

"The United Nations cannot end conflicts unilaterally, but only when all warring parties call for peace."

These examples demonstrate that the motivation of states or warring factions in any U.N. peacekeeping operation would be to maximize security and political gain or to reduce the possibility of political instability or loss. Whether a U.N. peacekeeping operation is successful will be determined by the outcome of this political calculus and will be little affected by the commitment of states to some preconceived international order, ideal or cooperative effort. Indeed, the states comprising the international community as a whole will become involved in or support U.N. peacekeeping operations only so long as they do not conflict with state-specific interests. International stability and cooperation are welcomed by most states in the world, only because most states support the international status quo, but this does not mean that their commitment to some ideal of international cooperation supersedes or contradicts their attachment to their own state interests.

Notwithstanding the high expectations of the global democracy of the new world order concept, the fact remains that wars are still "politics by other means," as Carl von Clausewitz believed. People fight and die for a variety of reasons, but the organized violence of a military operation, whether sponsored by a state or a guerrilla movement, still aims for a state-specified political goal. If the political goals of the warring factions are ignored—if they are seen as a politically neutral, humanitarian tragedy, for example—then no peacekeeping operation sponsored by the United Nations or any multinational organization will succeed. Peacekeeping will meet resistance by local fighters who have more to lose than the U.N. forces, and more to gain if the United Nations fails.

The United Nations Should Stress Prevention over Intervention

by Thomas G. Weiss

About the author: *Thomas G. Weiss, associate dean of faculty at Brown University, Providence, Rhode Island, is executive director of the Academic Council on the United Nations System.*

Euphoria surrounding the Cold War's demise and optimism about the possibilities for democratization have given way to a more sober appraisal of continuing and even increasingly violent civil wars in "peacetime" that were hardly imagined by the framers of the United Nations (UN) Charter. The search for order may be no less quixotic at present than it was earlier as decolonization gives way to micronationalism and self-determination goes to its logical extremes.

The end of the Cold War has reinvigorated the UN Security Council and enhanced the prospects for international intervention, but at the same time it has unleashed pent-up violence. Rather than enabling the tabula rasa of Francis Fukuyama's "end of history" [*The End of History and the Last Man*], the removal of East–West tensions permits the brutal expression of historical grievances. Power vacuums permit the implosion of "failed states."

In areas such as Afghanistan, Angola, Mozambique, and Somalia, conflicts fueled largely by superpower rivalry have taken on lives of their own. Strife dampened for decades by the existence of the Cold War has been rekindled in the Balkans and the various republics of the former Soviet Union. In other conflicts with no direct links to East–West rivalry—such as the Sudan, Liberia, and Sri Lanka—ethnic, religious, and political cauldrons seethe.

Intervention figures prominently in the policy lexicon and is the subject for numerous international symposiums. Vigorous rhetoric in the early 1990s has also been backed by operational decisions from the Security Council in the Persian Gulf and Somalia and to a lesser degree in the former Yugoslavia.

Abridged from *The Washington Quarterly*, vol. 17, no. 1 (Winter 1994), Thomas G. Weiss, "Intervention: Whither the United Nations?" by permission of The MIT Press, Cambridge, Mass., and the Center for Strategic and International Studies.

Although geopolitics are never irrelevant, humanitarian concerns are driving people, parliaments, and policymakers to intervene.

We are groping toward arrangements by which egregious aggression, life-threatening suffering, and human rights abuses become legitimate international concerns more routinely. We are moving in fits and starts from a controlling paradigm in which state sovereignty served as an all-purpose rationalization for narrowly defined raisons d'état toward a world in which states and armed opposition groups, as well as other less traditional actors, are challenging conventional notions of territorial sovereignty and insisting upon greater accountability.

More particularly, some members of the international community are beginning to argue that they have a right to intervene for humanitarian purposes. This situation is starkly distinct from the conventional wisdom of the past. In the words of Adam Roberts, "Humanitarian war is an oxymoron which may yet become a reality.". . .

Analysis of recent interventions and the examination of policy propositions leads to three recommendations. They represent choices for decision makers and citizens regarding future UN interventions in the humanitarian arena. Judgments about the feasibility and costs of each recommendation would lead an optimist to speculate that they are presented in the order of their desirability, the pessimist in reverse order of their likelihood.

The Costs of Civil Wars

The magnitude of the present humanitarian and human rights tasks resulting from civil wars is staggering. Until recently, armed conflict was supposed to be a third world phenomenon, but no longer. There are, by the most conservative estimates, at least 1 million refugees from the former Yugoslavia and probably three times that number displaced within the boundaries of that former Balkan republic. There are approximately the same number of refugees already from one clash between two former Soviet republics, Armenia and Azerbaijan. There are officially 20 million refugees worldwide and at least the same number of internally displaced persons.

Recent media coverage easily conjures up appalling images of those represented by these statistics. It is more difficult perhaps to conceive the total costs in terms of ruined economies and postponed development prospects as well as of the UN's growing bills for peacekeeping and humanitarian operations.

> ***"Strife dampened for decades by the existence of the Cold War has been rekindled."***

The billions spent by the United Nations in trying to mitigate the human costs of war are increased substantially by adding those of other private and public relief agencies. The United Nations is dramatically overextended—as he was leaving office in late 1992, Dick Thornburgh, former UN under secretary general for administration, called the continuing expansion of activities a "financial bungee jump." If civil wars are growing and their consequences becoming more dire, would not it be more reasonable to act earlier and head them off?

1: Give Priority to Prevention

The international community desperately requires a new strategic concept. It should stress taking as many steps as possible to prevent violence and war in addition to dealing with their consequences. The conceptual situation is not totally bleak. New thinking is appearing along with proposals to deal with the debris of violence in the post–cold war era. At their January 1992 summit, members of the UN Security Council perhaps recognized the frustrations and failures of the new era when requesting that the then newly elected UN secretary general evaluate the promise of the United Nations in a changed world. Boutros Boutros-Ghali's report, *An Agenda for Peace*, covers much ground, but perhaps one of its most striking features is its advancement of the concept of conflict prevention.

What is required is nothing less than a shift in the dominant way that the international community attacks problems. In formulating responses, new policy lenses should be tinted with preventive peacebuilding rather than intervention in and management of conflicts once they have erupted. The root causes of many conflicts—poverty, the unjust distribution of available resources, and the legacy of colonial boundaries in many multiethnic societies—should be addressed before they explode.

> ***"There are officially 20 million refugees worldwide and at least the same number of internally displaced persons."***

Governments normally think of preventive actions as the advance deployment of UN soldiers to settings like Macedonia or the expanded use of fact-finding, human rights monitors, and early-warning systems. These are certainly worthwhile. But effective prevention would include basic investment in economic and social development in poor countries as well as reforms to distribute the benefits of future growth more equitably. It also would include reform of the global financial and trading systems.

This is of course more easily written than done. We generally react more quickly and effectively to urgent and obvious crises than to long-simmering and less visible ones. Frequently we postpone dealing with what UNICEF has called silent crises until tomorrow, in favor of today's loud ones. Yet, this tall order is the alternative to either international intervention or spreading chaos. Although it may be unrealistic, it is not Pollyannaish to begin to think in this radically new fashion.

2: Do It Right or Not at All

There is clearly a growing requirement to employ military might to help quell ethnic violence, create humanitarian space, and protect fundamental human rights. Political pressures at present point toward skimping on UN operations that deal with the humanitarian debris of the post–cold war era, but international intervention in such civil wars as Somalia and the former Yugoslavia should be timely and robust or shunned altogether. While Western citizens, parliaments, and governments seek to avoid commitments, poignant media coverage sometimes elicits halfway measures when massive human rights abuses and starvation become particularly unpalatable. This is what many observers have dubbed the "CNN factor," and it often provokes useful action. But it also encourages much wishful thinking, underestimates long-term realities, and overlooks crises in which journalists find no convincing copy or footage for their editors. In the face of widespread suffering and less than adequate resources, the visceral reaction is to seek a magical "quick fix" or alternatively to respond incrementally, hoping that belligerents will somehow come to their senses. Neither is workable policy. Both can in fact be counterproductive.

"[Policy should be based on] preventive peacebuilding rather than intervention in and management of conflicts once they have erupted."

In the U.S.-led and UN-approved intervention in Somalia in December 1992, for instance, Washington wanted out almost before it got in. The announcement was accompanied by George Bush's suggestion that some GIs might return home before Bill Clinton's inauguration, then less than two months away. This estimate was woefully inaccurate and misleading, as was the calculation that a narrowly circumscribed effort—excluding such essential tasks as disarmament, help in reconstituting a civil society, and assistance for reconstruction—would be fruitful in restoring hope in this hapless country. There have been heavy casualties among aid workers and soldiers in what became a UN chapter VII operation in May 1993. U.S. Cobra gunships returned to attack General [Mohammed Farah] Aideed's followers in Mogadishu and elite U.S. Army Rangers were deployed. The saga of retaliations and insecurity illustrates just how wishful the thinking was and just how short-lived and partial were the results from this U.S.-led operation. . . .

Half-Measures in Yugoslavia

The quintessential piecemeal action was European and American dithering about the breakup of the former Yugoslavia. The initial deployment early in 1992 of some 14,000 UN blue helmets as a buffer in newly independent Croatia was accompanied by a token presence in Sarajevo. Symbols have obviously been of extremely limited value in staving off ethnic cleansing and other atrocities in Bosnia and Herzegovina. Subsequent ad hocery in 1992 and 1993 included: 1,500 soldiers to the area, followed later by 6,500 NATO forces, no-flight zones, and other saber rattling; vast humanitarian efforts; countless Security Council resolutions; and a seemingly endless number of cease-fires and negotiating sessions.

Such half-measures under UN auspices fostered Serbian war aims. Given their traditional operating procedures and constraints, UN soldiers were not strong enough to deter the Serbs, but they deterred the international community from more assertive intervention because the troops, along with aid workers, were vulnerable targets. Although assistance to refugees saved lives, it also helped foster ethnic cleansing by stimulating the movement of unwanted populations. Air drops of food made it seem that people counted and salved consciences, while massive and unspeakable human rights abuse and war crimes continued unabated.

Inadequate military and humanitarian action, combined with half-hearted sanctions and a negotiating charade, thus constituted a powerful diversion. They collectively impeded more vigorous Western diplomatic and military pressure or lifting the arms embargo for Muslims to help level the killing fields.

The United Nations has provided a means for governments to appear to be doing something without really doing anything. The urge to "do something" in troubled regions around the world should be resisted unless the measures taken have a reasonable chance of success. The moral of early post–cold war interventions is that hollow gestures can turn out to be worse than no action at all.

3: Be Prepared for Triage

One of the most unsettling facts emerging from recent events is the growing disparity between available resources and the skyrocketing demand for intervention. "Donor fatigue" is often a shallow and ready-made excuse to avoid humanitarian responsibilities. Yet recessionary and budgetary pressures are obviously at loggerheads with the crying need for outside helping hands in chaotic hot spots on every continent. In the words of the UN's high commissioner for refugees Sadako Ogata, "The time has come for a major dialogue on the hard choices that will have to be made in the face of finite humanitarian resources and almost infinite humanitarian demands."

Triage, the term for an unthinkable process of selection, will soon be making a comeback. Much remains to be done to get more from existing humanitarian resources and machinery. Nevertheless, policymakers and citizens will soon confront painful moral dilemmas. Is it not compulsory to channel resources to save those who can be saved rather than spreading them inadequately to as many suffering souls as possible? Does it make more sense to spend monies temporarily sparing the lives of those who will be eliminated subsequently by shellings or to help those in countries where belligerents have agreed to a cease-fire? Would it be more sensible to switch those

"In the face of widespread suffering and less than adequate resources, the visceral reaction is to seek a magical 'quick fix.'"

humanitarian resources being spent on peacekeepers and on airlifting supplies to civilians trapped in war zones to persons dying from malnutrition and preventable diseases? Humanitarian practitioners have come to realize that 10 to 20 times more can be done with the same limited resources to attack poverty's silent emergencies rather than the loud crises resulting from wars.

Increased Intervention Is Predicted

Former President Bush's heralded "new world order" has obviously not materialized. But we are poised precariously between the Cold War and an embryonic order whose positive characteristics are not yet visible. One of the clearest needs in today's world is to intervene effectively when civilians are trapped by the war strategies of irresponsible and sometimes genocidal leaders. To return to our original question, however, no consensus yet exists about international intervention, but a fragile body of UN and state practice is emerging.

> ***"UN soldiers were not strong enough to deter the Serbs, but they deterred the international community from more assertive intervention."***

Major increases in the use of armed force in the name of humanitarianism must undoubtedly be expected. The United Nations is on the brink of acting upon its obligations and circumventing its numerous limitations. As Canada's permanent representative to the UN Louise Fréchette has recently argued:

> The principles of sovereignty and non-intervention in internal affairs of states no longer reign supreme in the UN. Indeed the pressure felt in the UN is for more intervention, not less and the debate of the future may revolve less around the question of whether the UN has the *right* to intervene than whether it has a *duty* to do so.

As the 1990s unfold, there are bound to be more humanitarian crises and more pressures on the United Nations to help stem the chaos and protect civilians. Priorities should be defined by intergovernmental discussions because the three recommendations here really represent options. Confronted with increasing chaos and a seemingly endless number of humanitarian emergencies, the choices are better prevention, better intervention, or triage.

The United Nations Should Not Use Military Force

by Michael Clough

About the author: *Michael Clough is a senior fellow at the Council on Foreign Relations in New York City.*

Editor's note: On April 6, 1994, in the African country of Rwanda, following the death of President Juvenal Habyarimana, renewed fighting broke out in a civil war begun in the fall of 1993. During this new outbreak of hostilities between a rebel army of the Tutsi ethnic minority (14 percent of Rwanda's population) and government forces of the Hutu ethnic majority (85 percent of population), Hutu militias killed at least 200,000 Tutsi civilians and caused an estimated 2 million refugees to flee to neighboring countries. A UN observer force stationed in Rwanda to observe a previous cease-fire in the civil war was forced to retreat in April 1994 in the face of the renewed violence. In late July 1994, the rebel Tutsi army succeeded in overthrowing the Hutu government of Rwanda.

On May 25, 1994, United Nations Secretary General Boutros Boutros-Ghali denounced the international community for not sending troops to end the fighting in Rwanda, where an estimated 200,000 people have died. He was right to condemn world leaders for their inaction, but wrong to believe that a U.N. peacekeeping force is—or was—the answer. Quite the contrary. The efforts of Boutros-Ghali and others to expand the military role of the United Nations are partly to blame for the failure of the international community to develop effective ways to prevent such violent conflicts as [the one] in Rwanda.

Problems with Proposed UN Reforms

The root cause of the problem is the belief that the end of the Cold War opens the door for the United Nations to take on ever more responsibility for international peace and security. This ambition is an article of faith among a small but outspoken group of internationalists who regard the U.N. Charter as a sacred

Michael Clough, "The U.N. Must Abandon Its New Military Role," *Los Angeles Times*, May 29, 1994. Reprinted by permission of the author.

text that was regularly defiled by superpower antics during the Cold War. It was also fostered by world leaders, especially by former President George Bush, who see the world body as a convenient way to conceal unilateral desires beneath a cloak of international legitimacy (as happened in the case of the [1991 Persian] Gulf War) and to shift responsibility for troublesome conflicts in non-strategic places to others (as happened in the case of Angola). Finally, the new role was embraced by many relief and human-rights organizations that saw it as a means to transform the body into a vehicle for humanitarian intervention.

"Unfortunately, the results of U.N. military adventures have been disastrous."

Unfortunately, the results of U.N. military adventures have been disastrous. The Bush administration's cynical manipulation of the Security Council during the Gulf conflict has greatly increased distrust of the United Nations in many Third World countries. The misguided humanitarian intervention in Somalia has created a general reluctance to get involved in other conflicts. The U.N.'s role in military decisions regarding Bosnia has complicated and endangered the organization's humanitarian operations there and weakened the credibility of NATO [North Atlantic Treaty Organization] threats to deter Serbian aggression. Disagreements over U.N. military-deployment plans and a lack of troop commitments have become an excuse for inaction in Rwanda.

Some analysts contend these problems can be solved by a series of reforms, among them, adding new permanent members to the Security Council; strengthening the U.N. Secretariat's ability to plan and supervise military operations; creating a standing U.N. military force; and establishing criteria for humanitarian intervention under Chapter Seven of the U.N. Charter, which authorizes military action in response to threats to international peace and security. This is wishful thinking. Few of these reforms are likely to be approved by the U.N. membership. Even if they were, it is doubtful that they would produce the outcome their proponents covet.

Problems with UN Use of Force

The effective use of force requires a degree of consensus and resolve that the Security Council can only muster in extreme circumstances. The Gulf War and intervention in Somalia were the exceptions that proved the rule. In both instances, without American leadership, the United Nations would not have acted—or been able to act—in the ways it did. None of the reforms now being recommended would change this reality.

But even if a significant U.N. military capability could be created, it would be a mistake to move down this path. If an attempt were made to use such a force to stop the fighting in Rwanda, or Angola, or any of the other civil wars now raging, it would risk involving the United Nations in protracted guerrilla wars.

To believe otherwise would require a naive faith that the parties to these conflicts would be prepared to give up their objectives and bow to U.N. demands without a fight. At the same time, it would be equally naive to believe that a U.N. force would have any more success in ending civil wars than the United States had in Vietnam.

Just as important, military intervention would make it impossible for U.N. officials to maintain the impartiality that is usually essential to the success of diplomatic mediation efforts and humanitarian-relief operations. These are the areas where the United Nations has achieved most of its greatest successes. As we have seen in Bosnia, however, once the Security Council approves military actions, U.N. mediators and relief workers lose the shield of neutrality.

U.S. Opposition to UN Military Intervention

What can be done? The Clinton administration has taken a series of steps in the right direction. A presidential directive in May 1994 establishes criteria that will greatly restrict the kinds of peacekeeping operations Washington will support. One result is that the administration has been reluctant to back deployment of soldiers in Rwanda. But it has not gone far enough.

> ***"It would be . . . naive to believe that a U.N. force would have any more success in ending civil wars than the United States had in Vietnam."***

Over the long run, the only kind of policy that is likely to succeed is one that combines a blanket prohibition against U.N. military intervention in combat situations with serious efforts to bolster the non-military operations of the United Nations to head off violent conflict and alleviate human suffering.

It may be necessary for the United States and other countries to intervene for humanitarian reasons in conflicts such as Rwanda. And, over time, it may be possible for regional organizations to develop the military capabilities and decision-making structures needed for intervention. But these interventions are likely to be far more timely and successful if the United Nations is not involved. For example, the only opportunity to stop the violence in Rwanda through armed action was probably in the first hours after Rwandan government forces began to slaughter their opponents in Kigali. If the United States, France and Belgium had been willing to send troops in then, they probably could have prevented the killing from reaching such horrific proportions. Waiting for Security Council authorization would scuttle any such undertaking. As it is, the idea that such interventions are a U.N. responsibility provides a convenient rationale for Washington and other powers to stay on the sidelines.

Preventing Future Conflicts

Rather than decry the international community's failure to support his calls for military action in Rwanda, Boutros-Ghali should direct his attention to developing ways to prevent future Rwandas. One would be to push for the creation of an international criminal court that would be responsible for investigating crimes against humanity and gross human-rights violations. If such a court were created and its decisions accepted and enforced by the world's governments, it would provide a significant deterrent against the kinds of atrocities occurring in Rwanda.

In addition, Boutros-Ghali should take the lead in calling on the United Nations and all other international organizations to bar any government that comes to power through violence or commits gross human-rights abuses from receiving international assistance. Finally, he should devote greater effort to getting the international community to focus on the deteriorating situation in countries like Kenya and Zaire, which are already sliding down the same slippery slope that led to hundreds of thousands of deaths in Rwanda and Somalia.

These measures will not produce quick results, nor will they end the fighting in Rwanda. But they would help to create the kind of political environment that will discourage future slaughters and make military intervention unnecessary. By contrast, another quixotic U.N. military operation would only set the stage for more disasters.

Chapter 4

When and Where Should the United States Intervene?

U.S. Intervention: An Overview

by Stephen Engelberg

About the author: *Stephen Engelberg is a staff writer for the* New York Times.

If Somalia, why not Bosnia? If Bosnia, why not Rwanda? Or the Sudan? Or Haiti? Or Afghanistan?

After the Cold War

More than five years after the grand retreat of Communism, the list of plausible candidates for military intervention grows ever longer. Yet neither President Clinton nor other Western leaders have articulated a clear standard for distinguishing among victims of brutality and aggression.

The major post–cold war intervention, in the Persian Gulf, was not about Iraqi brutality (the Iraqi dictatorship had been brutal long before it invaded Kuwait), but about oil and alliances. Vital Western interests—the old standard for intervention—would have been at stake even if Iraq had scrupulously observed the Geneva Conventions.

And things were simpler in the cold war, when arguments over whether to commit forces to faraway conflicts were framed by the confrontation between Moscow and Washington. The world had no problem pragmatically averting its gaze from humanitarian catastrophes like Pol Pot's genocidal but diplomatically isolated regime in Cambodia.

But there is no oil in Haiti or Bosnia. There are no Communists in Rwanda. There is only murder and torture and genocide, without any meter of horrors that can calibrate one country's suffering against another's.

And where there are Western interests, they are subtle. Perhaps, for example, it is not Serbian atrocities that should motivate action in Bosnia, but issues of European stability.

Gone are the traditional hawks and doves. In their place stand the new globalists, who argue that the West has an overriding stake in encouraging international order and should do so as a coalition wherever the conflict, and, on the other side, the thinkers who oppose almost any intervention unless it can be justified by the familiar definitions of national interest.

If the search for high philosophical principles has yielded these appealingly coherent theories, there also remains an enormous middle ground where various flavors of political or policy experts are trying to improvise a practical way to guide America's use of power while recognizing its limits—notably the needs for domestic consensus and reasonable prospects of success.

Here is a sampling of the schools of thought, signposts to the debate on how to use American power in an unfamiliar world:

Acting to Stem Chaos

John Steinbruner, director of foreign policy studies at the Brookings Institution, is among the more forceful advocates of Western engagement. With the increasing interconnection of the world economy, he argues, the United States and its allies have a powerful interest in preventing the virus of chaos from infecting wider swaths of the globe.

"We live in an integrated world," Mr. Steinbruner said. "A serious infection that gets out of control in one place is threatening to the whole organism. If you live in the shoulder, and you've got gangrene of the feet, you'd better worry."

Intervention, Mr. Steinbruner contends, can be launched only by a coalition of forces from various nations, but he said the United States has a leading role. "If we don't undertake it," he said, "nobody else will."

He suggests a broad standard: That citizens of any country should be accorded basic human rights, which include the freedom from wholesale slaughter because their country's government has collapsed or because a group has unleashed an ethnic war (although, he adds, "I don't mean the right of a dissident to thumb his nose at a dictator.")

He acknowledges that such a standard, whether enforced through the United Nations or by the West, would have to be applied to every case, from Afghanistan to Rwanda.

"Once you espouse these doctrines," he said, "you have to apply them to places you aren't used to caring about, and that's why everyone shrinks away from it."

> ***"If we don't undertake it, nobody else will."***

Mr. Steinbruner said that the world now lacks the rationale, the coalition and the military planning for such operations. And he said that the main emphasis should be on early prevention of conflicts, rather than military intervention.

But he said that ultimately, aggressors will be deterred only by credible threats of countervailing force.

"Massive breakdowns of the civil order are too dangerous for the entire system," he said. "We are very slow to get on to this. But ultimately we won't have a lot of choice. It we want to run a coherent society ourselves, we will have to defend legal order at the far reaches of the globe."

Avoiding Entanglements

Ted Galen Carpenter, director of foreign policy studies at the Cato Institute, sees few, if any, humanitarian tragedies that justify American military intervention.

"We can express moral outrage as citizens, or as a government," he argues, "but that cannot be a criterion for intervention."

He worries that intervention is a slippery slope and that deployment of American troops to countries like Somalia builds the pressure for wider commitments.

"There are so many potential arenas," he said, "that even if we pursued it multilaterally, the U.S. would be involved in a great many conflicts, incurring great costs and substantial risks. A global security system is impractical."

Mr. Carpenter has little use either for those who call for intervention to quell selected instances of humanitarian abuses, usually the most egregious.

American forces, he said, should be placed in harm's way only if this country's survival is at stake, or when the international order is threatened by something like Hitler's rise to power.

"Those who come down in the middle end up getting into a lot of different enterprises, peacekeeping operations, and then find out, as we did in Somalia, that the task is much more difficult than we anticipated," he said. "At that point, all but the most ardent lose interest, or go into opposition."

For him, Bosnia is the classic example of a place in which the United States has no real interests and no reason to meddle. "Serbia is a third-rate economic and military power," he asserts, "with no territorial ambitions beyond the borders of Yugoslavia."

"As tragic as the situation is—and it is obviously horrible—the best solution is probably to let the various factions fight it out. To intervene there raises the obvious question. It there, why not the Sudan, where more than a million have perished, or Angola, where the U.N. says 1,000 a day are perishing, or the chaos of Afghanistan?

"There are a lot of tragedies in the world," he added, "and we can't intervene in all of them."

"American forces should be placed in harm's way only if this country's survival is at stake."

Mr. Carpenter dismissed the notion that a strong stand in, say, Bosnia, might deter aggressors elsewhere.

"Most conflicts have local roots; they're due to local factors," he said. "Just because an aggressor is hammered halfway around the world doesn't mean that competing factions in another region will be intimidated."

Zbigniew Brzezinski, who was President Carter's national security adviser, agrees it is impractical to intervene in every conflict. But he said the West cannot stand by when atrocities become as severe as the massacres in Rwanda, where as many as 200,000 people may have been killed, according to the U.N. Secretary General, Boutros Boutros-Ghali. The indifference to this staggering carnage, Mr. Brzezinski said, is a "total blemish on the international community and the international organizations."

America tends "to interfere as little as possible in foreign wars, civil wars," he said. "And that's the tendency of this President [Clinton]. Yet even he can't get away with it."

Mr. Brzezinski said it is a useless exercise to define when—and for what reason—foreign conflicts require intervention.

"It's not a mathematical question," he said. "It's a matter of common sense. At a certain point, disasters become something bigger, and people cannot stand aside.

"Is it a thousand people killed? A million?

"It depends somewhat on the traditions of the country. In a country like China, a million disappear, and this is taken rather stoically."

All of the people who call themselves pragmatists—from the hawkish to the dovish—say humanitarian interventions should be limited to those cases in which the West can make a difference at a reasonable cost.

But James R. Schlesinger, a former Director of Central Intelligence and Defense Secretary under Presidents Nixon and Ford, says this misses the point. Intervention implies a decision to, if necessary, use substantial force. That must be decided at the outset.

Are there cases of genocide where the United States and its allies should take action, even if no national interest is at stake? "Probably yes," Mr. Schlesinger says, "But it has to go over many hurdles."

Pressed on whether intervention ever becomes a moral imperative, he said:

"Those who would act on behalf of morality had better think through the entire moral fabric, including imposing those views on an indifferent body politic in America."

To Mr. Schlesinger, the most crucial hurdle is American public opinion.

"If people see enough horrors on TV, that can be enough," he said.

"This country is still the most democratic of democracies, in which foreign policies well up, to a large extent, from the general public. You can't do things as if you were the Imperial German Government. I don't believe you can go into a costly humanitarian operation solely as a result of ruminations by the executive branch."

He also cautioned against the notion of firing shots across the bow of an aggressor. "Don't do these little signals," he said. "That's an American illusion: 'If we only send a signal to Ho Chi Minh that his important assets are at risk, he will see that the rational thing to do is desist.' "

The United States Must Lead Interventions to Prevent Aggression

by Stanley R. Sloan

About the author: *Stanley R. Sloan is senior specialist in international security policy for the Congressional Research Service.*

During the cold war, the United States provided leadership and key military capabilities to deter an attack by the Soviet-led Warsaw pact. Today, the United States seems to be emerging as a self-deterred power—a country preventing itself from using force. This leaves the international system without the political credibility and military force needed to discourage aggressors.

The first victims of self-deterrence may be in obscure places like Gorazde, Bosnia. The long-term consequences, however, may strike at the heart of US interests and the hope for a stable world.

The Mood of the American Public

One could lay sole responsibility for this phenomenon on the Clinton administration. But self-deterrence is rooted in the mood of the public, reinforced by a perception of this mood in Congress, and given voice in the White House interpretation of its mandate.

At the end of the cold war, Americans were eager to focus on a wide range of domestic problems. The "peace dividend" was to be spent on America's future.

Well before the 1992 campaign, it was clear to most politicians that the public, suffering from cold-war leadership fatigue, did not want the United States to be the post-cold-war world's policeman. Then-President Bush had sought to justify the response to the Iraqi invasion of Kuwait in terms of a "new world order" in which US-Soviet cooperation could make the United Nations and the international system work to deter aggression. The concept was critiqued from many perspectives. The most telling was that a new world order wouldn't work

Stanley R. Sloan, "From U.S. Deterrence to Self-Deterrence," *The Christian Science Monitor*, May 3, 1994. Reprinted by permission of the author.

without US leadership, but Americans weren't willing to accept this burden.

President Clinton's election mandate therefore was to turn the government toward issues like jobs, crime, and health care. His political advisers told him (and continue to tell him) that "the economy, stupid" will determine a successful first term and reelection. International commitments pose a potential threat to such a scenario. They can be expensive, and costly in human terms when young Americans die in combat. Vietnam and the fate of President Johnson's Great Society initiative seem burned into the administration's political vision.

Restrictions on the Use of Force

The Clinton White House first hoped multilateral organizations could relieve the United States of overseas burdens and protect a domestic agenda. The White House seemed disinclined to use force unilaterally. In May 1993, a high-ranking State Department official told reporters that the United States had neither the inclination, the will, nor the money to respond militarily to behavior that did not directly threaten US interests.

Congress was wary of foreign military commitments after the cold war. When the humanitarian mission in Somalia became difficult, and particularly when 18 US soldiers were killed, it became evident that most members of Congress had less faith in the United Nations than did Clinton. Congressional critics suggested the United States should not put its own forces under UN command and should not make any commitment to supply the United Nations with forces. Members also suggested that, for every case in which US forces might be used for peace operations, the administration should be able to specify the purposes of this proposed use of military forces, present an estimate of the costs of such operations, and project the likely date for completion of the mission.

> ***"A new world order wouldn't work without US leadership, but Americans weren't willing to accept this burden."***

The administration's acceptance of such restrictions by repeating them in numerous official statements has reinforced the tendency toward self-deterrence. The consequence is that there are very few circumstances in which the administration could use force, even if it decided to do so.

Some would say this leaves the United States where it ought to be: ready to tend to domestic woes. This is not unreasonable. But, as with any approach, it may have costs.

Lack of US Leadership

Events in Bosnia demonstrate the consequences of self-deterrence. Very limited and largely symbolic uses of air power were insufficient to overcome the Bosnian Serbs' assumption that the United States, and thus the United Nations and NATO [North Atlantic Treaty Organization], did not have the stomach to use sufficient force to prevent them from taking Gorazde. "Might" therefore made "right."

It is becoming more clear that, in the post-cold-war world, as goes the United States, so goes the United Nations and NATO, particularly when it comes to the use of force. Without US leadership and military capabilities, the international system has a very limited capacity for responding to threats to the peace.

> ***"At what point of international lawlessness does the United States say 'Stop'?"***

As long as the United States remains a self-deterred power, therefore, there will be no disincentive (deterrent force) in the international system to discourage leaders and states with aggressive intent from using force when they believe it will serve their interests—whether to change borders, to seek revenge, or to gain access to natural resources.

The green light may be on—not just for the Serb military, but for potential aggressors in the Middle East and elsewhere. UN and NATO arrangements designed to organize responses to aggression will look increasingly like a modern Potemkin village—an impressive security façade with nobody at home.

US Interests

Today, tomorrow, and next month it may still be possible to say that such aggressions are tolerable in terms of US interests.

The question, however, is at what point of international lawlessness does the United States (and therefore the international community) say "Stop"? At what point does the United States start losing critical leverage in international relations when other countries stop paying attention to US views and interests? And at what point does the inability of the United States to act start undercutting the meaning of professed US principles and purposes in the international system?

The Chinese proverb says that the longest journey begins with a single step. America, having taken the first step toward self-deterrence may be on a journey toward a world in which the rule of the jungle begins to overtake the rule of law. This law must be policed in order to be effective.

The United States Should Intervene to Preserve International Order

by Robert G. Neumann

About the author: *Robert G. Neumann, former U.S. ambassador to Afghanistan, Morocco, and Saudi Arabia, is senior adviser at the Center for Strategic and International Studies in Washington, D.C.*

A specter is haunting the world—the specter of uncertainty, of aimless drift. After the short-lived euphoria caused by the collapse of communism, people face a world void of ideas. Western leaders, only yesterday so triumphant, seem burned out, while the widespread application of national self-determination, hallowed especially in the United States since Woodrow Wilson's day, has imposed large-scale death, dislocation, and misery on the world.

The United States Must Lead

We simply cannot wait until all the cobwebs have been cleared out of our minds. We must try to discern at least a preliminary analysis and establish a list of priorities.

One positive development of recent history is that the United Nations (UN), despite all its shortcomings and constraints, has become an important and viable organization. But to say "let the UN do it" is a cop-out. The UN is an international, not a supranational organization. "It" can do little, only its members can, especially the veto-carrying members of the Security Council. If they are to act collectively—the only way in which they can act—there has to be a catalyst. That catalyst is, and for a long time to come can only be, the United States, as European irresolution in the face of the civil wars in former Yugoslavia has underscored.

A catalyst for what? For making peace, ultimately. For stopping wholesale slaughter now. Using the catastrophe in former Yugoslavia as a laboratory example, it seems clear that an ongoing and spreading military conflict cannot be

Abridged from *The Washington Quarterly*, vol. 16, no. 1 (Winter 1993), Robert G. Neumann, "This Next Disorderly Half Century: Some Proposed Remedies" by permission of The MIT Press, Cambridge, Mass., and the Center for Strategic and International Studies.

stopped by the traditional peacekeeping efforts practiced by the UN. Peacekeeping is possible only when the belligerent parties are ready to keep the peace and to tolerate a UN force to keep them apart, to calm down the scene, perhaps even to allow some refugees to return. When there is an aggressive will on one or perhaps more than one side to change existing borders drastically, to create new realities, UN peacekeepers confront superior forces prepared to push them aside, not to accept them. In such a situation, aggression may have to be stopped by a military threat significant enough to instill respect. To do this, there has to be a political will to use military force if necessary. In fact it could be argued that the UN's concentration on probably fruitless peace-*keeping* prevents it from serious efforts at peace-*making*.

"There has to be a political will to use military force if necessary."

This cannot be the role of patched together, relatively small, multilingual UN peacekeeping forces. It is the role of a significant alliance of major nations, contributing sufficiently large national units to a sizable, functioning, military force.

North–South Conflict

Inevitably, much of the Third World, especially the Muslim and particularly the Arab world, sees in the assertiveness of the UN Security Council the replacement of the East–West conflict by a North–South one, with the North solidly in control, once more changing facts on the ground at the expense of the South. These are deeply, agonizingly felt, and widespread sentiments; they must be taken seriously. But as long as the South is as disunited as it is now, words are not easily followed by action, and, yes, active leadership must generally be the role of the North for a long time to come.

A former U.S. secretary of state, Dean Rusk, was once quoted as saying that people think differently, depending on whether they are thinking toward a conclusion or toward action. Rusk, who had his roots in both academe and statecraft, understood and respected both thinking tracks—and knew the difference. Yes, the West reacted more decisively against Iraq's invasion of Kuwait than against Israel's long occupation of Arab-inhabited land (conceding the considerable difference between these two situations). Yes, we would not have acted the same way if an African state had invaded another. Yes, we, the West, are not fair, not evenhanded.

But is there another way if future Kuwaits or Yugoslavias are to be avoided? Was an "Arab solution" to the Persian Gulf crisis ever anything other than a compromise that would have left Saddam Hussein triumphantly in Kuwait, ready to pounce again, almost certainly on Saudi Arabia?

To thinkers whose sole aim is conclusion, pointing an accusing finger at Western-dominated thinking comes only too naturally and is frequently justified. But to those whose preference is action, to make a difference in the concrete world, the road will be more complex and less theoretical.

If we agree that more Yugoslavias are intolerable, dangerous, and murderous, then, what do we do? Diplomacy first, of course. But if declarations and warnings, UN or other resolutions, do not succeed in deterring an aggressor or several aggressors, then more direct action has to be contemplated and organized to be credible to deter or restore. And if the issue is viewed that way, the only catalyst for collective action will in the foreseeable future be found to be the United States.

In the Yugoslav crisis, the U.S. government deliberately held back to give the Europeans an opportunity to act. Disunity in the European Community (EC) and its dismal failure were the result. Further action within a UN setup still seems possible, because Washington has begun, belatedly and still hesitatingly, to get into the act.

A U.S. initiative is not going to be simple. The mood of the American people is now rather inward-directed and the president will have to show strong leadership to arouse broadly shared willingness to shoulder that considerable burden. Americans will never be willing to shoulder it alone and should not be. That makes it easier, but not by much. The United States will have to keep a sufficient military establishment to act when needed and on short notice. Also there will be many other calls for action; if Yugoslavia, why not Haiti or West Irian, not to speak of the West Bank or Somalia or South Africa? Perfect justice, far-reaching evenhandedness, will always be elusive. But does the inability of the United States to act everywhere have to mean that it should intervene nowhere? Is unevenly applied action not better than no action?

"Active leadership must generally be the role of the North for a long time to come."

There is much for the American people to ponder. One must surely be sympathetic with the difficulty a large population experiences in wrestling with such complexities. Americans will have to learn painfully that powerful as they are, they will not be able to rise to every good cause and will not always choose wisely. And it is really quite good that U.S. public opinion is remarkably reluctant to police the world.

Willingness to Act Deters Aggression

There is a slightly brighter side. Once the above pattern of a clearly expressed willingness to act becomes more credible, future adventurers are likely to pause. As that happens, it will become easier for a future alliance to be formed, hold together, and pledge its resources and blood, if only over time. As Russia becomes reestablished as a democratic country, it will deem participation desirable. As important third world countries see that whining over injustice will avail them little, but that participation helps, their willingness to act constructively will increase. Firm, constructive leadership by an American president is capable of arousing, over time, pride in the role that the United States is called upon to take. This is not "manifest destiny," Heaven help us! It is only sheer necessity to move, gradually, haltingly, messily toward a somewhat more orderly and less murderous world.

This presents a diplomatic and operational dilemma. Yugoslavia has shown that aggression is more easily stopped by collective action in its earlier phase, before the aggressor is too successful, the aggressed too deeply hurt, and scores of refugees fled. But that is also the time when the coalition is new and fragile and when the political unity in each coalition country is not yet fully formed. "Let's give economic sanctions more time to work" is only one among the slogans of wavering politicians who lack the courage to tell their fellow citizens—and voters—that serious sacrifices will be demanded of them.

Nothing written above addresses itself to deeper, underlying causes of these and other conflicts such as great inequality of wealth and opportunity, of rampant overpopulation. But if one always insists on changing the underlying causes, one usually changes nothing. Jesus' words, "the poor will always be with us," are a somber warning. If the obstacles to keeping people from killing each other are formidable, redistributing the world's wealth is infinitely harder. But it seems to me that the need to stop, or at least diminish, this growing bloodletting and destruction of the Yugoslavias is urgent enough to make early action imperative, even if some of the deeper causes cannot be immediately addressed now, or even, for that matter, ever. . . .

Growing Zones of Order

The world of the next fifty years is going to be a dangerously disturbed one. If the end of the Cold War has brought new opportunities for cooperation across old East–West and North–South divisions, it has also stripped away a rigid structure of international relations that channeled and contained conflicts because of the horrible risks associated with their escalation to nuclear conflagration. In lieu of that structure today we find a potpourri of weak states struggling with fragile democratic institutions, renascent nationalism, and religious forces that in many parts of the world pose radical challenges to the secular status quo.

The situation in the former Yugoslavia is the epitome of this problem: state disintegration, the effort to "protect" by brutal force Serbian minorities whatever the consequences for others, and the utter absence of governance. It is also the harbinger of the future. The Lebanonization [government breakdown due to factional violence] of the world is proceeding apace. There are signs of it to be found on every continent, although the sharpest fears are in the post-Communist world, where many of these factors converge.

> ***"The only catalyst for collective action will in the foreseeable future be found to be the United States."***

To ignore this process of Lebanonization would be foolhardy. To quote Winston Churchill, "the war of the giants" has been followed by the "war of the pygmies"—but their wars will not be easily ignored. At the end of the twentieth century, even weak and underdeveloped states are arming themselves with weapons of mass destruction. Their conflicts will be very destabilizing and will touch directly the interests and security of the United States, not least through the threats they pose to U.S. friends and allies in Europe and the security interests Europeans and Americans share there. Moreover, their murderous repressions at home will also call into question the very purposes for which civilized states band together to defend common values. It is simply too dangerous to let these menacing trends continue. A serious attempt must be made at creating order, or at least growing "zones of order."

The United States Should Intervene to Promote Democracy

by Anthony Lake

About the author: *Anthony Lake is President Bill Clinton's assistant for national security affairs.*

I believe our nation's policies toward the world stand at a historic crossroads. For half a century, America's engagement in the world revolved around containment of a hostile Soviet Union. Our efforts helped block Soviet expansionism, topple communist repression, and secure a great victory for human freedom. Clearly, the Soviet Union's collapse enhances our security. But it also requires us to think anew because the world is new.

Foreign Interests vs. Isolationism

In particular, with the end of the Cold War, there is no longer a consensus among the American people about why, and even whether, our nation should remain actively engaged in the world. Geography and history always have made Americans wary of foreign entanglements. Now, economic anxiety fans that wariness. Calls from the left and right to stay at home rather than engage abroad are reinforced by the rhetoric of Neo-Know-Nothings.

Those of us who believe in the imperative of our international engagement must push back. For that reason, as President Clinton sought the presidency, he not only pledged a domestic renaissance but also vowed to engage actively in the world in order to increase our prosperity, update our security arrangements, and promote democracy abroad. . . .

Let us begin by taking stock of our new era. Four facts are salient.

First, America's core concepts—democracy and market economics—are more broadly accepted than ever. Over the past ten years, the number of democracies has nearly doubled. Since 1970, the number of significant command

Abridged from "From Containment to Enlargement" by Anthony Lake, *U.S. Department of State Dispatch*, September 27, 1993.

economies dropped from ten to three.

This victory of freedom is practical, not ideological: Billions of people on every continent are simply concluding, based on decades of their own hard experience, that democracy and markets are the most productive and liberating ways to organize their lives.

Their conclusion resonates with America's core values. We see individuals as equally created, with a God-given right to life, liberty, and the pursuit of happiness. So we trust in the equal wisdom of free individuals to protect those rights: through democracy—as the process for best meeting shared needs in the face of competing desires—and through markets—as the process for best meeting private needs in a way that expands opportunity. Both processes strengthen each other: Democracy alone can produce justice but not the material goods necessary for individuals to thrive; markets alone can expand wealth but not that sense of justice without which civilized societies perish.

Democracy and market economics are ascendant in this new era, but they are not everywhere triumphant. There remain vast areas in Asia, Africa, the Middle East, and elsewhere where democracy and market economics are at best new arrivals—most likely unfamiliar, sometimes vilified, often fragile. But it is wrong to assume these ideas will be embraced only by the West and rejected by the rest. Culture does shape politics and economics. But the idea of freedom has universal appeal. Thus, we have arrived at neither the end of history nor a clash of civilizations but a moment of immense democratic and entrepreneurial opportunity. We must not waste it.

America's Dominant Power

The *second* feature of this era is that we are its dominant power. Those who say otherwise sell America short. The fact is, we have the world's strongest military, its largest economy, and its most dynamic, multi-ethnic society. We are setting a global example in our efforts to reinvent our democratic and market institutions. Our leadership is sought and respected in every corner of the world. . . . Around the world, America's power, authority, and example provide unparalleled opportunities to lead.

> ***"Democracy and market economics are ascendant in this new era, but they are not everywhere triumphant."***

Moreover, absent a reversal in Russia, there is now no credible near-term threat to America's existence. Serious threats remain: terrorism, proliferating weapons of mass destruction, ethnic conflicts, and the degradation of our global environment. Above all, we are threatened by sluggish economic growth, which undermines the security of our people as well as that of allies and friends abroad. Yet none of these threats holds the same immediate dangers for us as did Nazi conquest or Soviet expansionism. America's challenge today is to lead on the basis of opportunity more than fear.

The *third* notable aspect of this era is an explosion of ethnic conflicts. As Senator Daniel P. Moynihan and others have noted, the end of the Cold War and the collapse of various repressive regimes have removed the lid from numerous cauldrons of ethnic, religious, or factional hatreds. In many states of the former Soviet Union and elsewhere, there is a tension between the desire for ethnic separatism and the creation of liberal democracy, which alone can safely accommodate and even celebrate differences among citizens. A major challenge to our thinking, our policies, and our international institutions in this era is the fact that most conflicts are taking place within rather than among nations. These conflicts are typically highly complex; at the same time, their brutality will tug at our consciences. We need a healthy wariness about our ability to shape solutions for such disputes, yet at times our interests or humanitarian concerns will impel our unilateral or multilateral engagement.

The *fourth* feature of this new era is that the pulse of the planet has accelerated dramatically—and with it the pace of change in human events. Computers, faxes, fiber-optic cables, and satellites all speed the flow of information. The measurement of wealth, and increasingly wealth itself, consists in bytes of data that move at the speed of light. The accelerated pace of events is neither bad nor good. Its sharp consequences can cut either way. It means both doctors and terrorists can more quickly share their technical secrets. Both pro-democracy activists and skinhead anarchists can more broadly spread their views. Ultimately, the world's acceleration creates new and diverse ways for us to exert our influence if we choose to do so—but increases the likelihood that if we do not, rapid events, instantly reported, may overwhelm us. As President Clinton has suggested, we must decide whether to make change our ally or allow ourselves to become its victims.

"A major challenge . . . is the fact that most conflicts are taking place within rather than among nations."

From Containment to Enlargement

In such a world, our interests and ideals compel us not only to be engaged but to lead. And in a real-time world of change and information, it is all the more important that our leadership be steadied around our central purpose. That purpose can be found in the underlying rationale for our engagement throughout this century. As we fought aggressors and contained communism, our engagement abroad was animated both by calculations of power and by this belief: To the extent democracy and market economics hold sway in other nations, our own nation will be more secure, prosperous, and influential, while the broader world will be more humane and peaceful.

The expansion of market-based economics abroad helps expand our exports and creates American jobs, while it also improves living conditions and fuels demands for political liberalization abroad. The addition of new democracies makes us more secure, because democracies tend not to wage war on each other or sponsor terrorism. They are more trustworthy in diplomacy and do a better job of respecting the human rights of their people. These dynamics lay at the heart of Woodrow Wilson's most profound insights; although his moralism sometimes weakened his argument, he understood that our own security is shaped by the character of foreign regimes. Indeed, most presidents who followed, Republicans and Democrats alike, understood we must promote democracy and market economics in the world—because it protects our interests and security and because it reflects values that are both American and universal.

"Our interests and ideals compel us not only to be engaged but to lead."

Throughout the Cold War, we contained a global threat to market democracies; now we should seek to enlarge their reach, particularly in places of special significance to us. The successor to a doctrine of containment must be a strategy of enlargement—enlargement of the world's free community of market democracies.

During the Cold War, even children understood America's security mission. As they looked at those maps on their schoolroom walls, they knew we were trying to contain the creeping expansion of that big, red blob. Today, at great risk of oversimplification, we might visualize our security mission as promoting the enlargement of the "blue areas" of market democracies. The difference, of course, is that we do not seek to expand the reach of our institutions by force, subversion, or repression.

A Strategy of Enlargement

We must not allow this overarching goal to drive us into overreaching actions. To be successful, a strategy of enlargement must provide distinctions and set priorities. It must combine our broad goals of fostering democracy and markets with our more traditional geostrategic interests. And it must suggest how best to expend our large but, nonetheless, limited national security resources—financial, diplomatic, and military.

In recent years, discussions about when to use force have turned on a set of vital questions, such as whether our forces match our objectives, whether we can fight and win in a time that is acceptable, whether we have a reasonable exit if we can not, and whether there is public and congressional support. But we have overlooked a prior, strategic question—the question of "where"—which sets the context for such military judgments.

I see four components to a strategy of enlargement.

- First, we should strengthen the community of major market democracies—

including our own—which constitutes the core from which enlargement is proceeding.

- Second, we should help foster and consolidate new democracies and market economies where possible, especially in states of special significance and opportunity.
- Third, we must counter the aggression—and support the liberalization—of states hostile to democracy and markets.
- Fourth, we need to pursue our humanitarian agenda not only by providing aid but also by working to help democracy and market economics take root in regions of greatest humanitarian concern.

A host of caveats must accompany a strategy of enlargement. For one, we must be patient. As scholars observe, waves of democratic advance are often followed by reverse waves of democratic setback. We must be ready for uneven progress, even outright reversals.

Our strategy must be pragmatic. Our interests in democracy and markets do not stand alone. Other American interests at times will require us to befriend and even defend non-democratic states for mutually beneficial reasons. Our strategy must view democracy broadly—it must envision a system that includes not only elections but also such features as an independent judiciary and protections of human rights. Our strategy must also respect diversity. Democracy and markets can come in many legitimate variants. Freedom has many faces. Let me review two of the four components of this strategy in greater detail. . . .

Fostering New Democracies

Beyond seeing to our base, the second imperative for our strategy must be to help democracy and markets expand and survive in other places where we have the strongest security concerns and where we can make the greatest difference. This is not a democratic crusade; it is a pragmatic commitment to see freedom take hold where that will help us most. Thus, we must target our efforts to assist states that affect our strategic interests, such as those with large economies, critical locations, nuclear weapons, or the potential to generate refugee flows into our own nation or into key friends and allies. We must focus our efforts where we have the most leverage. And our efforts must be demand-driven—they must focus on nations whose people are pushing for reform or have already secured it.

"[Our policy] must suggest how best to expend our large but, nonetheless, limited national security resources."

The most important example is the former Soviet Union—and it fits the criteria I just noted. If we can support and help consolidate democratic and market reforms in Russia and the other new independent states, we can help turn a former threat into a region of valued diplomatic and economic partners.

In addition, our efforts in Russia, Ukraine, and the other states raise the likelihood of continued reductions in nuclear arms and compliance with international non-proliferation accords. The new democracies in Central and Eastern Europe are another clear example, given their proximity to the great democratic powers of Western Europe. And since our ties across the Pacific are no less important than those across the Atlantic, pursuing enlargement in the Asian Pacific is a third example. In July 1993, President Clinton underscored that point in Japan and Korea with his descriptions of a New Pacific Community.

Continuing the great strides toward democracy and markets in our emerging Western Hemispheric community of democracies also must be a key concern. And we should be on the lookout for states whose entry into the camp of market democracies may influence the future direction of an entire region; South Africa and Nigeria now hold that potential with regard to Sub-Saharan Africa.

How should the United States help consolidate and enlarge democracy and markets in these states? The answers are as varied as the nations involved, but there are common elements. We must continue to help lead the effort to mobilize international resources, as we have with Russia and the other new states. We must be willing to take immediate public positions to help staunch democratic reversals, as we have in Haiti, Guatemala, and Nigeria. We must give democratic nations the fullest benefits of integration into foreign markets, which is part of why NAFTA [North American Free Trade Agreement] and the GATT [General Agreement on Tariffs and Trade] rank so high on our security agenda. We must link wider access to technology markets with commitments to abide by non-proliferation norms. And we must help these nations strengthen the pillars of civil society, improve their market institutions, and fight corruption and political discontent through practices of good governance.

"Our efforts . . . must focus on nations whose people are pushing for reform or have already secured it."

In all these efforts, a policy of enlargement should take on a second meaning, we should pursue our goals through an enlarged circle not only of government officials but also of private and non-governmental groups. Private firms are natural allies in our efforts to strengthen market economies. Similarly, our goal of strengthening democracy and civil society has a natural ally in labor unions, human rights groups, environmental advocates, chambers of commerce, and election monitors. Just as we rely on force multipliers in defense, we should welcome these "diplomacy multipliers," such as the National Endowment for Democracy.

The "Backlash" States

The third element of our strategy of enlargement should be to minimize the ability of states outside the circle of democracy and markets to threaten it. Democracy and market economics have always been subversive ideas to those who rule without consent. These ideas remain subversive today. Every dictator, theocrat, kleptocrat, or central planner in an unelected regime has reason to fear their subjects will suddenly demand the freedom to make their own decisions.

We should expect the advance of democracy and markets to trigger forceful reactions from those whose power is not popularly derived. The rise of Burma's democracy movement led to the jailing of its most vocal proponent, Aung San Suu Kyi. Russia's reforms have aroused the resistance of the *nomenklatura* [the former Communist Party elite].

> ***"We should expect the advance of democracy and markets to trigger forceful reactions from those whose power is not popularly derived."***

Centralized power defends itself. It not only wields tools of state power such as military force, political imprisonment, and torture but also exploits the intolerant energies of racism, ethnic prejudice, religious persecution, xenophobia, and irredentism. Those whose power is threatened by the spread of democracy and markets will always have a personal stake in resisting those practices with passionate intensity.

When such leaders sit atop regional powers, such as Iran and Iraq, they may engage in violence and lawlessness that threaten the United States and other democracies. Such reactionary, "backlash" states are more likely to sponsor terrorism and traffic in weapons of mass destruction and ballistic missile technologies. They are more likely to suppress their own people, foment ethnic rivalries, and threaten their neighbors.

U.S. Policy Toward Backlash States

In this world of multiplying democracies, expanding markets, and accelerating commerce, the rulers of backlash states face an unpleasant choice. They can seek to isolate their people from these liberating forces. If they do, however, they cut themselves off from the very forces that create wealth and social dynamism. Such states tend to rot from within, both economically and spiritually. But as they grow weaker, they also may become more desperate and dangerous.

Our policy toward such states, so long as they act as they do, must seek to isolate them diplomatically, militarily, economically, and technologically. It must stress intelligence, counter-terrorism, and multilateral export controls. It also must apply global norms regarding weapons of mass destruction and ensure their enforcement. While some of these efforts will be unilateral, international rules are necessary and may be particularly effective in enforcing sanctions, transparency, and export controls, as the work of the IAEA [International Atomic Energy Agency] in Iraq demonstrates.

When the actions of such states directly threaten our people, our forces, or our vital interests, we clearly must be prepared to strike back decisively and unilaterally, as we did when Iraq tried to assassinate former President Bush. We must always maintain the military power necessary to deter or, if necessary, defeat aggression by these regimes. Because the sources of such threats will be diverse and unpredictable, we must seek to ensure that our forces are increasingly ready, mobile, flexible, and smart. . . .

While some backlash states may seek to wall themselves off from outside influence, other anti-democratic states will opt to pursue greater wealth by liberalizing their economic rules. Sooner or later, however, these states confront the need to liberalize the flow of information into and within their nation and to tolerate the rise of an entrepreneurial middle class. Both developments weaken despotic rule and lead, over time, to rising demands for democracy. Chile's experience under General Augusto Pinochet proves market economies can thrive for a time without democracy. But both our instinct and recent history in Chile, South Korea, and elsewhere tell us they cannot do so forever.

We cannot impose democracy on regimes that appear to be opting for liberalization, but we may be able to help steer some of them down that path while providing penalties that raise the costs of repression and aggressive behavior. . . .

Ultimately, it is through our support for democracy and sustainable development that we best enhance the dramatic new winds of change that are stirring much of the developing world.

The United States Should Intervene to Protect American Interests

by James A. Baker III

About the author: *James A. Baker III was the U.S. secretary of state under President George Bush.*

With the eclipse of communism and the collapse of the Soviet Union, the United States has, in a real sense, lost its paradigm for international affairs. As we look to the future, we must learn to do without the explanation of international affairs that the Cold War provided and the tool for problem-solving, known as "containment," that saw us through ultimate victory in it.

From Disengagement to Engagement

Today, I believe, we are moving into the century's third great period in American foreign policy.

The first lasted until 1941, with a brief interregnum during World War I. During this period, American foreign policy was guided by the principle of *disengagement*. I believe that the term is more accurate than the usual one, "isolationism," because it better captures the historic folly of the period. This is because America, as World War I demonstrated, never was truly isolated.

The United States' size, large domestic market, and relative geographic remove, however, allowed America to indulge in the fantasy of isolation. By the 1930s, the fantasy had grown frayed. World-wide depression, the emergence of fascism, and the development of new weaponry had begun to erode even further the already shaky foundations of isolationism. Still, it took the shock of Pearl Harbor and the rigors of world war to rid America of its illusion. By disengagement we had sought to isolate ourselves—and failed.

The second period began with America's entry into World War II. In it, American foreign policy was driven by what could be termed *compulsory engagement*.

Abridged from James A. Baker III's speech "Selective Engagement," *Vital Speeches of the Day*, March 1, 1994. Reprinted by permission of the author and the James A. Baker III Institute for Public Policy, Rice University, Houston, Texas.

First fascist, then communist aggression thrust the United States onto the world scene. The advent of nuclear weapons raised the international stakes for America to unprecedented heights. Not only our way of life, but our lives themselves were at risk. We had no choice but to accept this reality. It was hard to argue the case for disengagement with tens of thousands of nuclear warheads targeted on the United States by a hostile Soviet Union.

> ***"America, as World War I demonstrated, never was truly isolated."***

In addition to the magnitude of the Soviet threat, there was its pervasiveness. Communist aggression made the entire world a field of contention. West and East competed, not just politically and militarily, but economically, technologically, and socially.

Selective Engagement and Interests

Today, with the end of the Cold War, we are entering yet a third distinct era in American foreign policy. That policy, I believe, should be guided by the principle of *selective engagement*—a principle that embraces the freedom of action that we enjoy with the end of the Cold War but recognizes the continued imperative of American leadership in the global arena. . . .

[Selective engagement] depends on a careful assessment of American interests.

On one level, of course, America's interests are simple and largely uncontested. Based upon the well-being of our citizens, they include security, prosperity, and promotion of America's values. Move from generalization to specificity, however, and we enter at once a far more complex area.

Preventing, containing and, where possible, resolving regional conflict is, for instance, clearly a general American interest. Just as plainly, however, America's specific interest in avoiding conflict on the Korean peninsula differs in type and magnitude from our interest, for example, in promoting a peaceful settlement in Angola. War in Korea would immediately involve thousands of American troops, and, given North Korea's dangerous game of nuclear hide-and-seek, the potential use of atomic weapons.

A Sense of Proportion

In short, all interests are not equal. Specific policies must reflect this fact. Above all, they must be proportionate to the American interests involved.

Fiascos in Haiti and Somalia can be traced, at least in part, to the lack of such proportion. In Somalia, especially, we saw what could be called "mission creep." What began as a limited humanitarian mission grew to an ill-considered exercise in nation-building with deadly consequences.

I do not say that we had or have no interests in either country. Clearly, the United States does have an interest in encouraging democracy in Haiti, just as we do in averting human suffering in Somalia. But those interests are not of sufficient importance to squander American lives or fritter away American prestige.

Only a sense of proportion, I believe, permits us to craft appropriate policies. We cannot solve every one of the world's problems. What we can and must do is focus our attention and resources on the key challenges to our real vital interests. . . .

They include consolidating democracy and free markets in Eastern Europe and the former Soviet Union, containing regional conflicts and stemming the proliferation of weapons of mass destruction, strengthening an open global economic system, redefining the Western Alliance, and renewing American leadership.

All these challenges share one common characteristic: our success or failure in meeting them will directly affect the lives of Americans for years and decades to come. I know of no better definition of a vital American interest.

Conflicting Interests

As we pursue American interests, however, we must recall that our approach to a specific country, region, or issue can possess competing, sometimes contradictory objectives. Often our interests themselves will conflict; sometimes our long and short-term goals.

It is important that we recognize these competing objectives. By doing so, we can make an informed choice among them, or, preferably, craft a policy that balances them.

"In short, all interests are not equal."

American policy towards China is a case in point. Any list of American interests in China would include protection of human rights, market access for American firms, and Chinese cooperation on a range of international security issues, especially non-proliferation. Yet, given the regime in Beijing, an absolutist American policy on human rights would undercut both our commercial interest and, to pick a topic from [the] headlines, our interest in denying North Korea nuclear weapons.

Moreover, American efforts to promote human rights in China by diplomatic isolation and economic sanctions risk a backlash by the Chinese regime that would actually damage our long-term goal of Chinese democratization.

Faced with such a circumstance, the Bush administration developed a China policy that pursued, through a mix of incentives and disincentives, all our major interests in China. That policy seemed unsatisfactory to many, especially in the human rights community, but we had no real alternative without surrendering other important American interests. Balance in our policy towards China was and remains critical. . . .

Three Sources of American Power

Assessing interests and balancing objectives, however, are not enough. There must also be a firm understanding of the nature and exercise of American power.

Today, the United States enjoys a preeminence in world affairs unique in history. That preeminence is perhaps most decisive in the military sphere. With the collapse of the Soviet Union and the demise of the Warsaw Pact, the United States no longer faces a global enemy. Our victory in the Gulf War demonstrated a capacity to project overwhelming military force half a world away. In short, American military supremacy today goes unchallenged. Any aggressor contemplating action against the United States must include the certainty of defeat in his calculations.

America's international stature is also rooted in its economic strength. The recent recession and current restructuring of American industry have tended to obscure the underlying vitality of the American economy. Contrary to popular belief, our workers remain the world's most productive. Our export sector is the world's largest. And, with congressional approval of NAFTA [North American Free Trade Agreement], the United States stands poised with Mexico and Canada to enjoy a market of over 350 million consumers.

But the wellsprings of American influence transcend military might and economic vitality. They include a third, intangible source: credibility. America's allies look to us with trust for a reason. Three times during this century, in two world wars and one cold one, the United States stood forthrightly with its friends against aggression and for freedom. More recently, President Bush declared that Saddam Hussein's invasion of Kuwait would not stand and made good on America's pledge.

Economic strength and military might are necessary but not sufficient causes of American power. There must also be a willingness to use that power consistently, decisively, and effectively. That willingness—that credibility—has been a crucial element of American leadership since World War II.

However, if any American leadership is to be sustained, American military might, economic power, and credibility must be maintained. . . .

Means of Exercising Power

I suspect that lack of resolve in our foreign policy derives, not only from confusion over our interests in this new era, but also a fundamental uneasiness with the concept of American power. Comfort with American power is a precondition to its competent exercise.

> ***"What we can and must do is focus our attention and resources on the key challenges to our real vital interests."***

During the Cold War, virtually every use of American power could be understood and explained to the American people as a response to the danger of Soviet totalitarianism. Today, of course, that argument is obsolete—and no similarly compelling calculus of force has emerged to replace it.

Whether America uses its power alone or with others must be based on pragmatic considerations. Alliances, whether formal or informal, and multilateral organizations, such as the United Nations (U.N.), all represent means, not ends, in the pursuit of American interests. Properly understood, multilateralism, coalition-building, and unilateral action constitute instruments by which a strategy of selective engagement can be pursued.

> ***"Often our interests themselves will conflict; sometimes our long and short-term goals."***

We need a choice, not just of policies, but of instruments to implement them. Sometimes, as in support for a settlement in Cambodia, the U.N. will be the most appropriate vehicle. Other times, as in support for reform in the former Soviet Union, we will have to form *ad hoc* coalitions with like-minded states. And, as it did in Panama, the United States must always be prepared to act unilaterally when necessary, the oldest and still surest test of a great power.

I believe that American action against Iraqi aggression in the Gulf provides a model for the effective use of American power. It included unilateral action in our decision to dispatch troops to Saudi Arabia in the immediate aftermath of the invasion of Kuwait. It embraced the creation of an *ad hoc* coalition first to enforce economic sanctions, then to finance and fight the war against Saddam Hussein. And it included resort to multilateral institutions like the U.N. to rally world opinion and ensure universal compliance with Iraq's political and economic isolation.

The Meaning of Selective Engagement

When we speak of "selective engagement," the term itself explains much.

First, it recognizes the idea of an America actively engaged in international affairs. It embraces the concept of an America not just in the world, but of it. Soviet expansion may have compelled American engagement after World War II, but post-war America's achievements were not limited to fighting and winning the Cold War.

A global liberal economic regime, partnership with former adversaries like Germany and Japan, and the creation of a truly international community of democratic values spanning three continents and two great oceans were all, in a sense, part of the Cold War. But, in another sense, they transcended it.

All were the products of American engagement. And American engagement remains no less imperative in today's world of fierce economic competition, burgeoning instability, and renascent fascism. In sum, the "engagement" aspect of selective engagement recognizes that disengagement today is simply not an option.

Second, selective engagement stresses that American engagement means making choices—that is, selecting how, when, and where we will engage. With America's emergence as the world's sole superpower, we enjoy unprecedented freedom of action. In stark contrast with the Cold War, we confront today no single overwhelming threat to our interests. Ironically, America can do so much today that we are tempted to attempt everything—or do nothing at all.

This freedom makes it all the more imperative that our nation's leaders set clear, coherent, and comprehensive criteria for making these vital decisions. Above all, we need to act in proportion to our interests, seek balance in our objectives, and remain credible in the exercise of our policies.

U.S. Interventions Should Balance Moral and Practical Principles

by James Chace

About the author: *James Chace is editor of the* World Policy Journal.

Whatever happened to the moral center of American foreign policy? When Bill Clinton was elected, he appeared to be trying to balance realism with morality. But he never presented a strategy of what that would mean concretely for United States foreign policy. The president said during the campaign that he believed that "no American foreign policy can succeed if it slights our commitment to democracy." Yet that is precisely what has happened in Bosnia: we slighted our commitment to democratic ideals by allowing one country, Serbia (or one faction within it), to impose its will on another, Bosnia. In Somalia, we declared that our intervention there was for humanitarian reasons, but when warring factions were not prepared to allow a democratic process to take place, the United States was not prepared to enforce the peace that was necessary for any democratic tendency to have a chance to succeed.

Balancing Interests and Morals

The problem that bedevils any American president, of course, is the need to balance the national interest—wherever that may lie—to the American belief in a democratizing mission. President Clinton, unfortunately, has failed to define our national interest in either Somalia or Bosnia; and if there is a national interest involved—arguably so in former Yugoslavia in the light of our half-century commitment to the stability of Europe—he should have acted decisively to wed the concept of the national interest to the moral commitment to prevent the genocidal slaughter that has now taken place in Bosnia-Herzegovina.

Americans are, after all, most comfortable with a foreign policy that is imbued with moral purpose. Even when the pursuit of justice has led to unin-

James Chace, "The American Conscience," *World Policy Journal*, Fall 1993. Reprinted by permission of the World Policy Institute, New York.

tended consequences, even when our ideals have concealed from ourselves—as well as from others—motivations of a darker and more complex nature, we have preferred a policy that invokes moral purpose rather than self-interest. Whether as simply the champion of freedom in a benighted and sinful world, or as a crusader seeking to establish a Jeffersonian empire of freedom, America has viewed itself as exceptional, ordained to play a singular role in world affairs.

> ***"Americans are, after all, most comfortable with a foreign policy that is imbued with moral purpose."***

America's assumption that it has a redemptive mission was forcefully expressed eleven years before the Declaration of Independence, when John Adams wrote in his diary, "I always consider the settlement of America with reverence and wonder, as the opening of a grand scene in providence for the illumination of the ignorant, and the emancipation of the slavish part of mankind all over the Earth." Ours then was to be a unique destiny. As the historian Henry Adams described Jefferson's idea of an American mission, the third American president "aspired beyond the ambition of a nationalist, and embraced in his view the whole future of man."

Against "Perfectionism"

Not all the Founding Fathers were so convinced that the American experiment was either unique or sufficiently protected by geography to allow us the luxury of moral virtue that somehow set us apart from the rest of mankind. Alexander Hamilton rejected those "idle theories which have amused us with promises of an exception from imperfection, weaknesses and evils incident to society in every shape." In *The Federalist* he asked, "Is it not time to awaken from the deceitful dream of a golden age and to adopt as a practical maxim for the direction of our political conduct that we, as well as the other inhabitants of our globe, are yet remote from the happy empire of perfect wisdom and perfect virtue?"

But Hamilton's warning against the search for moral perfection in an imperfect world seldom became part of the rhetoric—or even the reality—of American foreign policy. It was not until the election of the two Roosevelts that the country found presidents who combined the idealistic aspirations of Adams and Jefferson with the worldly realism of Hamilton. "Perfectionism," Franklin D. Roosevelt counseled, "no less than isolationism or imperialism or power politics, may obstruct the paths to international peace."

Time and again to further the national interest, presidents have had to appeal to our sense of moral obligation. When they have failed to do this, as Richard Nixon did when he and Henry Kissinger pursued a foreign policy largely devoid of moral content, they left behind no structure. As between justice and order, Nixon and Kissinger preferred order; indeed they believed that order was a precondition for justice. Despite their short-term successes, their policy of manipulating the balance of power left a legacy of disasters waiting to happen.

Defending Realism with Morality

Both Jimmy Carter and Ronald Reagan, on the other hand, displayed their foreign policy in moral wrappings, though both men fawned over dictators when their definition of the national interest contravened their moral convictions. Less idealist than realist, George Bush seemed to understand the need to wed a realist position to moral ends. At the time of the Gulf War, Bush was not successful in garnering public support for U.S. military intervention until he justified the use of American troops on the grounds that it was America's job to punish aggression. Closer to the truth was the need to ensure the flow of oil at reasonable prices. But Bush could not defend an American policy in such coldly realist terms. Instead, he articulated our role as the enforcer of a latter-day pax americana, declaring that "we have a disproportionate responsibility for the freedom and security of various countries." Despite his rhetorical commitment to a balanced foreign policy, however, he remained a reactive defender of the status quo.

That supreme realist, Walter Lippmann, after the Kennedy administration's misguided attempt to overthrow Cuba's Fidel Castro at the Bay of Pigs, wrote an enduring truth of what goes into the making of an effective American foreign policy: "A policy is bound to fail which deliberately violates our pledges and our principles, our treaties and our laws." He reminded us—and it is a good time to be reminded again—that "the American conscience is a reality. It will make hesitant and ineffectual, even if it does not prevent, an un-American policy."

"Time and again to further the national interest, presidents have had to appeal to our sense of moral obligation."

Now that the ideological struggle against communism is no longer relevant, and furthering the transition to democracy in countries emerging from the long night of totalitarianism is paramount, we need most of all a sense of proportion. Clinton will surely be confronted with failure in his own foreign policy unless he is able to balance the democratizing mission with the pursuit of the national interest. When this balance fails to be struck, our foreign policy falls into crisis. For without such a balance, no *American* policy can succeed.

And if we finally choose to intervene in the affairs of others in order to further the democratic ideal, then we would do well to heed once again the words of Alexander Hamilton that "the means employed be proportional to the extent of the mischief." This is the real message of Bosnia and Somalia.

The United States Should Avoid Interventions

by David Fromkin

About the author: *David Fromkin is author of* A Peace to End All Peace.

"Isolation is no longer possible or desirable," the President said. It was September 1901, the speaker was William McKinley and the subject of his address at the opening of the Pan-American Exposition in Buffalo [New York] was the role the United States should play in the dawning 20th century.

McKinley's point was that modern technologies of transport and communications had abolished distance. It was obvious even then. So internationalism evolved into the dominant theme of American foreign policy. Today, though, with the collapse of the Soviet Union, internationalism is losing its way as we stumble from the narrow and chaotic streets of Somalia to Haiti and, possibly to the quagmire of Bosnia.

Pursue Selfish Goals

Even in its isolationist years, Washington often sent expeditions to deal with trouble spots abroad—from the shores of Tripoli (to suppress the Barbary pirates) to the coast of China. Freed from preoccupation with the Soviet threat, should the United States do more of this sort of thing? Should it right wrongs—in Somalia, Bosnia, Haiti?

This is not the early 1900s, when the United States treated the mini-countries of the Caribbean and Central America like colonies. American motives are now largely humanitarian rather than selfish; and yet, for that very reason, it may be even more of a mistake to send in soldiers. For humanitarian goals tend to be broad, while selfish goals tend to be narrow. And armed interventions seem to be most successful when they are aimed at a narrow objective, tangible and clearly defined, so that the troops, having accomplished it, can get out fast—before the local population has time to turn against them as an occupying force.

The armies we dispatch to foreign soil for humanitarian reasons can try to

David Fromkin, "Don't Send in the Marines," *The New York Times Magazine*, February 27, 1994.

save people from others or from themselves. In either case, the results are nearly always perverse and disappointing.

Sending in an army rarely saves a nation that can't defend itself; it often just postpones defeat until our forces are withdrawn. Thus the Persian Gulf war saved Kuwait and perhaps Saudi Arabia from invasion by a predatory and much more powerful neighbor; but in a few years, when United Nations forces and pressures are removed, the problem of the imbalance of power in that region will recur. President Bush could have solved the problem by allowing the heart of the invading army, the Republican Guard, to be destroyed; but he did not, perhaps for fear of lessening Iraq's ability to defend against the Iranians on the other side, possibly giving rise to a new problem calling for yet another United States–led military intervention.

"Sending in an army rarely saves a nation that can't defend itself."

The great danger in sending armed expeditions abroad to defend the weak is that there will be no end to interventions: dispatching them will become the country's everyday occupation. United States armies will routinely shuttle back and forth to the Middle East to quell fire fights; or else, as with American forces sent in 1950 to defend the South Korean frontier, they will stand guard half a world away forever.

To police the globe in this fashion is beyond our means. But even were that not so, such a program of continuous intervention would not result in a moral new world order. For we can protect the weak only against the weak; we cannot protect against the strong. We are powerful enough to liberate Kuwait from Iraq but not to liberate Tibet from China. So at the very best, the regime we could impose on the world would be morally hypocritical, bringing the petty thief to justice while leaving the master criminal at large.

When the Troops Are Withdrawn

Nor are the results more satisfactory when we interfere between a foreign people and its own government. In the twilight of the Bush Administration, Americans, rightly horrified by the starvation in Somalia, and correctly perceiving that it was caused by the country's rival warlords, sent in not only food but also troops to insure that the food was distributed to the needy. But President Bush did not face the question of what would happen when the troops were withdrawn: would not the warlords go back to warlording and the Somalis back to starving?

When the mission of the United States–United Nations expedition broadened for a time to include the overthrow of a particular warlord, yet another question was raised: Who should replace him? Unless we are prepared to provide an alternative government, and to dedicate to it, over the course of years or decades, the support and guidance it needs to establish itself, we should stay our hand. It is irresponsible of us to destroy even a wicked regime if we cannot replace it. That is the behavior of a repairman who comes to the home or office, takes apart all the machinery and plumbing, leaves the parts lying on the floor and then goes away.

Military intervention, even if undertaken for purely humanitarian reasons, is inescapably a political act. It implies that the country in question is being governed either in the wrong way or by the wrong people—otherwise why did we have to send in not food and medicine, experts or advisers, but troops and guns and airplanes?

Yet *can* we offer a better alternative? Our record of leaving honest, decent, democratic new local leaders behind after we intervene is not a good one: Somoza in Nicaragua, Duvalier in Haiti, Trujillo in Panama and Batista in Cuba are the first names that come to mind. It seemed that everyone in America from Errol Flynn to intensely radical postgraduate students at Columbia University were enthusiasts for Fidel Castro when he took power in Havana.

Do we have the alternative of exercising a United Nations–mandated trusteeship until the locals become capable of self-government? As Britain, France, Spain, Portugal, Holland and Belgium had to learn at midcentury, when they still ruled colonial empires, people will accept bad government but not foreign government—and that is even more true in the 1990s than it was a half century ago.

Vital National Interests

The American public was right to want to scuttle the Somalia expedition as soon as American corpses appeared on the television screen. When the tools we choose to use are soldiers, tanks, guns and bombs, we are going to be killing people, and some of our troops are going to be killed, too. If the issue is not important enough to be worth the lives of United States service personnel, we should not be sending in the armed forces. Doctors, the Peace Corps, technical advisers, yes; but not the troops. When, then, *should* we order our forces into combat?

The answer is clearest with countries our own size, for to war against them is to risk our national existence. We should not do so unless America's life is at stake. The Founding Fathers wrote not of dispatching invasion forces or of going to war, but of providing for the common defense; and historically, the United States did not go to war unless it thought itself attacked. For all of the moral fervor against Spanish rule in Cuba, it was not until Americans believed that Spain had sunk the battleship *Maine* that they clamored for war.

"It is irresponsible of us to destroy even a wicked regime if we cannot replace it."

The coming of the Second World War taught us to take a larger view of self-defense. We saw that Hitler was picking off countries one by one, going from strength to strength as he exploited the resources of those he had conquered. If we had waited until he attacked us, it might have been too late. We applied this lesson in a muddled sort of way to containing the expansion of the Soviet sphere, taking stands in South Korea and South Vietnam as the only alternative to taking a stand closer to home. However wrong in its application to those two conflicts, the theory is sound: if necessary, we should fight to protect our *vital* interests abroad—those interests essential to our ability to protect ourselves.

"People will accept bad government but not foreign government."

But today none of our vital interests are at risk. Nobody is cutting the flow of Middle Eastern oil. Nobody threatens the Panama Canal. No single power is on the march to dominate the whole of Europe or the whole of Asia. If the world were to remain as it is today, the United States never would need to go to war again.

Humanitarian Interests

Yet, the temptation to use our armed forces in less-than-war situations is strong now that we are so much more powerful than other countries. We have national and humanitarian interests all over the globe, and often are told that we can have our way at little cost. If we can bring humane and honest government to Haiti, why not do so? It would be a good deed, and might solve our Haitian refugee problem besides. If we can bring an end to the strife in Bosnia, why not? It would not only rescue victims of terrible suffering, but also would prevent a wider war that might draw in Greece, Turkey and Bulgaria, threatening international stability.

Unfortunately, there are limits to what outsiders can do to solve a domestic quarrel, and limits, too, to what can be done by armed force. If air strikes are all it takes to get the contending parties in Bosnia to make peace, fine; but if it takes an army, then, with due regard to the ruggedness of the terrain and the ferocity of the inhabitants, surely what is required is hundreds of thousands of troops.

And since the essential problem is that the intermingled peoples, driven by blood feuds, will not live with one another in peace, how long will the troops have to stay until a new generation grows up with a changed attitude? Ten years? Twenty years?

There is nothing wrong with using force in pursuit of a national interest if the interest is of sufficient importance, so long as armed intervention will solve the problem, and at an acceptable cost. Our successful in-and-out raids in Grenada and Panama were misleading precedents, chosen precisely because they were exceptions: in the usual case, we sink in a quagmire.

Our commanding lead in weaponry, however useful in making war, does not necessarily equip us to impose a lasting peace. Ascribed to more than one wit, the wise 19th-century saying was, "You can do everything with your bayonets . . . except sit on them."

The United States Should Let Its Allies Defend Themselves

by Pat Buchanan

About the author: *Pat Buchanan, who sought the Republican nomination for president in 1992, is a nationally syndicated columnist.*

We may pay a heavy price for ignoring the wise counsel of our most famous generals.

As Richard Reeves relates in *President Kennedy: Profile of Power*, "Dwight Eisenhower told his successor it was time to start bringing the troops home from Europe. 'America is carrying far more than her share of free world defense,' he said." We are creating dependencies, said Ike; and our trade balance is suffering.

Previous Doctrines Ignored

In his 1951 farewell address, Douglas MacArthur counseled America to erect her Pacific defense perimeter on the "islands extending in an arc from the Aleutians to the Marianas, held by us and our free allies. . . . From this island chain, we can dominate with sea and air power every Asiatic port from Vladivostok to Singapore." Ignoring MacArthur's advice, John F. Kennedy and Lyndon B. Johnson sent ground troops into Vietnam.

Seeing America overextended, Richard Nixon proclaimed the "Guam Doctrine" in 1969 declaring that our Asian allies must begin to assume primary responsibility for their own defense. Because the Nixon doctrine was not implemented, Americans will be among the first to die in any second Korean war.

Protecting South Korea

Since the Cold War ended, some of us have begged Washington to urge Seoul to use her huge trade surplus to purchase U.S. weapons, so we might pull our

Pat Buchanan, "U.S. Doesn't Have to Be Involved in Every War," *Conservative Chronicle*, April 20, 1994. Reprinted by permission: Tribune Media Services.

36,000 troops off the DMZ [demilitarized zone]. In July 1993, addressing the U.S. policy of risking war to prevent North Korea from acquiring an atomic bomb, this writer asked:

"(W)hen did this become our responsibility? Why is it our duty, when it is not America who is threatened, first or foremost, by such regimes? How long are we to carry this responsibility? How many attacks must we launch, how many wars fight, as extremism captures one nation after another which then decides it cannot live without the bomb? Or would America be better off if her allies built their own arsenals, and deterred their enemies themselves?"

In March 1994, we learned that South Korea sought in 1991 to build her own nuclear deterrent. She was blocked by Washington. Nor was this the first time. As far back as the '70s, South Korea sought to build her own nuclear deterrent. Washington would not permit it.

Why? Why did we oppose Seoul's initiative when it could have meant redeploying U.S. troops, and maintaining our alliance with MacArthur's trumps: sea and air power? Why do we insist on being the ones to destroy North Korea, if she attacks the South?

Let Others Pick Up the Burden

If British and French nuclear arsenals helped deter Moscow in the Cold War, why should not small nuclear arsenals in South Korea, Japan, Taiwan and Australia help deter the neighborhood bullies of East Asia who reside in Pyongyang [North Korea] and Beijing [China]?

The United States cannot hold back the tide of history, but we can, with imagination, devise a strategy to preserve our security, and that of our allies, without being engaged in every crisis from the outset, or involved in every war from the first shot.

How? During the Cold War, one nation aligned with us made a defense effort comparable to ours: Israel. Though relying on U.S. aid, Israel maintained her superiority over all potential enemies. There is no reason great nations like Germany and Japan, and regional powers like Taiwan and South Korea, that are five-to-ten times as large as Israel, cannot maintain similar defense efforts, say 5 or 6 percent of GNP. Were they to do so, the net increase in allied power would be enormous; the United States could bring home its troops, and use the income from arms sales to finance a missile defense for the entire West.

"Why is it our duty, when it is not America who is threatened?"

What prevents this vision from being realized is that too many Americans will not let go. As was said of Theodore Roosevelt, they insist on being the bride at every wedding and the corpse at every funeral. These gurus cannot abide the idea of the United States taking a supporting role. And too many friends, for historic reasons, reject any major role for Germans or Japanese.

But unless we are willing to permit Germany and Japan, both democracies now for half a century, to assume their natural roles in the global balance of power, America will have to play not only her own role as the world's preeminent power in the air, on the seas, and in space, but assume their duties as well—with U.S. troops.

Yet, anyone in touch with the heartland knows Americans do not want to fight a fourth Asian war in fifty years, nor do Americans believe the Balkans or Eastern Europe are vital U.S. interests.

If Americans have to fight a second Korean war, Bill Clinton, who blustered and backed down from Somalia to Bosnia to Haiti, will not alone be responsible. So, too, will be those who forgot that it is the duty of a statesman not to expend the precious lives of his soldiers in wars where no vital interest is at stake.

All U.S. Interventions Should Be Opposed

by Stephen R. Shalom

About the author: *Stephen R. Shalom is a professor of political science at William Paterson College in New Jersey and is the author of* Imperial Alibis: Rationalizing U.S. Intervention After the Cold War.

A debate currently rages over the issue of U.S. military intervention abroad. Unlike previous debates on this issue over the past fifty years, today the Left is sharply divided. There have been calls for particular intervention in *In These Times* and *Dissent* and exchanges in the pages of *The Nation, The Boston Review, Peace and Democracy News*, and *The Progressive*. Left conferences in New York and Washington have grappled with the issue, as have many panels at the recent Socialist Scholars' Conference and numerous radio debates.

Bad Interventions During the Cold War

It is somewhat puzzling why this issue of intervention is being raised now. Sure the world has changed in rather substantial ways and it would be foolish to ignore these changes. But it is not at all clear why these changes ought to revise the standard Left presumption against U.S. intervention.

If one believed that the reason for bad U.S. interventions in the past was because of a paranoid fear of the Soviet Union, then the end of the Cold War would indeed mean the end of bad interventions. But Moscow has always served as an excuse for U.S. interventions motivated by quite other considerations, considerations of imperial domination. So when the CIA engineered the overthrow of the elected government of Guatemala in 1953, Washington used a Soviet bloc arms shipment as its justification, even though the planning for the intervention began before the arms shipment occurred. When the United States wanted to support death squads in El Salvador, it issued a White Paper falsely charging that the Soviet Union was a major source of weapons to the Salvadoran guerrillas. And when Washington wanted to crush the Sandinista govern-

Abridged from Stephen R. Shalom, "The Debate on Intervention," *Z Magazine*, June 1994. Reprinted by permission of the author.

ment, it manufactured evidence that Soviet MiGs [military fighter jets] were being sent to Nicaragua. The United States was engaged in imperial interventions long before the Bolsheviks came to power. So the demise of the Soviet Union hardly means the end of interventions rooted in the structures of U.S. society.

"Moscow [during the Cold War] served as an excuse for U.S. interventions motivated by quite other considerations."

When the Soviet "bear was on the loose," the Pentagon devoured about $300 billion a year; today spending has only gone down to $260 billion, giving some indication of just how little Moscow really mattered. Even when one corrects for inflation, Clinton is spending more on the military today than Richard Nixon did in 1974 in the midst of the Cold War. The end of the Cold War will change the excuses that U.S. policy-makers will use for future interventions, but it won't end the urge to intervene.

Interventions at the Cold War's End

This, of course, doesn't explain why some on the Left, in particular, are urging a rethinking of intervention. Why does the end of the Cold War make U.S. intervention more acceptable? To be sure, if the Cold War had ended because the Left had taken power in the United States, our assessment of U.S. intervention would be different. But even if Clinton had not violated so many of his campaign promises, his election would not have signified a decisive break in U.S. foreign policy.

U.S. interventions are militarily more possible today because there is little danger of provoking an all-out nuclear war. No rational person would have urged that U.S. troops intervene in Czechoslovakia in 1968 because nuclear conflagration would have been the likely result. But it's hard to imagine that Washington would have considered intervening to defend Prague's "socialism with a human face" had there been no danger of wider war. To put it another way, the only thing that might have propelled a U.S. intervention would have been the desire to weaken an adversary—the Soviet Union—whose military power placed some check on U.S. ability to intervene elsewhere. So if there were, hypothetically, no danger of nuclear war from a U.S. intervention, there would also not have been any incentive for U.S. intervention. During the Cold War, there have been many places where the United States might have intervened without any risk of nuclear escalation: to promote democracy, for example, in Haiti under Duvalier or the Philippines under Marcos, or to stop massacres, say, in East Pakistan in 1971 or Indonesia in 1965. But the United States was supporting the dictators and the butchers in these cases, and far from contemplating intervention, it refrained from even withdrawing U.S. support for tyranny and terror.

I suspect that one reason some Leftists have become more inclined towards

U.S. intervention is that they have concluded that intervention will no longer be a danger to movements for social justice around the world because such movements no longer exist. The end of the Cold War, in this view, has meant that the opportunity for revolutionaries to receive arms and aid from the Soviet bloc has dried up, making the prospects for social change more difficult than before. This is probably true, despite the strings that Soviet aid usually entailed. But that prospects are dimmer doesn't mean they are nonexistent. The miseries of living in the New World Order will surely generate new struggles for social change. I am going to argue that in general the Left should continue to oppose U.S. military interventions because:

1. By making good interventions possible, we make bad interventions more likely: this is the precedent argument;
2. Bad countries don't make good interventions;
3. Outsiders are inherently incapable of bringing self-determination to others (as argued by John Stuart Mill);
4. The pacifist argument that military force is counterproductive.

Precedent

The precedent argument holds that even if there were a good intervention, it would serve to weaken the taboo against intervention in general. Obviously, there have been many other violations of this taboo before, but there remains a reasonably widespread presumption against foreign intervention. For the Left to endorse the precedent of interventions, even for a good cause, may well help open the floodgates to many other bad interventions.

Likewise, to develop or maintain the capabilities to undertake good interventions, one has to build up the same Pentagon budget, the same interventionary weapons systems, and the same foreign base structure that facilitate bad interventions.

Intervening for the good hinges on the very contestable notion of what is good. Once intervention for the good becomes legitimized, the Left will often lose the contest over the definition of what is good and bad. Allowing countries to intervene when they consider that certain rights have been transgressed is a prescription for disaster. It is better to prohibit all interventions than to allow the U.S. government to decide which interventions are good.

> ***"U.S. interventions are militarily more possible today because there is little danger of provoking an all-out nuclear war."***

Consider the analogy to the hate-speech issue. Some on the Left assert that the government ought to legislate speech for the good. Others, including me, insist that if we legitimize government regulation of speech, we will end up making it easier for the government to ban good speech. It is better to establish as a principle that there should be no government regulation of speech and take the bad with the good, rather than risk having the government decide what is good and what is bad.

Bad Countries, Good Interventions

Even if the United States intervenes in a case where the Left agrees evil is being done, the government will further its own interests, not those of the local victims. World opinion was rightly horrified by Spanish treatment of the Cuban people in 1898, but U.S. intervention resulted in a half century of dictatorship and U.S. domination.

Let me be clear, when I refer to the United States as a "bad government," I mean that the United States can be shown to be a bad government by clear objective measures, by looking at what the United States has done and is doing in the world. Consider a place where some 200,000 people—one third of the population—have been killed: namely, East Timor. Leave aside that in the past Washington gave Indonesia the green light for its invasion and provided 90 percent of its arms; leave aside that for years the United States worked in the UN to give diplomatic support to the invasion. Consider only U.S. policy today, while the killing and conquest continue. In 1992, Congress ended military training aid to Indonesia in protest over a massacre in East Timor's capital of Dili. In December 1993 it was revealed that Indonesian soldiers were being trained at U.S. military bases under the technicality that Indonesia was paying for the training. The previous June, the heads of the Senate Foreign Relations Committee and the Foreign Operations Subcommittee had written to the Department of State that allowing Indonesia to purchase U.S. military training "would be directly contrary to the intent of Congress." But that's precisely what has been going on. Note that no one is calling on the United States to risk the lives of its young men and women by invading Indonesia or bombing Jakarta, but even the minimal step of cutting off military training is unacceptable to the Clinton administration. And it is this administration that some are hoping will intervene for a good cause—sort of like approaching muggers on the street and asking them if they wouldn't mind protecting another mugging victim on the next block.

> ***"It is better to prohibit all interventions than to allow the U.S. government to decide which interventions are good."***

Some reject this argument as merely pointing out a double-standard, which might be true but irrelevant. We don't, after all, reject out of hand all good actions that are performed by those with a double standard. But the point is not (just) that U.S. concern for some victims of atrocities is hypocritical, but also, as a practical matter, it is not very realistic to expect those who turn a blind eye to, and even participate in, some mass murder to become morally engaged in preventing some other mass murder.

Obviously, if major social change took place in the United States so that it was no longer a bad government, this argument would not apply. Nor does the argument apply to the case of international brigades which are independent of bad governments. Neither of these considerations, however, are relevant to the current debate on U.S. intervention.

Mill's Argument

A third argument against intervention is one that goes back at least to John Stuart Mill. As Michael Walzer has summarized Mill's argument, self-determination is not the same as political freedom. The former term is more inclusive, covering also a political community's struggle for freedom—whether successful or not. Members of a political community cannot be set free by an external force. "It is during an arduous struggle to become free by their own efforts that [the virtues needful for maintaining freedom] have the best chance of springing up." Mill didn't believe that intervention fails more often than not to serve the purposes of liberty; he believed that, given what liberty is, it necessarily fails. The internal freedom of a political community can only be won by the members of that community, just as in the Marxian view the liberation of the working class can come only from the workers themselves. Thus, for Mill, there can be evil social systems, with much oppression, where revolution is justified but where intervention is not, for the former is an act of self-determination, while the latter undermines self-determination.

Related to this argument is another liability that outsiders have in bringing freedom to others: outsiders are often uninformed of local conditions and thus ill-suited to bring social benefit. Consider the case of Somalia. U.S. forces charged headlong into the complex web of Somali politics, bringing to bear their special blend of arrogance and ignorance. Before the U.S. intervention there had been signs that Muhammad Farah Aidid was waning in power within his sub-clan. But first the U.S. promoted Aidid by treating him as a key leader, and then it demonized him, driving even members of his sub-clan who disagreed with him to his support, fearing that they were, in the words of the Operations Director for the U.S.-led Command, "on the edge of a clan eradication." Now, Aidid has become one of the most powerful figures in the country, which is a real tragedy, because he is a brutal thug.

> ***"The internal freedom of a political community can only be won by the members of that community."***

Is it contradictory to damn the United States on the one hand for embracing Aidid and on the other for demonizing him? No. The fact is that there is no easy way for outsiders to reconstitute Somali society, particularly when they disdain the opinions of Somalis. No Somalis were consulted before Operation Restore Hope, and many of the policies carried out by outsiders marginalized and ignored Somalis, and have bred dependence and demoralization. It is thus extremely doubtful that U.S. Marines can bring Somalia what it most needs, which is precisely the participation and empowerment of Somalis.

The fourth argument against military intervention is the pacifist critique. Whatever one thinks about absolutist pacificism, there is little doubt that pacifists have identified many ways in which military action undermines the values we hope to promote: it makes reconciliation more difficult, it lessens the taboo around killing, it is almost invariably organized in hierarchical structures and thus undermines democracy. The means one uses to attain certain ends invariably influence the ends that are actually achieved.

Moreover, military action almost never deals with the root causes of problems and thus using it encourages quick fix solutions that ignore the underlying sources of conflict. And because various domestic constituencies benefit from military intervention, there is a tendency to champion military action in situations where it is inappropriate, especially by those whose careers or profits or testosterone depend on war.

There are also a whole host of very real practical and logistical obstacles to military intervention. As Richard Falk has reminded us, even in cases where the U.S. government seems to have had strong strategic motives for intervention, as in Lebanon in 1983, "success" from the point of view of the intervenor has been elusive.

> ***"Using [military action] encourages quick fix solutions that ignore the underlying sources of conflict."***

Precision military operations are especially difficult. The destructive potential of military technology is immense, but its ability to achieve precise goals is still very remote. When Marine F/A-18 planes attacked Serbian armored vehicles near Gorazde on April 11, 1994, for example, two of three bombs dropped failed to explode and a fourth became hung up on the wing of one of the planes.

Exceptions

There are exceptions to each of these four arguments against intervention. The precedent argument assumes that the clearest place to draw the line between acceptable and unacceptable state behavior, particularly by the United States, is between intervention and no intervention and that drawing the line anywhere else weakens the general presumption against intervention. Precedents and taboos matter: but if there were a case where a particular intervention seemed uniquely good, couldn't we educate people to see why this case was not like most of the other cases we rightly oppose?

The argument that bad governments don't undertake good interventions likewise has an exception. That is, it is possible that the net consequence of an intervention might be positive even where the motives of the intervenor were bad.

During World War II, the United States government did not care about the plight of Europe's Jews—as shown by its failure to do a number of easy things that could have saved thousands. Nevertheless, a consequence of defeating Hitler was that the death camps were closed down. And it is possible to make a case that despite all the horrendous consequences of World War II—the millions of lives lost, the undermining of revolutionary movements, the re-imposition of colonialism (in Vietnam, for example)—on balance it was still better that the United States intervened than had it not.

Mill recognized two exceptions to his basic non-interventionist position, exceptions that he claimed flowed logically from his general argument: (1) secession and (2) counter-intervention. Michael Walzer suggests a third exception: namely, massacre. In the case of secession, said Mill, the political community whose self-determination we care about no longer exists; the boundary of the political community is in doubt and intervention might help the secessionists achieve their independence and hence self-determination. When an outside country or countries have intervened in a civil war, then counter-intervention might restore the balance so that the domestic struggle can be resolved domestically. And finally when widespread massacres are taking place, the notion of a political community no longer applies.

There are exceptions, too, to the pacifist paradigm. Although the usual effects of military force are counter-productive, there are circumstances where human suffering might be substantially reduced by resort to arms. I doubt, for example, that there were any pacifist strategies that would have had much impact on the German *Einsatzgruppen* who machine-gunned hundreds of thousands of unarmed Jews.

Limiting Exceptions

So each of these four basic arguments against intervention has exceptions, but in order for an intervention to be justified it has to fall under an exception to all four arguments. Most U.S. interventions historically have been objectionable on all four grounds, but even one ground would be sufficient for us to oppose an intervention.

> ***"There is good reason to be very stingy with exceptions to non-intervention."***

There is good reason to be very stingy with exceptions to non-intervention. Take Mill's exceptions: secession, counter-intervention, and massacre—each one of them involves a great many subjective judgments. Moreover, since almost every society has some number of individuals who would like to secede, some measure of intervention by other outsiders, and some degree of mistreatment of its citizens, every country could claim justification for intervention wherever it wanted. Where does one draw the line? Serbia could claim, for example, that Croatia mistreated some of its citizens or was preventing secession and that either of these justified its intervention. Washington claimed that its intervention in Vietnam was a counter-intervention to that of North Vietnam and that its support for the [Nicaraguan] *Contras* was to protect Miskito Indians.

It is true that in domestic law we don't reject, for example, the plea of self-defense just because it is often falsely claimed, but in domestic law we at least have some authoritative mechanisms for evaluating claims, namely courts of law that can hear evidence and establish guidelines. A world in which countries determined for themselves when any of these three exceptions to the principle of non-intervention ought to apply would be a very dangerous place indeed. Not everyone would invade everyone else (prudence would discourage the weak from attacking the strong), but certainly the strong would have a field day. For this reason, many smaller countries—often the victims of large neighbors—have taken the position that nothing justifies intervention by one country into the affairs of another. For example, Latin American nations were able to pressure Washington into signing a convention in Buenos Aires in 1936 agreeing not to intervene in the region for any reason (a pledge, of course, broken many times). And though the Latin American governments that took this absolute non-interventionist position may have wanted to shield themselves from interference with their own human rights abuses, my guess is that democratic opinion throughout Latin America supported the non-intervention convention. . . .

"From the fact that some sort of intervention in trade and aid policy is inevitable it does not follow that military intervention is justified."

Everything Is Intervention

Some argue that in the contemporary interdependent world it is impossible not to intervene: whether the United States trades with country X or doesn't trade with country X, it is intervening; whether the United States chooses to give economic aid to country Y or not to give aid, it is intervening. Since intervention is thus inevitable, we might as well make sure it is for the good.

It's true that it is impossible to avoid decisions on trade, aid, and diplomacy, and so whatever the United States does will be an intervention of sorts. Few progressives, for example, supported United States trade with South Africa or aid to Chile's Pinochet or El Salvador's Duarte. There are thus cases where the Left endorses using U.S. trade policy to influence the domestic policies of other countries. If Washington traded with South Africa, it helped apartheid; if it didn't trade it hurt apartheid: there was no way to avoid having an impact. Therefore, in these cases it makes sense for the Left to push to ensure that the intervention be for the good. . . .

But from the fact that some sort of intervention in trade and aid policy is inevitable it does not follow that military intervention is justified. Trade, aid, diplomacy—these are the normal, legal practices of international life. Every country has the right to decide who it wants to trade with or aid, and in deciding it is inevitably rewarding or penalizing other countries. But sending in the Marines is not the same thing. Countries do not normally have the right to invade other countries or to engage in covert operations abroad. Generally, it is not intervention to fail to dispatch troops or to refrain from covert operations. So there is nothing inconsistent with a position that says that U.S. trade and aid policy should favor human rights, democracy, and adherence to international law, while at the same time the United States should not engage in military intervention or covert CIA intervention. . . .

Isolationism

In arguing for non-intervention, we often find ourselves aligned with isolationists, those who oppose foreign adventures not because of the harm the United States is likely to do, but because of the costs to the United States and because of a basic indifference to foreign suffering. Though I opposed the dispatch of U.S. troops to Somalia, it was disheartening to read one U.S. citizen's argument for withdrawal, as quoted in the *New York Times:* "It's really very simple. If I have to choose between pictures of starving Somalian babies or dead American soldiers being dragged through the streets of Mogadishu, well, I don't want to see any more dead Americans. Sorry."

It is awkward to be on the same side of the Somalia intervention question as this racist. But there are no fewer racists on the other side, those who would incinerate large numbers of Somali civilians in their effort to capture Muhammad Farah Aidid. We need to distinguish our views from those of both groups of racists, the isolationists and the interventionists.

To some extent, the peace movement bears some responsibility for egocentric isolationism. Too often the anti-war movement resorted to the opportunist argument against intervention—that Americans would be coming home in body bags. We need to be much clearer and much more principled: it is because we are concerned for Somalis that we recommended (those of us who did) against intervention there. It was because of our support for Vietnam's struggle against U.S. imperialism that we opposed U.S. intervention there.

> ***"We [the Left] need to distinguish our views from those of both . . . the isolationists and the interventionists."***

When we hear Americans say "don't send U.S. troops to Haiti, who cares about them," we need to reply: "don't send U.S. troops to Haiti because we do care about the struggle of the Haitian people for justice and decent lives." And let us do what we can to help that struggle and its victims. Sure it's not easy to help the struggle; but U.S. Marines will definitely not help the struggle. When we hear others say, "Let's keep out of that Balkan quagmire where

American lives will be lost in behalf of one crazy fanatic or another," we have to respond, "We support the Bosnian struggle for preserving a multi-ethnic state, and that's why we want NATO to stay out." And let us do what we can to help that struggle and its victims, including working to lift the arms embargo. And let us also express our solidarity with and do what we can to support peace forces in Serbia and Croatia. Opposing U.S. intervention is not giving up on internationalism. It is almost always the best way to be an internationalist.

UN Interventions by World Region: September 1994

As of September 1994, there are over 72,000 peacekeepers stationed throughout the world—up from 11,500 in January 1992. As this statistic suggests, the number and scope of UN missions has increased dramatically in recent years. The following is a survey of UN interventions and their status as of September 1994, a month that witnessed, among other developments, a UN-sanctioned intervention by the United States to restore democracy in Haiti.

UN Peacekeepers by Country: September 1994

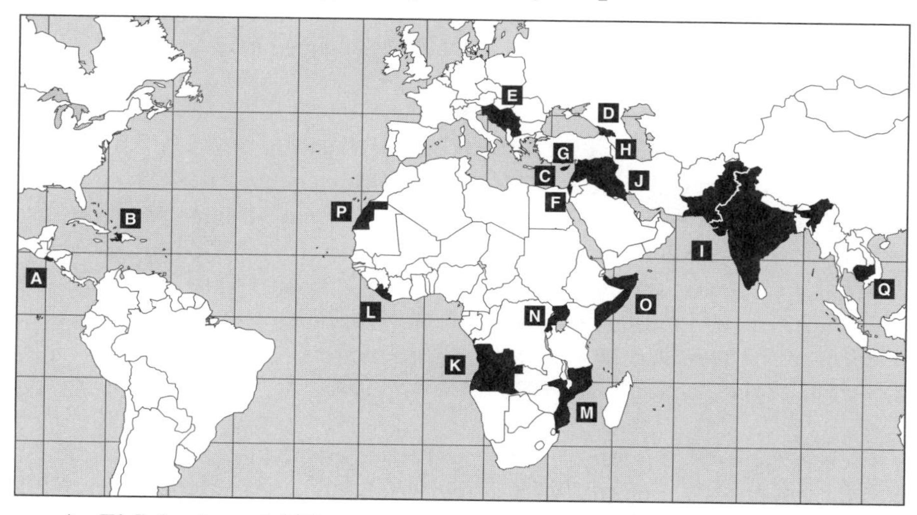

A. El Salvador—1,000
B. Haiti—17,000
C. Cyprus—1,235
D. Georgia—21
E. Former Yugoslavia—34,555
F. Israel/Palestine—220
G. Lebanon—5,315
H. Syria—1,035
I. India/Pakistan—39
J. Iraq/Kuwait—1,147
K. Angola—79
L. Liberia—426
M. Mozambique—5,760
N. Rwanda/Uganda—2,500
O. Somalia—20,000
P. Western Sahara—347
Q. Cambodia—20

Africa

Angola—Since 1975, when Angola gained independence from Portugal, the National Union for Total Independence of Angola (UNITA) has fought a civil war against the Marxist government of Angola and its Cuban allies. In December 1988, the United Nations intervened to observe the withdrawal of the Cuban troops, which was accomplished by June 1991. The United Nations subsequently was asked to observe the implementation of a cease-fire and peace agreement signed on May 1, 1991, by the government of Angola and UNITA. On September 29–30, 1992, democratic elections were held, in accordance with the peace agreement; UNITA, however, rejected the results of the election and resumed the civil war. Approximately 80 UN troops and observers remain in Angola to enforce sanctions against UNITA and reestablish the peace process.

Liberia—A peace treaty was signed on July 25, 1993, ending the civil war begun in 1990 between the Interim Government of National Unity of Liberia and the regional, ethnic-based factions the National Patriotic Front of Liberia and the United Liberation Movement for Democracy. A transitional government was put in place in March 1994 promising nationwide elections in September 1994. Three hundred UN observers and 65 UN troops supplement the forces from neighboring West African states engaged in disarming the three parties to the civil war and repatriating refugees.

Mozambique—In 1990, peace talks began between the Marxist government of Mozambique and the National Resistance Movement (RENAMO), led by Jonas Savimbi, to end a civil war that had been waged since Mozambique gained independence in 1975. The result was an October 1992 peace agreement promising elections scheduled for October 1994. Over 5000 UN troops, 275 UN police, and 330 military observers are in Mozambique to monitor the disarmament of the two warring sides, the repatriation of refugees, and the implementation of the elections.

Rwanda/Uganda—Fighting in Rwanda between the ethnic majority Hutu-led government and the minority Tutsi-dominated Rwandese Patriotic Front (RPF) rebels first started in October 1990. Following the failure of a number of cease-fires negotiated by the Organization of African Unity, in February 1993 the governments of Rwanda and neighboring Uganda, where RPF rebels had established camps, requested UN intervention. In June 1993, a UN force of 81 military observers and 11 civilians was sent to Uganda's border with Rwanda. Following the August 1993 signing of the Arusha Peace Agreement promising elections in Rwanda, a further 2548 troops were sent to Rwanda. On April 6, 1994, the Hutu president of Rwanda, Juvenal Habyarimana, was killed in a plane crash. Suspicious about the crash, government soldiers started a new round of fighting that included the slaughter of tens of thousands of Tutsi and Hutu civilians and resulted in a mass exodus of refugees to neighboring countries. All but 270 UN observers retreated after 10 Belgian soldiers were killed. Following four months of fighting, the RPF rebels succeeded in overthrowing the government and ending the fighting, and in June 1994, 2500 French soldiers resumed the peacekeeping operation in Rwanda. The 81 troops on the Uganda border were withdrawn in September 1994.

Somalia—In 1991, the United Somali Congress, an ethnic clan-based rebel faction led by Mohammed Farah Aideed, succeeded in overthrowing the military dictatorship of Mohammed Siad Barre, who had ruled Somalia since 1969. A civil war between Aideed's forces and other factions who had opposed Siad Barre quickly ensued. In April 1992, 3000 UN troops began a humanitarian operation to bring relief supplies to victims of a famine caused by the civil war. Because humanitarian efforts were blocked by the factions, the United States sent more than 27,000 military personnel in December 1992 to protect the relief supplies. In March 1993, in the face of growing violence in Somalia, the United Nations took the unprecedented step of authorizing the use of force by those protecting the relief supplies. The U.S. forces were replaced by those of other countries in March 1994, and the United Nations is scheduled to withdraw the remaining 18,400 troops by March 1995, though it has not been successful in scheduling elections.

Western Sahara—In 1976, Spain ceded its colony in Western Sahara to Morocco. Since that time, the Polisario Front has sought independence for Western Sahara, establishing a government in exile in neighboring Algeria. A cease-fire in the war between Morocco and the Polisario Front, promising a democratic referendum on independence, was agreed upon in late 1991. The United Nations has posted 350 military personnel (out of a proposed force of 3000) in Western Sahara to monitor the cease-fire, but lack of progress in implementing the referendum is prompting some countries to threaten to withdraw their troops.

Americas

El Salvador—In July 1991, the United Nations established an observer mission in El Salvador to help negotiate a peace agreement between the government of El Salvador and the insurgent Marxist Frente Farabundo Martí para la Liberación Nacional (FMLN). The peace agreement was signed in January 1992, and the United Nations began monitoring human rights, the military, and the police. Democratic elections were held in March and April 1994, and despite some continuing violence, the election results were declared fair and acceptable by the UN observers. Nearly 300 UN police and observers remain in El Salvador to monitor human rights.

Haiti—In September 1991, the Haitian military overthrew Haiti's first democratically elected president, Jean-Bertrand Aristide. With the failure of efforts to negotiate a political settlement, the United Nations imposed economic sanctions on Haiti in June 1993. The United States succeeded in brokering the July 1993 Governor's Island Accord between Aristide and the Haitian military, ensuring Aristide's return to the presidency. The accord was broken in October 1993, however, when U.S. troops aboard the USS *Harlan County*, as the first contingent of UN military observers, were blocked from landing in Haiti. In response, the United Nations imposed stronger new sanctions on Haiti. UN human rights observers sent in September 1993 were expelled by the Haitian military in July 1994. The UN then authorized the use of force to restore democracy in Haiti, and a U.S.-led coalition of forces began preparing to invade. On September 18, 1994, the military junta agreed to step down and uphold the Governor's Island agreement, and U.S. military forces that had been poised to invade Haiti instead entered the country peacefully to ensure the transfer of power.

Asia

Cambodia (Kampuchea)—In January 1979, neighboring Vietnam invaded Cambodia to remove the communist Khmer Rouge dictatorship, which had overthrown the previous monarchy. Vietnam eventually withdrew its forces in 1989, as fighting between the Khmer Rouge, the former monarchy, and the Vietnam-backed government continued. In October 1991, all three groups signed a peace treaty that empowered the United Nations to administer the government of Cambodia until elections in May 1993. However, the Khmer Rouge boycotted the elections, which established a new constitution for Cambodia and a government headed by King Norodom Sihanouk. The United Nations withdrew its forces in September 1993. A 20-member team of observers was reestablished in November 1993 to monitor continuing violence between the Royal Cambodian Armed Forces of the government and the Khmer Rouge National Army of Democratic Kampuchea.

India/Pakistan—India and Pakistan have been fighting for control of the border area of Kashmir since both countries gained independence in August 1947. The United Nations first sent peacekeepers in January 1949 to observe a cease-fire that in July 1949 became a formal peace agreement. In 1971–1972 the peace agreement was broken and a new cease-fire established. Hostilities in the form of threats and minor armed clashes between the two countries continue, and 39 UN military observers remain in the area.

Europe

Cyprus—A civil war between Greek and Turkish Cypriots began in December 1963, three years after Cyprus gained independence from Britain in August 1960. UN peacekeepers intervened in March 1964 to observe a cease-fire, which was broken in July 1974. Despite the lack of a formal cease-fire, 1188 UN peacekeepers currently patrol an agreed-upon buffer zone dividing the Greek and Turkish areas of the island. The United Nations is currently negotiating the implementation of an agreement on confidence-building measures signed by the two sides in June 1993.

Georgia—Georgia became independent from the former Union of Soviet Socialist Republics in April 1991. In August 1992, a civil war began after the region of Abkhazia attempted to secede from Georgia. The first members of a UN observer mission were sent to Georgia in August 1993 to monitor a cease-fire negotiated between the government of Georgia and the Abkhaz separatists. The cease-fire quickly broke down, and although agreements were negotiated between the two sides in April 1994 the conflict has not been settled. The UN mission was to have included 55 military observers but has never been fully deployed.

Former Yugoslavia—In June 1991, the republics of Slovenia, Croatia, and Macedonia declared independence from Yugoslavia. A war between the breakaway Croatia and what was left of the federal Yugoslav government in the Serbian republic was settled by a UN-brokered cease-fire in January 1992. Following that settlement, Bosnia and Hercegovina declared its independence, precipitating a civil war among the Serb, Croat, and Muslim groups of that republic. Worsening the situation, both Croatia and Serbia have been accused of sending their armed forces to fight in Bosnia, and all sides in the conflict have been accused of "ethnic cleansing"—the use of rape, murder, terror, and concentration camps to force the evacuation of particular ethnic groups from certain areas. In March 1992, the United Nations sent 22,000 peacekeepers to the former Yugoslavia to observe the cease-fire between Croatia and the federal government (now composed of Serbia and Montenegro), to prevent Serbian aggression against Macedonia, and to protect civilians and humanitarian relief supplies in Bosnia. With the Bosnian war escalating, the United Nations in April 1993 established six cities in Bosnia, including the capital, Sarajevo, as "safe havens" where civilians could get humanitarian aid. In response to continuing attacks on Sarajevo, in February 1994 the United Nations took the unprecedented step of authorizing North Atlantic Treaty Organization forces to conduct air strikes to defend the safe havens. With each new initiative and resolution, the United Nations has raised the number of troops in former Yugoslavia to its present level of 33,300, but the three parties to the conflict have not been able to agree on a partition of the territory of Bosnia, and fighting continues.

Middle East

Iraq/Kuwait—In August 1990, Iraq invaded neighboring Kuwait and attempted to annex it. In response, the United Nations approved the use of force to remove Iraq's army from Kuwait, and in January–February 1991 a U.S.-led multinational force defeated Iraq's army and liberated Kuwait. UN troops and military observers were deployed to a demilitarized zone along the Iraq/Kuwait border established in April 1991. As of April 1994, they numbered 900 troops and 250 military observers, though there could eventually be as many as 3000 troops. Further, in accordance with UN resolutions, UN inspectors are monitoring the dismantling of Iraq's nuclear and chemical weapons manufacturing capabilities. Also, the United States and its Gulf War allies are enforcing a ban on Iraqi military flights over the Kurd-inhabited north and Shia-dominated south of Iraq. The flight ban is a continuation of Operation Provide Comfort begun in April 1991 to provide humanitarian aid to Iraqi Kurds, who were victims of aggression before and after the Gulf War by the regime of Saddam Hussein.

Israel/Palestine—War quickly broke out between Israel and its Arab neighbors following Israel's independence in May 1948. A UN observer mission was established in Jerusalem in June 1948 to monitor a truce between Israel and its Arab neighbors. The 220 observers in Jerusalem are part of a network of UN missions in the Middle East region monitoring the results of a series of wars between Israel, Lebanon, Syria, Jordan, and Egypt.

Lebanon—In 1975, various Christian and Muslim militias in Lebanon began a civil war that left the country without a government for over fifteen years. In 1978, a UN peacekeeping force was sent to separate the militias and work to restore government. However, when 241 U.S. Marines were killed in a terrorist attack in October 1983, and many other European soldiers were killed in similar attacks, the forces were withdrawn. Since 1991, a new government in Lebanon has successfully worked to restore order and defeat or disarm the militias.

During the anarchy of the civil war years, terrorist groups used Lebanon as a base from which to attack Israel, and Israel invaded Lebanon twice, in March 1978 and June 1982. Since the 1978 invasion, Israel has controlled a nine-mile-wide "security zone" in southern Lebanon along their shared border. The current contingent of 5300 UN troops remaining in Lebanon is monitoring the withdrawal of Israeli troops, but terrorist attacks on Israel continue, and Israel continues to direct military action against targets in this "security zone."

Syria—In October 1973, war once again broke out between Israel and its neighbors Egypt and Syria. During this war Israel seized and annexed the Golan Heights from Syria. Since June 1974, over 1000 UN troops have monitored the Golan Heights in cooperation with the UN mission in Israel.

Bibliography

Books

American Friends Service Committee	*Dollars or Bombs: The Search for Justice Through International Economic Sanctions.* Philadelphia: AFSC Peace Education Division, 1993.
Richard J. Bloomfield and Gregory F. Treverton	*Alternative to Intervention: A New U.S.–Latin American Security Relationship.* Boulder, CO: Lynne Rienner Publishers, 1990.
Boutros Boutros-Ghali	*An Agenda for Peace: Preventive Diplomacy, Peacemaking and Peace-keeping.* New York: United Nations, 1992.
Zbigniew Brzezinski	*Out of Control: Global Turmoil on the Eve of the Twenty-First Century.* New York: Maxwell Macmillan International, 1993.
Carnegie Endowment for International Peace	*Changing Our Ways: America and the New World.* Washington: Brookings Institution, 1992.
Ted Galen Carpenter	*A Search for Enemies: America's Alliances After the Cold War.* Washington: Cato Institute, 1992.
Richard Michael Connaughton	*Military Intervention in the 1990s: A New Logic of War.* New York: Routledge, 1992.
Francis M. Deng and Larry Minear	*The Challenges of Famine Relief: Emergency Operations in the Sudan.* Washington: Brookings Institution, 1992.
Paul Diehl	*International Peacekeeping.* Baltimore: Johns Hopkins University Press, 1993.
Elizabeth G. Ferris	*The Challenge to Intervene: A New Role for the United Nations?* Uppsala, Sweden: Life and Peace Institute, 1992.
Jeffrey R. Gerlach	*Providing a Haven for Refugees: An Alternative to U.S. Military Intervention in the Balkans.* Washington: Cato Institute, 1993.
Ernst B. Haas	*Beware the Slippery Slope: Notes Toward the Definition of Justifiable Intervention.* Berkeley: University of California Press, 1993.
Richard Haass	*Intervention: The Use of American Military Force in the Post–Cold War World.* Washington: Carnegie Endowment for International Peace, 1994.

Ralph A. Hallenbeck — *Military Force as an Instrument of U.S. Foreign Policy: Intervention in Lebanon, August 1982–February 1984.* New York: Praeger, 1991.

Graham Hancock — *Lords of Poverty: The Free-Wheeling Lifestyles, Power, Prestige and Corruption of the Multi-Billion Dollar Aid Business.* London: Macmillan, 1989.

Alan James — *Peacekeeping and International Politics.* London: Macmillan, 1990.

Ariel E. Levite, Bruce W. Jentleson, and Larry Berman, eds. — *Foreign Military Intervention: The Dynamics of Protracted Conflict.* New York: Columbia University Press, 1992.

Douglas J. MacDonald — *Adventures in Chaos: American Intervention for Reform in the Third World.* Cambridge: Harvard University Press, 1992.

Samuel M. Makinda — *Seeking Peace from Chaos: Humanitarian Intervention in Somalia.* Boulder, CO: Lynne Rienner Publishers, 1993.

Lisa Martin — *Coercive Cooperation: Explaining Multilateral Economic Sanctions.* Princeton, NJ: Princeton University Press, 1992.

John H. Maurer and Richard H. Porth — *Military Intervention in the Third World: Threats, Constraints, and Options.* New York: Praeger, 1984.

Laura W. Reed and Carl Kaysen, eds. — *Emerging Norms of Justified Intervention.* Cambridge: Committee on International Security Studies, American Academy of Arts and Sciences, 1993.

Linda Robinson — *Intervention or Neglect: The United States and Central America Beyond the 1980s.* New York: Council on Foreign Relations Press, 1991.

Nigel S. Rodley — *To Loose the Bands of Wickedness: International Intervention in Defence of Human Rights.* New York: Macmillan, 1992.

John Roper et al. — *Keeping the Peace in the Post–Cold War Era: Strengthening Multilateral Peacekeeping.* New York: Trilateral Commission, 1993.

Peter J. Rowe and Christopher J. Whelan — *Military Intervention in Democratic Societies.* Dover, NH: Croom Helm, 1985.

David J. Scheffer, Richard N. Gardner, and Gerald B. Helman — *Post–Gulf War Challenges to the U.N. Collective Security System: Three Views on the Issue of Humanitarian Intervention.* Washington: United States Institute of Peace, 1992.

Peter J. Schraeder, ed. — *Intervention into the 1990s: U.S. Foreign Policy in the Third World.* Boulder, CO: Lynne Rienner Publishers, 1992.

Stephen R. Shalom — *Imperial Alibis: Rationalizing U.S. Intervention After the Cold War.* Boston: South End Press, 1993.

David R. Smock, ed. — *Making War and Waging Peace: Foreign Intervention in Africa.* Washington: United States Institute of Peace Press, 1993.

Keith Somerville — *Foreign Military Intervention in Africa.* New York: St. Martin's Press, 1990.

John D. Steinbruner, Ashton B. Carter, and William J. Perry	*A New Concept for Cooperative Security.* Washington: Brookings Institution, 1992.
Antonio Tanca	*Foreign Armed Intervention in Internal Conflict.* Boston: M. Nijhoff Publishers, 1993.
United Nations	*The Blue Helmets: A Review of United Nations Peace-Keeping.* New York: United Nations, 1990.
Bruce W. Watson and Peter G. Tsouras	*Operation Just Cause: The U.S. Intervention in Panama.* Boulder, CO: Westview Press, 1991.
Thomas G. Weiss and Larry Minear	*Humanitarianism Across Borders: Sustaining Civilians in Times of War.* Boulder, CO: Lynne Rienner Publishers, 1993.

Periodicals

Kenneth L. Adelman	"Can the UN Do the Job?" *The World & I*, April 1993. Available from 2800 New York Ave. NE, Washington, DC 20002.
Madeleine K. Albright	"Agenda for Dignity," *U.S. Department of State Dispatch*, November 22, 1993.
Richard L. Armitage	"The Importance of U.S. Leadership," *The World & I*, June 1994.
Doug Bandow	"Avoiding War," *Foreign Policy*, Winter 1992–93.
Doug Bandow	"Keeping the Troops and the Money at Home," *Current History*, January 1994.
Henry S. Bienen	"The New Isolationism," *Society*, September/October 1992.
Boutros Boutros-Ghali	"An Agenda for Peace: One Year Later," *Orbis*, Summer 1993.
Christopher Caldwell	"Aristide Development," *The American Spectator*, July 1994.
CQ Researcher	"Economic Sanctions," October 28, 1994. Available from 1414 22nd St. NW, Washington, DC 20037.
CQ Researcher	"Foreign Policy Burden," August 20, 1993.
Chester A. Crocker	"The Rules of Engagement in a New World," *The Washington Post National Weekly Edition*, May 16–22, 1994. Available from 1150 15th St. NW, Washington, DC 20071.
Robert Cullen	"Human Rights Quandary," *Foreign Affairs*, Winter 1992–93.
Terry L. Deibel	"Internal Affairs and International Relations in the Post–Cold War World," *The Washington Quarterly*, Summer 1993. Available from MIT Press, Journals Div., 55 Hayward St., Cambridge, MA 02142.
Bogdan Denitch	"Bosnia, Dying While the World Watches," *The Washington Post National Weekly Edition*, February 21–27, 1994.
Larry Diamond	"The Global Imperative: Building a Democratic World Order," *Current History*, January 1994.

Larry Diamond — "Promoting Democracy," *Foreign Policy*, Summer 1992.

Michael W. Doyle — "Forcing Peace: What Role for the United Nations?" *Dissent*, Spring 1994.

Jan Eliasson — "Confronting Reality: The UN Prepares for Expanded Duties," *Harvard International Review*, Fall 1993. Available from P.O. Box 401, Cambridge, MA 02238.

Richard Falk — "Hard Choices and Tragic Dilemmas," *The Nation*, December 20, 1993.

Marrack Goulding — "The Evolution of United Nations Peacekeeping," *International Affairs*, July 1993. Available from Cambridge University Press, 40 W. 20th St., New York, NY 10011-4211.

Tony P. Hall — "The Humanitarian Agenda in the New World Order," *Mediterranean Quarterly*, Fall 1992. Available from Mediterranean Affairs, Inc., National Press Building, Suite 984, Washington, DC 20045.

Rosalyn Higgins — "The New United Nations and Former Yugoslavia," *International Affairs*, July 1993.

John F. Hillen III — "Peacekeeping Is Hell," Policy Review, Fall 1993.

Stanley Hoffmann — "Out of the Cold: Humanitarian Interventions in the 1990s," *Harvard International Review*, Fall 1993.

James C. Ingram — "The Politics of Human Suffering," *The National Interest*, Fall 1993. Available from 1112 16th St. NW, Suite 540, Washington, DC 20036.

Michael Johns — "How to Save Bosnia," *The World & I*, July 1994.

Max M. Kampelman — "Secession and the Right of Self-Determination: An Urgent Need to Harmonize Principle with Pragmatism," *The Washington Quarterly*, Summer 1993.

Robert D. Kaplan — "A Reader's Guide to the Balkans," *The New York Times Book Review*, April 18, 1993.

Catherine M. Kelleher — "Soldiering On," *The Brookings Review*, Spring 1994.

Jeane Kirkpatrick — "Facing a World Without Threats," *New Perspectives Quarterly*, Summer 1992.

Anthony Lake — "A Strategy of Enlargement and the Developing World," *U.S. Department of State Dispatch*, October 25, 1993.

Joanne Landy — "Magical Thinking About Intervention in Haiti," *Peace & Democracy*, Summer 1994.

William Lewis — "Suffering from Overload," *The World & I*, June 1994.

Edward C. Luck — "Making Peace," *Foreign Policy*, Winter 1992–93.

Thomas G. Mahnken — "America's Next War," *The Washington Quarterly*, Summer 1993.

Michael Mandelbaum	"The Reluctance to Intervene," *Foreign Policy*, Summer 1994.
Larry Minear	"Humanitarian Intervention in a New World Order," *Overseas Development Council Policy Focus*, February 1992. Available from 17th St. & Constitution Ave. NW, Washington, DC 20006.
Yehudah Mirsky	"Democratic Politics, Democratic Culture," *Orbis*, Fall 1993. Available from Foreign Policy Research Institute, 3615 Chestnut St., Philadelphia, PA 19104.
Joshua Muravchik	"Beyond Self-Defense," *Commentary*, December 1993.
Andrew S. Natsios	"Food Through Force: Humanitarian Intervention and U.S. Policy," *The Washington Quarterly*, Winter 1994.
Robert Oakley et al.	"A UN Volunteer Force—the Prospects," *The New York Review of Books*, July 15, 1993.
Ralph Peters	"Vanity and the Bonfires of the 'Isms'," *Parameters*, Autumn 1993. Available from the U.S. Army War College, Carlisle, PA 17013-5050.
Adam Roberts	"Humanitarian War: Intervention and Human Rights," *International Affairs*, July 1993.
Randall Robinson	"Get Ready to Go into Haiti," *The Washington Post National Weekly Edition*, May 23–29, 1994.
Peter W. Rodman	"Intervention and Its Discontents," *National Review*, March 29, 1993.
Alvin Z. Rubinstein	"In Search of a Foreign Policy," *Society*, September/October 1992.
John Gerard Ruggie	"Wandering in the Void: Charting the U.N.'s New Strategic Role," *Foreign Affairs*, November/December 1993.
Stephen R. Shalom	"Reflections on Intervention," *Peace & Democracy News*, Winter 1993/94.
Patrick J. Sloyan	"The Secret Path to a Bloodbath," *The Washington Post National Weekly Edition*, April 18-24, 1994.
Stephen John Stedman	"The New Interventionists," *Foreign Affairs*, America and the World Edition, 1992/93.
Evan Thomas	"Playing Globocop," *Newsweek*, June 28, 1993.
Alan Tonelson	"Clinton's World," *The Atlantic Monthly*, February 1993.
Robert W. Tucker and David C. Hendrickson	"America and Bosnia," *The National Interest*, Fall 1993.
Thomas G. Weiss	"New Challenges for UN Military Operations: Implementing an Agenda for Peace," *The Washington Quarterly*, Winter 1993.
Carol J. Williams	"The Shadow of a Shield," *Los Angeles Times Magazine*, July 25, 1993. Available from Times Mirror Square, Los Angeles, CA 90053.

Timothy E. Wirth — "Redefining Human Rights: Commitment and the Enforcement Dilemma," *Harvard International Review*, Spring 1994.

Warren Zimmerman — "Why America Must Save Bosnia," *The Washington Post National Weekly Edition*, May 2–8, 1994.

Organizations to Contact

The editors have compiled the following list of organizations concerned with the issues debated in this book. The descriptions are derived from materials provided by the organizations. All have publications or information available for interested readers. The list was compiled on the date of publication of the present volume; names, addresses, and phone numbers may change. Be aware that many organizations take several weeks or longer to respond to inquiries, so allow as much time as possible.

American Defense Institute (ADI)
1055 N. Fairfax St., 2nd Fl.
Alexandria, VA 22314
(703) 519-7000

This educational organization studies international issues related to national defense. It opposes deployment of American troops in foreign crises and opposes committing U.S. troops to a U.N. armed force. It publishes a quarterly newsletter, *ADI News*, and occasional *ADI Briefing* papers.

Amnesty International USA
322 Eighth Ave.
New York, NY 10001
(212) 807-8400

Amnesty International is a nongovernmental organization founded on the conviction that governments must not deny individuals their basic human rights as outlined in the United Nations Universal Declaration of Human Rights. It publishes numerous books, *The Amnesty International Newsletter*, *Country Reports* on individual countries, and an *Annual Report*.

The Brookings Institution
1775 Massachusetts Ave. NW
Washington, DC 20036-2188
(202) 797-6000

Founded in 1927, this think tank conducts research and provides education in foreign policy, economics, government, and the social sciences. It publishes the *Brookings Review* quarterly, as well as numerous books and research papers.

Campaign for Peace and Democracy
PO Box 1640, Cathedral Station
New York, NY 10025
(212) 666-5924

The campaign is a network of activists from the peace, labor, and minority and women's rights movements who oppose military interventions and believe that an internationally organized grassroots effort provides the only genuine foundation for achieving peace, freedom, economic justice, and ecological survival. It publishes *Peace & Democracy* twice per year.

CARE
151 Ellis St.
Atlanta, GA 30303
(800) 521-CARE
(404) 681-2552

CARE is the world's largest private, nonprofit, nonsectarian relief and development organization. It operates programs in disaster relief, food distribution, primary health care, agriculture and natural resource management, population, and small business support. It publishes the quarterly *CARE World Report* and occasional *CARE Briefs*.

Cato Institute
1000 Massachusetts Ave. NW
Washington, DC 20001-5403
(202) 842-0200

The institute is a libertarian public policy research foundation dedicated to stimulating debate on foreign and domestic policy issues. Its *Policy Analysis* on current topics is published periodically and *Cato Policy Review* is published every other month.

Center for War/Peace Studies
218 E. 18th St.
New York, NY 10003
(212) 475-1077

This organization seeks to reform the United Nations to create a legislative body that will move the world toward cooperation under international law rather than by violent conflict. Its Binding Triad proposal for a new voting system in the UN General Assembly would give more importance to states with larger populations or that contribute more to the UN budget. It publishes *Global Report: Progress Toward a World of Peace and Justice* four times per year.

Council on Foreign Relations
58 E. 68th St.
New York, NY 10021
(212) 734-0400

The council is a group of individuals with specialized knowledge of international affairs that was formed to study the international aspects of American political, economic, and strategic concerns. It publishes *Foreign Affairs* six times per year.

Foreign Policy Association
729 Seventh Ave.
New York, NY 10019
(800) 628-5754

This national, nonprofit, nongovernmental, educational organization believes that in a democracy a concerned and informed public is the foundation for an effective foreign policy. It publishes annually the *Great Decisions* briefing book on current foreign policy issues. Interventionism was addressed in the 1993 edition.

Global Exchange
2017 Mission St., #303
San Francisco, CA 94110
(415) 255-7296

Founded in 1988, this nonprofit research, education, and action center seeks to link people in the North (First World) and South (Third World) who are promoting social justice and democratic development. Global Exchange promotes a U.S. foreign policy that is noninterventionist. It publishes *Global Exchanges* quarterly.

Human Rights Watch
485 Fifth Ave.
New York, NY 10017
(212) 972-8400

Founded in 1978, this nongovernmental organization conducts regular, systematic investigations of human rights abuses in countries around the world. It publishes many books and reports on specific countries and publishes *Africa Watch*, *Americas Watch*, *Asia Watch*, *Helsinki Watch*, and *Middle East Watch* as well as *The Human Rights Watch Quarterly*.

Institute for Policy Studies
1601 Connecticut Ave. NW, 5th Fl.
Washington, DC 20009
(202) 234-9382

This nonpartisan center for research and education sponsors critical examination of the assumptions and policies that define America's stance on domestic and international issues and offers alternative strategies. It publishes guides, brochures, books, policy papers, and the quarterly *Global Communities*.

Liberty Lobby
300 Independence Ave. SE
Washington, DC 20003
(202) 546-5611

This political lobby opposes U.S. intervention in the affairs of sovereign nations unless there is a threat to America's regional security interests. The lobby publishes the monthly *Liberty Letter*.

National Democratic Institute for International Affairs (NDI)
1717 Massachusetts Ave. NW
Washington, DC 20036
(202) 328-3136

This organization seeks to promote and strengthen democratic institutions and values in new and emerging democracies. It conducts nonpartisan political development programs in more than sixty countries focusing on election processes, legislative training, and civic education. It publishes *NDI Reports* quarterly.

Overseas Development Council
1875 Connecticut Ave. NW, Suite 1012
Washington, DC 20009
(202) 234-8701

The council is a public policy institute that focuses on U.S./developing country issues such as poverty, economic development, and political development. It publishes *Policy Focus* seven to ten times per year and *U.S.-Third World Policy Perspective* quarterly.

Peaceworkers
721 Shrader
San Francisco, CA 94117
(415) 751-0302

This organization encourages the creation of an unarmed United Nations Peaceworkers Service composed of persons trained in the diplomatic skills necessary for peaceful resolution of conflicts. It provides information to interested individuals on its efforts to reform the United Nations.

Reason Foundation
3415 S. Sepulveda Blvd., Suite 400
Los Angeles, CA 90034
(310) 391-2245

The foundation promotes individual freedoms and free-market principles. It opposes interventionism in U.S. foreign policy. Its publications include the monthly *Reason* magazine as well as books, research reports, and newsletters.

Resource Center for Nonviolence
515 Broadway
Santa Cruz, CA 95060
(408) 423-1626
fax (408) 423-8716

The center offers a wide-ranging educational program on the history, theory, methodology, and practice of nonviolence as a force for personal and social change. It publishes the *Resource Center for Nonviolence—Center Update* and *Newsletter*, each semiannually.

Trilateral Commission
345 E. 46th St., Suite 711
New York, NY 10017
(212) 661-1180

The commission encourages closer cooperation among North America, Western Europe, and Japan. It meets annually to analyze major issues confronting the trilateral group. It publishes many books in addition to the annual magazine *Trialogue*.

United Nations Association of the United States of America
485 Fifth Ave., 2nd Fl.
New York, NY 10017
(212) 697-3232

A nonpartisan, nonprofit research organization dedicated to strengthening the United Nations and U.S. participation in it. Its publications include the bimonthly newspaper the *Interdependent*.

United States Institute of Peace
1550 M St. NW, Suite 700
Washington, DC 20005-1708
(202) 457-1700

The institute is an independent, nonpartisan organization established by Congress to support and promote the peaceful resolution of international conflict. It publishes the monthly *In Brief* and *Journal* newsletters.

World Policy Institute
65 Fifth Ave., #4
New York, NY 10008-3003
(212) 490-0010

The institute is the foreign policy department of the New School for Social Research, a private college in New York City. It formulates policy recommendations on U.S. and world security issues. It publishes *World Policy Journal* quarterly.

Index

Adams, Henry, 208
Adams, John, 208
Adamson, Peter, 104-105
Afghanistan, 79, 107
Africa
  arms race in, 105-106
  hostility to colonialism, 90-91
  responsibility for peace/democracy in, 102-106
  some states not fit to govern, 93
  UN should foster self-government, 88-94
An Agenda for Peace (Boutros-Ghali), 79-80, 145, 160, 165-66, 172
aid. *See* foreign aid
Aideed, Muhammad Farah, 56, 58, 59, 121, 128, 173, 221
Algeria, 119
altruism, national interests versus, 70
Amin, Idi, 91
Amnesty International, 75
Anderson, Kenneth, 68
Angola, 105, 183, 202
Aristide, Jean-Bertrand, 131
Aung San Suu Kyi, 199
Avakian, Bob, 127-30

"backlash states," U.S. and, 198-200
Baker, James A., III, 201
Balaguer, Joaquin, 132
Barley, Nigel, 104
Barre, Mohamed Siad, 24, 58
Barzani, Massoud, 19
Batista, Fulgencio, 212
Bay of Pigs invasion, 209
Beckman, David, 165
Beijing, China, 43
Bhartiya Janata Party, 113
Bir, Cevik, 28
Bismarck, Otto von, 146
Bloomfield, Lincoln P., 139
blue helmets, 98, 149, 173
Bosnia. *See* Yugoslavia (the former)
Boutros-Ghali, Boutros, 122, 136, 138, 141, 147
  An Agenda for Peace, 79-80, 145, 160, 165-66, 172
  on development, 153-56
  on peacekeeping, 149-53
  Rwanda crisis and, 176, 178-79
  on sovereignty, 81
  "a white man's war," 103
Bradley, Bill, 131
Brzezinski, Zbigniew, 183-84
Buchanan, Pat, 214
Burundi, 105, 147
Bush, George, 115
  Bosnia and, 36, 124
  Gulf War and, 118, 125, 177, 204, 209, 211
  "new world order" and, 175, 185
  Somalia and, 24-25, 36, 57, 121, 173

Cambodia, 43, 50, 79, 83
  UN peace process in, 80, 84-85, 98-99, 165
CARE, 65
Carpenter, Ted Galen, 183
Carr, Caleb, 57
Carter, Jimmy, 107-108, 133, 209
Castro, Fidel, 109, 209, 212
Catholic Relief Services (CRS), 62
Catholics
  humanitarian intervention and, 29-34
  National Conference of Catholic Bishops, 70
cease-fire enforcement units, 153
Chace, James, 207
change, pace of, 195
Charter of Paris for a New Europe, 38, 97
chemical warfare, 20, 23
Chile, 76, 200, 224

China, 184
  conflicting U.S. policies toward, 203
  sanctions against, 132
Christian duty to intervene, 29-34
Churchill, Winston, 148, 192
civil wars, 147
  costs of, 171-72
  see also Korea; Somalia; Yugoslavia (the former)
Clarke, Jonathan, 117
Clausewitz, Carl von, 57
Clinton, Bill, 115, 127, 184, 186, 195
  Bosnia and, 124
  foreign policy issues, 68, 75, 132, 207, 209, 216
  Haiti and, 122, 125
  military expenditures, 218
  New Pacific Community and, 198
  Somalia and, 28, 47, 61, 122, 173
Clough, Michael, 176
coercive enforcement, 146
Cold War
  bad interventions during, 217-18
  end of, multiple crises since, 23, 170, 191, 195, 218-19
  foreign aid during, 78-79
  nonintervention and, 37-38
colonialism
  hostility to, 90-91
  new, 88-89
Common Market, 30
compulsory engagement, 201-202
Conference on Security and Cooperation in Europe (CSCE), 37-38, 97
Conference on the Human Dimension, 97
Congo, 50, 90-91
  failed UN involvement in, 168
Conry, Barbara, 116
conservatorships, 82-84
  objections to, 86-87
  three models of, 83-84
  trusteeships
    roots of, 89-90
    should be resurrected, 86, 92-93
containment, 69
  to enlargement, 195-96
Convention on the Prevention and Punishment of the Crime of Genocide, 37, 38
Cornforth, F.M., 148
Cuba
  Bay of Pigs invasion, 209
  sanctions against, 109
Cuban Democracy Act (Torricelli-Graham measures), 109
Czechoslovakia, 41, 50, 218

Dallaire, Romeo, 106
Declaration on the Rights of Minorities (UN), 97
democracy
  as an American core concept, 193-94
  characteristics of, 115
  democratic rights, 96-97
  minority rights, 97-98
  U.S. should foster new democracies, 197-98
  viewpoints on,
    intervention for, overview, 68-76
    promotion has encouraged violence, 113-15
    U.S. should intervene to promote, 193-200
    U.S. should protect, 95-101
development (economic/social), 153-56
  mounting needs for, 153-54
  origins of Third World development, 154-55
  social development and stability, 155-56
de Waal, Alex, 48
disengagement. *See* isolationism
Dominican Republic, 50, 132
donor fatigue, 174
Duarte, José Napoleón, 224
Duvalier, François, 212, 218

East Timor, 220
  U.S. helped cause starvation in, 26
economic sanctions. *See* sanctions
Eisenhower, Dwight, 214
Eland, Ivan, 107
Elliott, Kimberly, 131
El Salvador, 217
  UN peace process, 99-100, 168
Elshtain, Jean Bethke, 68
The End of History and the Last Man (Fukuyama), 170
enforcement. *See under* peacekeeping
engagement
  compulsory, 201-202
  disengagement (isolationism), 201, 210, 225-26
  selective, 202, 205-206
Engelberg, Stephen, 181
enlargement, 69, 73

from containment, 195-96
strategy of, 196-200
Ethiopia, 50, 52, 53, 108, 112
ethnic cleansing, 33, 37-38, 106, 173
European Community (EC), 36, 37, 190
European Free Trade Area, 37
European Human Rights Convention, 38
executive agent, 147

failing states
intervention to save, 77-87
Falk, Richard, 222
Farabundo Martí National Liberation Front (FMLN), 99, 168
The Federalist, 208
fifth column effect, 110-11
foreign aid
alternatives are not discussed, 65-66
during Cold War, 78-79
from aid to intervention, 91-92
undermines self-sufficiency, 62-66
Foreign Policy magazine, 127
Fréchette, Louise, 175
Fromkin, David, 210
Fukuyama, Francis, 170

Galtung, Johan, 109-10
General Agreement on Tariffs and Trade (GATT), 198
Geneva Conventions, 56, 181
genocide, 27, 51, 118
as greatest crime, 71-72
prevention and punishment of, 37-38
Geymmayel, Amin, 120
Gingrich, Newt, 131
Governors Island accord, 121
Greenwood, Christopher, 36
Grenada, 41, 92, 100
Group of *77*, 81
Guam Doctrine, 214
Guarantee Clause
international clause needed, 101
of U.S. Constitution, 96, 101
guardianships. *See* conservatorships

Habyarimana, Juvenal, 105, 119, 176
Haiti, 52-53, 119
as case from hell, 142
economic sanctions against, 110, 131-33
twenty years of U.S. occupation, 121-22
U.S. helped cause starvation in, 26
Halperin, Morton H., 95
Hamilton, Alexander, 208, 209
Hansen, Peter, 137
Harcourt, W.V., 50
Harper's Magazine, 68
Harries, Owen, 122-23
Harvard International Review, 19
Hauser, Rita, 136
Havel, Václav, 139
Helman, Gerald B., 77
Hersi, Mohammed Siad ("Morgan"), 58, 59
Himes, Kenneth R., 29
Hitler, Adolf, 27, 74, 108, 112, 146, 212
Hitt, Jack, 68
Ho Chi Minh, 184
Holmes, Kim R., 68, 163
Hufbauer, Gary, 131
humanitarian intervention
arguments against
"lending-respectability," 26-27
"they're-dead-anyway," 25-26
Catholics and, 29-34
defined, 19
limits to what can be accomplished, 213
military force and, 22-23
morality and, 22-23
new era of, 140-41
pacifism and, 32-33
problems and defects of, 46-47
sovereignty issue and, 19-20
United Nations and
charter, 42-43
doctrine, absence of, 44-45
double standards, 43-44
leadership is essential, 21
problems with intervention, 41-46
vague goals of, 45-46
viewpoints on
aid undermines self-sufficiency, 62-66
can protect human rights, 19-23
can save lives, 24-28
Christian duty to intervene, 29-34
is not effective, 39-47
is problematic, 48-56
see also intervention; military intervention
Humanitarianism and War Project, 137, 138
human rights
as above sovereignty, 34
humanitarian intervention can protect, 19-23

minority rights, 97-98
theory of, and intervention, 31, 34
Human Rights Watch, 105-106
Huntington, Samuel, 142
Hussein, Saddam, 22-23, 35, 45, 109-110, 128, 132, 146, 189

imperialism
is not a policy, 127
U.S. must desist from, 124-30
Imperialism (Lenin), 90
Independent, 104
interests. *See* national interest
international issues
international cooperation, 143-44
international (world) community
central dilemma of, 144
as difficult term, 74-75, 142-43
International Atomic Energy Agency (IAEA), 141, 146, 199
International Herald Tribune, 35
International Monetary Fund (IMF), 81-82, 155
International Red Cross, 82, 104
intervention
from aid to intervention, 91-92
causes anti-American sentiment, 121-22
creates new problems, 122-23
forms of, 51-53
idealism in, 118-19
impartiality is impossible in, 120-21, 127
increase in is predicted, 175
morality above politics, 35-38
prevention over intervention, 170-75, 178-79
revival of, 50-51
rule of nonintervention and, 40-41
rules of, 100-101
viewpoints on
Christian duty to intervene, 29-34
to save failing states, 77-87
should not be used in regional conflicts, 116-23
United Nations and, an overview, 135-38
see also democracy, intervention for; humanitarian intervention; military intervention; sanctions
In the Cause of Peace (Lie), 162
Iraq, 42, 140-41
Operation Desert Storm, 21, 36
sanctions against, 108-110, 111
isolationism (disengagement), 201, 210, 225-26
national interests versus, 193-94
Israel, 157-58, 215

Jackson, Jesse, 25
Jefferson, Thomas, 208
John Paul II, 33-34
Johnson, Lyndon B., 127, 214
Johnson, Paul, 88
Johnston, Philip, 165
Jonah, James, 147
just war theory, 30-31

Karadzic, Radovan, 37
Keating, Colin, 135
Kennedy, John F., 127, 209, 214
Kerux newsletter, 32
Khmer Rouge, 78, 83, 99
Kipling, Rudyard, 90
Kissinger, Henry, 208
Korea, 147, 211
as failure of intervention, 120
North Korea's nuclear arms, 202-203
protecting South Korea, 214-15
Kurds, 19-23, 30, 34, 138
Operation Provide Comfort, as success, 22

Lake, Anthony, 193
League of Nations, 108, 112
Lebanon, 41, 119, 120
Lebanonization, 191-92
Lee, John M., 161
"lending-respectability" argument, 26-27
Lenin, Vladimir, 129
Imperialism, 90
Leonard, Terry, 104
less-developed countries (LDCs), 165
Liberia, 89
Lie, Trygve, 158
In the Cause of Peace, 162
Lippmann, Walter, 209
Lodge, Henry Cabot, 60-61
Luttwak, Edward, 25

MacArthur, Douglas, 214, 215
Marcos, Ferdinand E., 218
Maren, Michael, 62
market economics
as an American core concept, 193-94
Marshall, Will, 68
Marshall Plan, 70

Marx, Karl, 144
Marxism-Leninism-Maoism
  revolutionary science of, 125, 127, 129
McCloskey, Frank, 68
McKinley, William, 210
media. *See* press
Midden, Betsy, 35
military intervention
  arguments against U.S., 219-22
    exceptions to, 222-24
  humanitarian intervention and, 22-23
    historical review of, 49-50
  is always political, 57-61
  is counterproductive, 219, 222
  justifications for, 20
  national interests and, 212-13
  preconditions for, 52-56
  problems when troops withdraw, 211-12
  U.S. opposition to, 178
  U.S. restrictions on use of force in, 186
Mill, John Stuart, 219, 221-22
Minear, Larry, 137-38
minorities
  Declaration on the Rights of Minorities (UN), 97
  oppression by majorities, 113-14
  rights of, 97-98
Mobutu (Sese Seko), Joseph-Desiré, 93
morality
  avoiding moral perfection, 208
  balancing with practical principles, 207-209
  defending realism with, 209
  humanitarian intervention and, 22-23
  moral indications to intervene, 35-38
moral statism
  view of international relations, 33
Mouat, Lucia, 135
Moynihan, Daniel P., 195
multilateral sanctions, 111-12, 133
Mussolini, Benito, 108, 112
Myanmar, 43

Nasser, Gamal Abdel, 132
National Commission for the Consolidation of Peace (El Salvador), 99
National Conference of Catholic Bishops, 70
national interest
  altruism versus, 70
  conflicting (and unequal) interests, 202
  difficulty in defining, 72
  intervention and, 212-13
    to protect U.S. interests, 201-206
  isolationism versus, 193-94
  U.S. interests are not at risk, 213, 216
national sovereignty. *See* sovereignty of nations
Natsios, Andrew, 165
Ndadaye, Melchior, 105
Neier, Aryeh, 69, 113
Neumann, Robert G., 188
New Pacific Community, 198
New Republic, 25
"new world order," 175, 185, 219
New York Times, 65, 116, 225
Nixon, Richard, 208, 214, 218
nomenklatura, 199
nongovernmental organizations (NGOs)
  United Nations and, 84
nonintervention, rule of, 40-41
nonviolence, 27
  pacifism and, 31-32
Noriega, Manuel, 128
North American Free Trade Agreement (NAFTA), 198, 204
North Atlantic Treaty Organization (NATO), 37, 141, 177, 186-87
North Korea. *See* Korea
North-South conflict, 189-90
Nuclear Non-Proliferation Treaty (NPT), 143

Oakley, Robert, 118
O'Brien, Thomas, 37
Ogata, Sadako, 174
Omaar, Rakiya, 48
Operation Desert Storm, 21, 36
Operation Lifeline, 52
Operation Provide Comfort
  as resounding success, 22
  see also Kurds
Operation Restore Hope. *See under* Somalia
Organization for Economic Development, 154
Organization of American States (OAS), 95

pacifism, 27
  humanitarian intervention and, 32-33
  nonviolence and, 31-32
  pacifist critique of military force, 219, 222

Panama, 100
Paris accord (1991, on Cambodia), 98-99
Parmelee, Jennifer, 102
Pax Christi, 32
peacekeeping, 149-53, 157-62
  cease-fire enforcement units, 153
  coercive enforcement, 146
  defined, 166-67
  limits of, 167-68
  new role for, 150-51
  peace enforcement, 145, 151-53, 159-60, 167
  peacemaking, 189
  post-conflict peace-building, 79-80
  principles of, 150
  responses must be quick, 152-53
  warmaking and, 167
Peru, 130
Pinochet, Augusto, 76, 200, 224
Pius XII, 30-31
poison gas. *See* chemical warfare
"politics by other means" (Clausewitz), 57, 169
Pol Pot, 27, 181
post-conflict peace-building, 79-80
power
  means of exercising, 204-205
  sources of American power, 194-95, 203-204
precedent argument, 148, 219-20
President Kennedy: Profile of Power (Reeves), 214
press (media)
  powerlessness of, 106
  role in interpreting humanitarian needs, 64-66
Principle of the Dangerous Precedent, 148

rally-around-the-flag effect, 109
Ratner, Steven R., 77
Reagan, Ronald, 92, 107, 120, 133, 209
realism view of international relations, 33
Red Cross, 82, 104
Reeves, Richard, 214
Refugee Policy Project, 137
refugees, number in world, 171
regional conflicts
  definition of, 116-17
  intervention should not be used in, 116-23
  see also civil wars
relief agencies
  are businesses, 63-64
Revolutionary Communist Party, USA, 124
Revolutionary Worker, 124
Roberts, Adam, 39, 171
Robinson, Randall, 25
Roosevelt, Franklin D., 127, 208
Roosevelt, Theodore, 215
Rothschild, Matthew, 24
Rusk, Dean, 189
Rwanda, 102-106, 119, 135-36, 147, 176-79

Sahel, 53
sanctions
  economic
    are not effective, 131-33
    can be effective, 107-112
  fifth column effect of, 110-11
  goals of, 107-108
  multilateral sanctions, 111-12, 133
  rally-around-the-flag effect of, 109-110
  selective use of, 109-110
San José Agreement on Human Rights, 100
Schlesinger, James R., 184
Schott, Jeffrey, 131
Schroeder, Paul W., 118
selective engagement, 202, 205-206
self-determination
  Mill's argument for, 219, 221-22
  the right of, 77-78
Serbia. *See* Yugoslavia (the former)
Shalom, Stephen Rosskamm, 25, 26, 217
Sharp, Jane, 35
Sihanouk, Norodom, 85
silent crises, 172
Singh, V.P., 113
"slippery slope," 20-21, 179, 183
Sloan, Stanley R., 185
Slovenia. *See* Yugoslavia (the former)
social development. *See* development (economic/social)
Somalia, 42-43, 57-61, 92, 121, 173, 225
  as case from hell, 141
  failure to intervene early in, 161
  intervention was justified, 24-28
  Operation Restore Hope, 22, 28, 44-46
Sommer, Theo, 119
Somoza, Anastacio, 212
South Africa, sanctions against, 111
South Korea. *See* Korea

sovereignty of nations
  absolute, exceptions to, 81-82
  current forces working against, 29-30
  human rights are above, 34
  issue of, 19-20, 27
  no longer prime issue, 175
  redefinition of, 164-65
  roots of, 48-49
  traditional, 80-81
  weakening of, 29-30
Speer, Albert, 108
Stanley, Timothy W., 161
Steinbruner, John, 182
Sudan, 43, 52

Tanzania, 91
"Terrorism Futures" (Pentagon), 122
Thatcher, Margaret, 92
"they're-dead-anyway" argument, 25
Thornburgh, Dick, 171-72
Tienanmen Square massacre, 132
Time magazine, 116
Tito (Josip Broz), 36-37
Torricelli-Graham measures (Cuban Democracy Act), 109
To Unite Our Strength (Lee, Von Pagenhardt, and Stanley), 161
triage, necessity of, 174-75
Truman Doctrine, 69
trusteeships. *See* conservatorships

Uganda, 50, 91
United Nations
  Cambodian peace process and, 98-99
  Conference on Environment and Development, 143
  Covenant on Civil and Political Rights, 38
  Declaration on the Rights of Minorities, 97
  El Salvador peace process and, 99-100
  law enforcement process and, 145-47
  nongovernmental organizations (NGOs) and, 84
  number of peacekeeping missions in world, 135
  problems with intervention, 41-46
  sovereignty no longer primary, 175
  unanimity without force, 158-59
  Universal Declaration of Human Rights (1948), 38, 49, 51, 81, 96
  viewpoints on
    interventions, an overview, 135-38
    should be the world's policeman, 139-48
    should foster self-government in Africa, 88-94
    should have volunteer armed forces, 157-62
    should intervene to save failing states, 77-87
    should keep peace and promote development, 149-56
    should not use military force, 176-79
    should play limited role in interventions, 163-69
    should stress prevention over intervention, 170-75
  see also conservatorships; development (economic/social); peacekeeping; United Nations, units of
United Nations, units of
  Development Programme (UNDP), 78, 84
  High Commissioner for Refugees (UNHCR), 82
  Human Rights Commission, 20, 81
  Military Staff Committee (MSC), 166
  Observer Mission (El Salvador), 99
  Security Council
    Resolution 688 (repression of civilians), 20, 42-44
    Resolution 693 (Salvadoran observers), 99
    Resolution 794 (invasion of Somalia), 42
  Sub-Commission on Prevention of Discrimination and Protection of Minorities, 97
  Transitional Authority in Cambodia (UNTAC), 98
  United Nations Protection Force (UNPROFOR), 42, 45
United States
  Agency for International Development (AID), 63, 64, 96, 155
  "backlash states" and, 198-200
  conflicting (and unequal) interests, 202
  Constitution, Guarantee Clause of, 96, 101
  foreign policy, three periods of, 201-202
  interests and intervention and, 187
  lack of leadership by, 186-87
  restrictions on use of force, 186
  should foster new democracies, 197-98

sources of power, 203-204
viewpoints on
all U.S. interventions should be opposed, 217-26
intervention, an overview, 181-84
must cease imperialist interventions, 124-30
must lead to prevent aggression, 185-88
should avoid interventions, 210-13
should balance moral/practical principles, 207-209
should intervene for international order, 188-92
should intervene to promote democracy, 193-200
should intervene to protect interests, 201-206
should let allies defend themselves, 214-16
should protect new democracies, 95-101
Urquhart, Sir Brian, 157, 164

Vietnam War, 125
as costly, colossal failure, 120
Von Pagenhardt, Robert, 161

Walzer, Michael, 221, 223
war(s)
humanitarian war, as oxymoron, 171
major, defined and counted, 116
as "politics by other means" (Clausewitz), 57, 169
small, 145
theory of just war, 30-31
Washington Quarterly, 118
Weber, Max, 70
Weinberger, Caspar, 36
Weiss, Thomas G., 136, 138
on prevention, 170-75
welfare internationalism, 154
White Dominions, 90
"white man's burden" (Kipling), 90
"a white man's war" (Boutros-Ghali), 103
Wilson, Woodrow, 60-61, 89, 188, 196
World Bank, 155
world community. *See under* international issues
World Food Program, 64
"World Military and Social Expenditures," 116

Yeltsin, Boris, 76
Yugoslavia (the former), 33, 119, 151, 190
as case from hell, 141-42
half-measures in, 173-74
moral indications for intervention in, 35-38
refugees from, 171
results of self-deterrence, 186-87
sanctions against, 133
U.S. failure to intervene early in, 159, 207
U.S. has no reason to intervene, 183

Z Magazine, 25
zones of order, 191-92